SENSORY PROPERTIES OF FOODS

An industry–university co-operation Symposium organised under the auspices of the National College of Food Technology, University of Reading

THE SYMPOSIUM COMMITTEE

GORDON G. BIRCH, B.Sc., Ph.D., D.Sc. (Lond), F.R.I.C., M.R.S.H., F.C.S.
Reader at National College of Food Technology, Reading University, Weybridge, Surrey.

J. G. BRENNAN, M.Sc., F.I.F.S.T.
National College of Food Technology, Reading University, Weybridge, Surrey.

J. A. FORD, B.A. (Oxon)
Secretary at National College of Food Technology, Reading University, Weybridge, Surrey.

R. HARPER, M.Sc., D.Sc. (Manchester), Ph.D., F.B.Ps.S., F.I.F.S.T.
Reader at University of Reading, Department of Food Science, The University, London Road, Reading, Berks.

R. JOWITT, B.Sc. (Eng), D.L.C., Dip.Chem.Eng., C.Eng., F.I.,Chem.E., M.I.Mech.E.
Reader at National College of Food Technology, Reading University, Weybridge, Surrey.

K. J. PARKER, M.A., D.Phil. (Oxon)
General Manager, Tate & Lyle Ltd, Group Research & Development, Philip Lyle Memorial Research Laboratory, Reading University, PO Box 68, Reading, Berks.

E. J. ROLFE, B.Sc., M.Chem.A., F.R.I.C., F.I.F.S.T.
Principal, National College of Food Technology, Reading University, Weybridge, Surrey.

Mrs B. A. SHORE,
National College of Food Technology, Reading University, Weybridge, Surrey.

SENSORY PROPERTIES OF FOODS

Edited by

G. G. BIRCH, J. G. BRENNAN
and K. J. PARKER

APPLIED SCIENCE PUBLISHERS LTD
LONDON

APPLIED SCIENCE PUBLISHERS LTD
RIPPLE ROAD, BARKING, ESSEX, ENGLAND

ISBN: 0 85334 744 1

WITH 38 TABLES AND 99 ILLUSTRATIONS

© APPLIED SCIENCE PUBLISHERS LTD 1977

Printed in Great Britain by Galliard (Printers) Ltd, Great Yarmouth

List of Contributors

C. ÅKESSON
  The Swedish Food Institute, S-400 21 Göteborg, Sweden.

L. M. BARTOSHUK
  John B. Pierce Foundation and Yale University, 290 Congress Avenue, New Haven, Connecticut 06519, USA.

J. BEESLEY
  Confectionery Group Quality Control, Cadbury Limited, Bournville, Birmingham B30 2LU, England.

M. G. J. BEETS
  International Flavors and Fragrances (Europe), Liebergerweg 72–98, Postbox 309, Hilversum, The Netherlands.

G. G. BIRCH
  National College of Food Technology, St. George's Avenue, Weybridge, Surrey KT13 0DE, England.

J. G. BRENNAN
  National College of Food Technology, St. George's Avenue, Weybridge, Surrey KT13 0DE, England.

J. W. CHANDLER
  MPI Sensory Testing, Inc., 770 Lexington Avenue, New York, NY 10021, USA.

v

F. J. FRANCIS

Department of Food Science and Nutrition, University of Massachusetts, Amherst, Massachusetts 01003, USA.

R. HARPER

Department of Food Science, University of Reading, London Road, Reading RG1 5AQ, England.

J. D. HIGGINBOTHAM

Tate & Lyle, Ltd., Group Research & Development, Philip Lyle Memorial Research Laboratory, University of Reading, PO Box 68, Reading RG6 2BX, Berks., England.

C. A. M. HOUGH

Tate & Lyle, Ltd., Group Research & Development, Philip Lyle Memorial Research Laboratory, University of Reading, PO Box 68, Reading RG6 2BX, Berks., England.

P. HOWGATE

Ministry of Agriculture, Fisheries & Food, Torry Research Station, PO Box 31, 135 Abbey Road, Aberdeen AB9 8DG, Scotland.

J. B. HUTCHINGS

Unilever Research Laboratories, Colworth House, Sharnbrook, Bedford MK44 1LQ, England.

R. JOWITT

National College of Food Technology, St. George's Avenue, Weybridge, Surrey KT13 0DE, England.

E. KUGLER

Coca-Cola Europe, Essen, West Germany.

R. LANGLAIS

Coca-Cola Europe, Essen, West Germany.

M. LAUSTER

Coca-Cola Europe, Essen, West Germany.

C. K. LEE

Tate & Lyle, Ltd., Group Research & Development, Philip Lyle Memorial Research Laboratory, University of Reading, PO Box 68, Reading RG6 2BX, Berks., England.

G. LOHRE
Coca-Cola Europe, Essen, West Germany.

D. B. MacDOUGALL
Agricultural Research Council, Meat Research Institute, Langford, Bristol BS18 7DY, England.

H. R. MOSKOWITZ
MPI Sensory Testing, Inc., 770 Lexington Avenue, New York, NY 10021, USA.

H. E. NURSTEN
Department of Food Science, University of Reading, London Road, Reading RG1 5AQ, England.

L. G. PLASKETT
Biotechnical Processes Ltd., Skilmoor House, Cadmore End, High Wycombe, Bucks. HP14 3PJ, England.

A. RAY
National College of Food Technology, St. George's Avenue, Weybridge, Surrey KT13 0DE, England.

E. J. ROLFE
National College of Food Technology, St. George's Avenue, Weybridge, Surrey KT13 0DE, England.

R. S. SHALLENBERGER
New York State College of Agriculture & Life Sciences, Department of Food Science and Technology, New York State Agricultural Experiment Station, Cornell University, Geneva, New York 14456, USA.

P. SHERMAN
Queen Elizabeth College, University of London, Campden Hill Road, London W8 7AH, England.

E. VON SYDOW
The Swedish Food Institute, S-400 21 Göteborg, Sweden.

Contents

Session IV (Chairman: A. W. Holmes)

Introduction

E. J. ROLFE

National College of Food Technology, University of Reading, Weybridge, Surrey, England

Lord Zuckerman speaking at the Annual Lunch of the British Nutrition Foundation in 1975 expressed the opinion that:

'our understanding of taste physiology and of flavour technology is abysmal. If the next generation and generations beyond are going to be fed acceptably as well as adequately, we shall certainly need to do far more research and development in these fields of study than has been contemplated hitherto. The survival of our western civilisation is going to depend on a new food revolution—by which I mean a revolution in our methods of processing food, in increasing the shelf life of our food and in improving our methods of distribution. In practically all advanced countries agricultural research still attracts vastly greater resources than does food research. This imbalance will surely have to change.'

In making these remarks Lord Zuckerman has highlighted two very crucial issues which are inhibiting the development of food research and the optimum utilisation of our food resources.

1. *The disparity between resources devoted to food research and those devoted to agriculture*

Since the statement was made, this fact is being voiced increasingly, but it must be pressed more vigorously if any improvement is to be achieved in the extent of support given to studies in food science and technology. But there are real difficulties arising from misunderstanding. The introduction of high-yielding strains of cereals, e.g. rice and wheat, is acclaimed as revolutionary and as a

1

major development towards increasing world food supplies, and so it can be, provided the fertilisers are available, and the crop can be irrigated. By comparison, little impact is made when the development is that of devising acceptable and nutritious products from, e.g., vegetable proteins. The tendency is for the latter to be considered as mere technical advance, requiring little of the erudition and knowledge which the successful geneticist must have. This is, of course, a fallacy but the idea no doubt is one of the factors which colour the thinking when funds to support research are being considered.

2. *Our knowledge and understanding of taste physiology and of flavour technology is inadequate, and this thought can be extended to include all the sensory properties of food*

It can be argued that Britain is better fed than ever before. By applying the accumulated knowledge and principles of food science and food technology the food manufacturer, by means of food processing and preservation, provides the population with an unprecedented choice of foods throughout the year, irrespective of season, and at reasonable prices. Thus, we can always enjoy a varied diet, a point emphasised as desirable by nutritionists, and in general also the food we eat is more than sufficient to meet our physiological needs—indeed, obesity has become our dominant example of malnutrition.

But this very satisfactory state of affairs (excluding obesity) should not allow us to be complacent regarding our future food supplies. We can be certain for the first time in history that the future will be dramatically different from the present. The acceptance of this premise is readily apparent in our attitude towards energy. We have been forced to recognise that our known resources of fossil fuels will not last very long into the future, and as a consequence some effort is being directed towards the development of alternative and more permanent sources of energy such as the wind, sun, tides, etc. Also, attempts are made through fiscal and other means of persuasion to make the general public and industry energy conscious.

Similarly, with food it is becoming apparent now that we cannot go on enjoying indefinitely our present diet, particularly with its relatively-high content of protein foods of animal origin. The high cost of meat is already affecting the situation, and in the long term we shall be unable to afford and sustain, at the present level of production, the poor conversion of cereals, etc. by animals into more attractive foods.

If radical changes appear to be certain within the foreseeable future then it becomes prudent to plan for these changes in good time. Thus, we should now place emphasis on the development of new acceptable and equally-nutritious foods to replace those that will become prohibitively expensive or in short supply. Already much vigorous work is in progress in this area, e.g. production of single-cell protein, leaf protein, and textured vegetable protein. But there is a big and difficult gap to bridge between producing these basic food raw materials and their conversion into products acceptable to the consumer. The first essential is to know a great deal more about the sensory aspects of food, and it is hoped that this symposium will stimulate greater activity. The knowledge is needed to assist in the development of new foods from novel or otherwise neglected sources. Secondly, there is a need to educate the population in order to increase their awareness of nutrition. This opens up again the controversial question of whether some indication of the nutritional quality of a food should be included on the label. A large number of people can cope with tables of energy values of foodstuffs and plan their diets, and no doubt many could have their interest stimulated further. Opinions are offered such as the information would mean little or nothing to the housewife, or that the consumer is not interested. 'Housewife' and 'consumer' cover people with a broad spectrum of interests and abilities and such sweeping opinions as above are far too dogmatic. To adopt such opinions will effectively inhibit the development of a general interest in nutrition.

However, everybody believes himself or herself to be an expert on food at least to the extent of identifying his likes and dislikes and in reaching decisions regarding quality. It is the consumer's opinion of quality which is significant in the success or otherwise of a food manufacturer's products. In general when deciding on acceptability, the consumer integrates the contributions from appearance, taste, smell and texture. Though these characteristics may represent separate properties of the foodstuff, they certainly mutually interact to influence a consumer's assessment. For example, it has been reported that food tasters, presented with white chocolate flavoured ice cream and brown vanilla ice cream, almost without exception when asked to identify the flavour, pronounced the white ice cream as vanilla and the brown as chocolate. Similar tests have been carried out with children using red and yellow jellies variously flavoured. Irrespective of the real flavours they thought the red jellies were strawberry and those which were yellow lemon. Similar results have been obtained also with coloured sponge cakes. However, such results are not too surprising and must not be interpreted to mean either that the flavour of food is relatively unimportant, or that the consumer cannot discriminate. All the foods tested were of a texture and structure unrelated to any particular flavour. The consumers were used to meeting the identical texture and appearance associated with a wide variety of flavours. The only significant difference in the appearance of the samples which they tasted was colour, an attribute associated in their mind through long previous experience with a particular flavour, and not surprisingly it affected their judgement.

As has been said on many previous occasions, we eat food not nutrition, and food will be eaten only if it is palatable and attractive. It is far from being true that a hungry man will eat anything. The food technologist therefore sees as an important objective the improvement of methods of food processing and preservation so as to retain not only the nutritive value but also the desirable aspects of quality. He is therefore seeking means of reducing flavour loss in concentrated and dehydrated foods, and of minimising 'over cooked' flavours and deterioration in texture of canned foods, etc.

It is recognised that appearance and all the other sensory characteristics of a food are important regarding its acceptance and enjoyment. Research in this direction demands an understanding of such characteristics and means of quantitative measurement. The logical extension in the application of such knowledge is to the development of novel foodstuffs.

The objective of this symposium is to explore and discuss the present state of knowledge and thinking within this important area. Lord Kelvin once stated that when you can measure a thing and express it by a number then you know something about it. However, before any attempts at measurement can be made we have first the very difficult problem of identifying those properties which contribute to the attributes of appearance, flavour, texture. Using Lord Kelvin's yardstick it will be seen from consideration of the papers to be presented that we are moving towards knowing something about the sensory properties of foodstuffs.

1

Modification of Taste Quality

LINDA M. BARTOSHUK

*John B. Pierce Foundation and Yale University,
New Haven, Connecticut, USA*

ABSTRACT

*Modern psychophysical studies of taste support the functional
independence of the four taste qualities: sweet, sour, salty and bitter.
This functional independence plays a special role in taste modification.*

*One of the most common forms of taste modification is the use of
condiments or flavouring agents; this type of modification results from
mixture interactions among the four taste qualities. When substances
are mixed, their tastes change even when no chemical reactions occur
among the substances. Early studies compared taste mixtures to colour
mixtures but tastes actually mix in a very different way. Different taste
qualities do not fuse to produce a new taste the way colours fuse in
mixtures (e.g. red and green lights fuse into yellow). The component
taste qualities are recognisable in mixtures but are reduced in intensity.
These decrements appear to be predictable from the shapes of the
psychophysical functions relating taste intensity to stimulus
concentration. Substances tasted under certain circumstances produce
compressed psychophysical functions (i.e. successive concentration
increments produce smaller and smaller increments of perceived
intensity). The degree of compression predicts the amount by which the
taste of that substance will be suppressed in a mixture tasted under the
same conditions. Synergism can also occur with tasting conditions and
substances that produce expanded functions (i.e. successive
concentration increments produce successively larger perceived
intensities).*

*More dramatic modification effects result from the topical
application of substances from certain plants like* Synepalum

5

dulcificum (*miracle fruit*), Gymnema sylvestre *and* Cynara scolymus (*globe artichoke*). *Miracle fruit adds a sweet taste to substances that normally taste sour,* Gymnema sylvestre *selectively abolishes sweetness, and the globe artichoke causes water to take on a sweet taste.*

In all of the cases of taste modification, the nature of the qualities never changes. A new quality may be added, one may be subtracted or the perceived intensities of all qualities present may be shifted; but these changes can all be viewed as changes in intensity. The taste qualities perceived are still sweet, sour, salty and bitter.

INTRODUCTION

Belief in the four basic tastes, sweet, sour, salty and bitter, as the irreducible units of taste experience was the culmination of a considerable amount of 19th-century debate, but consensus on this point did not lead to consensus on other issues concerning taste quality. Friedrich Kiesow (1858–1940) and Hjalmar Öhrwall (1851–1929) were the major figures in a battle over the status of taste quality. Kiesow[1] argued that sweet, sour, salty and bitter are qualities within a single taste modality just as colours are qualities within vision. Öhrwall[2] argued that taste qualities are independent of one another and should really be considered to be separate modalities. He believed the four basic tastes were more analogous to the skin senses (touch, warmth, cold and pain) than they were to colours. Kiesow's view prevailed, possibly in part because his influential mentor, Wilhelm Wundt, produced many students who wrote textbooks. Kiesow's experiments produced a variety of taste analogies to known colour vision phenomena.[1,3,4]

This old controversy is of interest now because modern psychophysical studies challenge many of Kiesow's conclusions.[5,6] The unpopular opinions of Öhrwall now appear to have considerable merit; the four taste qualities appear to be remarkably independent of one another. It should be noted that the 'four basic tastes' discussed now are not as philosophically weighty as those of the 19th century. Current research focuses on establishing the functional properties of these qualities rather than debating the nature of quality itself. Perhaps the best illustration comes from studies of cross-adaptation. If the tongue is exposed to a constant concentration of NaCl, within seconds the salty taste will begin to diminish. If the concentration is not too high, the salty taste will eventually disappear and a subsequent NaCl stimulus will be tasteless. If the taste of some substance other than NaCl is diminished as well, cross-adaptation is said to have occurred. McBurney and his co-workers have shown that cross-adaptation occurs among salty,[7] sour,[8] and sweet[9] substances. Some bitter substances failed to cross-adapt.[8] McBurney and Bartoshuk[10,11] have shown that cross-adaptation fails to occur across qualities.

The independence of the four basic tastes is important to the concept of taste modification. Some 19th-century descriptions of taste phenomena suggest that one quality can be changed into another. In the opinion of this author, taste modification of that sort does not occur. When the taste of a substance is changed, careful analysis will show that the change is quantitative, not qualitative. Perceived intensities of the qualities present may be increased or decreased, a quality may be removed or a new one added, but one quality does not change into another. Students of the senses will note that his argument is akin to concluding that taste is analytic rather than synthetic.

TASTE MIXTURE INTERACTIONS

Classic View of Mixture Interactions

When substances with different taste qualities are mixed, the intensities of their tastes change even if no chemical reactions occur. These interactions play an important role in the use of condiments or flavouring ingredients in foods. For example, most people have probably noticed that the addition of salt to food not only adds a salty taste but also changes the perceived intensities of other tastes in the food.

Kiesow was the first to study taste mixture interactions systematically. His experiments were designed to find taste analogies with colour vision.[4] When opponent colours are mixed, hues cancel and the mixture is grey. Kiesow examined all possible pairs of the four basic taste qualities to try to find cancellation in taste. He found that the mixtures tasted less intense than the sum of the components but cancellation proved to be elusive. He found only one mixture (weak sucrose plus weak NaCl) in which neither component quality was recognisable.

Subsequent mixture research did not challenge Kiesow's basic philosophy, that is, the research was designed to find the laws by which pairs of qualities interacted with one another. Although more recent research tends to support Kiesow's main result, that a mixture is less intense than the sum of its parts,[12-14] a variety of studies have reported enhancement as well.[15-19]

Studies of mixtures of substances with similar tastes have followed a different tradition. Most of these studies dealt with sweet substances and produced formulae intended to permit the prediction of mixtures of various sweeteners from the sweetness of the components.[20-25] These studies, and the few additional studies not oriented toward sweet[26,27] bring up another extremely interesting issue: *synergism*. Synergism is customarily said to occur when a mixture has a taste intensity that is greater than the simple sum of the taste intensities of its components.

Moskowitz has published a series of experiments on mixtures of substances with different tastes as well as mixtures of substances with similar tastes. On the basis of his own data as well as a thoughtful review of the literature, Moskowitz[25] summarised the mixture research that derives both from Kiesow's colour analogies and the sweetness models. He concluded that suppression occurs between pairs of substances with different taste qualities while simple additivity or synergism occurs between pairs of substances with similar taste qualities.

An Alternate View of Mixture Interactions

It seemed to us that the last part of this summary could not be true for at least one case: the addition of a substance to itself. Figure 1 illustrates[28] the logic that led us to this conclusion. A, B, and C are three hypothetical psychophysical functions for taste. These particular functions are power functions but the following logic is not restricted to these. Consider adding A to itself. The perceived intensity of concentration 1·0 of A added to concentration 1·0 of A, that is, of concentration 2·0 of A, is 1·4. The same operation on B and C would produce perceived intensities of 2·0 and 2·8 respectively. Function A is said to show compression while C shows expansion. As this example illustrates, the shape of the psychophysical function determines how a substance adds to itself. Simple additivity would be predicted only for B. Synergism would be predicted for C and suppression would be predicted for A.

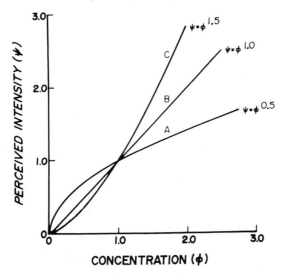

F<small>IG</small>. 1.   Power functions showing perceived intensity as a function of concentration for three hypothetical taste substances A, B and C. The function for A shows compression and the function for C shows expansion. (From Bartoshuk.[28])

Should this logic be extended to substances with similar qualities? Figures 2–4 show the results of an experiment designed to test this.[29] Mixtures were constructed in the following way: Concentrations of four substances (e.g. acids) were selected to have perceived intensities about equal to a standard NaCl solution (0·1M NaCl). These were

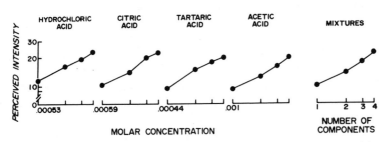

F<small>IG</small>. 2.   The four functions on the left show the perceived intensity (measured by magnitude estimation) of four acids as a function of concentration. Body-temperature stimuli were flowed across the tongue. The label at the left of the abscissa for each function gives the molar concentration of the weakest stimulus; the other stimuli were twice, three times and four times as concentrated, respectively. The function on the right is the mixture function (see text). The slopes of the best-fitting straight lines are: hydrochloric acid, 0·49; citric acid, 0·57; tartaric acid, 0·54; acetic acid, 0·54; and mixtures, 0·55. (From Bartoshuk and Cleveland.[29])

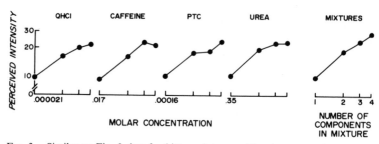

FIG. 3. Similar to Fig. 2, but for bitter substances. The slopes are: QHCl, 0·60; caffeine, 0·62; PTC, 0·56; urea, 0·60; and mixtures, 0·77. (From Bartoshuk and Cleveland.[29])

used to construct the six possible two-component mixtures, the four possible three-component mixtures, and the one possible four-component mixture. Of course, mixtures were not constructed by simply combining the component solutions, since this would dilute the solutes. For example, 0·07M sucrose contains 24·0 g of sucrose per litre of solution, and 0·12M fructose contains 21·6 g per litre of solution. A mixture of the two contains 24·0 g of sucrose and 21·6 g of fructose per litre of mixture. The average responses to the mixtures of one, two, three and four components make up the mixture function shown on the right side of each figure. The psychophysical functions constructed from one, two, three and four times each of the original concentrations of the four substances are shown on the left. The psychophysical functions of the unmixed components can be compared directly to the mixture function. In these figures, the psychophysical functions are plotted in log–log coordinates instead of linear coordinates. A log–log plot of a power function is a straight line with a slope equal to the exponent of the power function. The

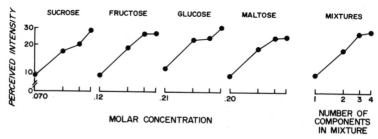

FIG. 4. Similar to Fig. 2, but for sugars. The slopes are: sucrose, 0·75; fructose, 0·78; glucose, 0·69; maltose, 0·70; and mixtures, 0·80. (From Bartoshuk and Cleveland.[29])

log–log plots in Figs. 2–4 are approximately straight lines, so the slopes of the lines approximately reflect the exponents of power functions relating concentration to perceived intensity. Thus in these figures a slope of less than one shows compression and a slope greater than one shows expansion.

Note that the mixture functions look much like the psycho-physical functions of the unmixed components. The slopes of the psychophysical functions and the mixture function are given in the legends under each figure. The mixture functions show suppression when their slopes are less than one just as the psychophysical functions of the unmixed components show compression when their slopes are less than one. These data suggest that the logic suggested in Fig. 1 extends at least to the substances tested here.

If the shapes of the psychophysical functions of the unmixed components predict mixture interactions, then changing the slopes should change the interaction. The slopes can be experimentally changed by changing the conditions under which the substances are tasted.[30] The data in Figs. 2–4 were collected by asking subjects to judge the taste of stimuli warmed to body temperature and flowed across the extended tongue. Figure 5 shows the results of repeating the experiment with sugars but with a different procedure: subjects sipped room temperature stimuli, judged them, then spit them into a receptacle. The slopes of the psychophysical functions in Fig. 5 are

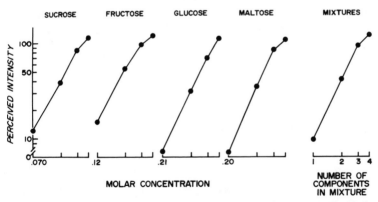

FIG. 5. The stimuli were the same as for Fig. 4, except that they were tasted with the sip-and-spit procedure; stimuli were at room temperature. The slopes are: sucrose, 1·67; fructose, 1·54; glucose, 1·97; maltose, 2·01; and mixtures, 1·87. The absolute values of perceived intensity for Figs. 4 and 5 cannot be compared directly but those in Figs. 2–4 can be so compared. (From Bartoshuk and Cleveland.[29])

greater than one, that is, they show expansion. The mixture function has a similar slope which means that the mixture tasted much stronger than the simple sum of the components (this is synergism). Thus, changing the slopes of the psychophysical functions for the unmixed sugars changed the mixture interactions. This is illustrated especially well by comparing the mixture of the four sugars with the simple sum of the unmixed sugars. The simple sum of the four unmixed sugars was 40 in both experiments. The perceived intensity of the mixture of all four sugars tasted with the flow procedure was 29. The perceived intensity of the same mixture tasted with the sip-and-spit procedure was 123. That is, the mixture was 0·7 times the simple sum with the flow procedure that produced compressed psychophysical functions, but was 3 times the simple sum in the sip-and-spit procedure which produced expanded psychophysical functions.

With hindsight, these results seem unsurprising. Pfaffmann[31] and Beidler[32] noted in the early sixties that magnitude of neural response did not usually increase in direct proportion to concentration. If substances with similar tastes affect the same receptor sites, then the neural responses to these substances would add along the concentration function typical of these receptor sites. If the function for the sites showed compression, then the mixture would show suppression. If the function for the sites showed expansion, then the mixture would show synergism.

On the other hand, a relation between compression and suppression in mixtures of substances with different qualities would be surprising indeed. Figures 6 and 7 show the results of experiments very similar to those above but conducted with mixtures of the four

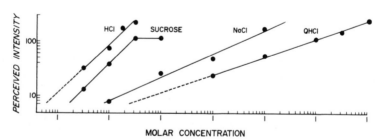

Fig. 6.   Perceived intensity of HCL, sucrose, NaCl, and QHCl as a function of concentration. The lowest concentrations are 0·003M HCl, 0·03M sucrose, 0·001M NaCl, and 0·00001M QHCL. Log units are marked along the abscissa. The slopes are: HCl, 0·89; sucrose, 0·67 (lower portion 0·94); NaCl, 0·43; and QHCl, 0·32. (From Bartoshuk.[28])

basic taste qualities. Figure 6 shows the psychophysical functions produced when hydrochloric acid (HCl), sucrose, sodium chloride (NaCl) and quinine hydrochloride (QHCl) are flowed across the tongue at body temperature. Note that all of the functions show compression (i.e. their slopes are less than 1·0) but HCl shows the least and QHCl the most compression. Figure 7 shows the perceived

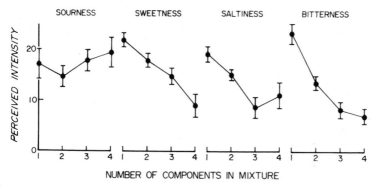

FIG. 7. Average perceived intensity ± 1 S.E.M. of each of the four taste qualities in mixtures of 1, 2, 3 and 4 components (see text). (From Bartoshuk.[28])

intensity of each of the four qualities in one- through to four-component mixtures. For example, the bitterness of QHCl alone is shown by the first point in the bitterness function, the average bitterness of all two-component mixtures containing QHCl is shown by the second point in the function, the average bitterness of all three-component mixtures containing QHCl is shown by the third point, and the bitterness of the four-component mixture is shown by the fourth point. The function shows that bitterness decreases as the number of components increases, that is, bitterness is suppressed in these mixtures. Note that HCl, which showed the least compression also showed the least suppression in the mixtures while QHCL which showed the greatest compression also showed the greatest suppression in the mixtures.

If these stimuli are tasted at room temperature with the sip procedure, the slope of the psychophysical function for HCl decreases and those for NaCl and sucrose increase to about 1·0. The mixture interactions change as well. Sourness decreases as the number of components increases and saltiness and sweetness remain about constant (Bartoshuk[33–35]).

The relation between the shape of the psychophysical function and mixture interactions requires much additional study. The shapes of the psychophysical functions can be altered in a variety of ways and the effects of the alterations on mixture interactions should be examined. The possibility of synergism in mixtures of substances with different taste qualities has not been investigated at all because no tasting conditions used in our laboratory have yet produced expanding functions for at least two substances with different taste qualities. This is an especially-important possibility to study. However, the results already reported show that Kiesow's 19th-century view of taste mixtures is inadequate. Kiesow believed that taste mixture interactions could be predicted from the perceived *qualities* of the components. We have shown instead that the *additive properties* of the components predict taste mixture interactions, that is, the way a substance adds to itself predicts how it will add to other substances.

The view of mixtures presented here may help explain some of the apparent contradictions in the mixture literature. Since investigators believed that the determinants of mixture interactions were the taste qualities of the components, they had no reason to control other variables like the method of tasting, temperature of solutions, and so forth. Since the conditions most important for interactions varied across experiments, conflicting results are not surprising. It should be noted that the suggested relation between mixture interactions and the shapes of the psychophysical functions of the unmixed components does not contradict previous experimental results. The experiments that led to the conclusion that simple additivity or synergism always occurs in mixtures of substances with similar tastes were run with tasting techniques that tend to produce power functions with exponents of 1·0 or greater. In our experiments, we deliberately chose some conditions that produce lower exponents in order to demonstrate that suppression would then result in the mixtures. In other words, we do not mean to contradict the existing data. We believe them to be sound and valuable; we offer an alternate interpretation of those data.

Taste-mixture interactions are obviously important because most taste stimuli outside of the laboratory are complex. Although no one can say for certain, the tasting conditions most often encountered outside the laboratory may well tend to produce psychophysical functions that are compressed. This would provide a kind of intensity constancy in taste experience. Complex tastes would not be systematically more intense than simple tastes. Conditions producing expanded functions would produce synergism but this phenomenon would be expected to be less frequently encountered than suppression.

TASTE MODIFIERS

Gymnema sylvestre

Gymnema sylvestre is a woody, climbing plant that runs over the tops of tall trees in parts of India and Tropical Africa.[36,37] Its effects on taste were first described to the Western world at a meeting of the Linnaean Society in 1847.[38] The description originated from a British Officer, Captain Edgeworth, and his wife who were located in India. They noted that chewing the leaves of this plant destroyed the ability to taste sweet substances for several hours but left intact the ability to taste other substances. This observation was challenged by laboratory studies[39-41] which suggested that the effects of *Gymnema sylvestre* were not specific to sweet; bitter and, to a lesser extent, salty were also affected.

The question of its specificity arose again when the effects of *Gymnema sylvestre* were re-examined with modern psychophysical methods.[42-46] The reduction of bitterness discovered by the 19th-century psychophysicists may well have been an artifact. Cross-adaptation was not understood in the 19th century so the tongue was not rinsed after exposure to the leaves. Thus, bitter substances in the leaves could have cross-adapted the bitter stimuli. Figure 8 shows that when the tongue was rinsed before stimuli were tested, *Gymnema sylvestre* substantially reduced the perceived intensity of sucrose but not QHCl, citric acid, HCl, or NaCl.[43,47] *Gymnema sylvestre* has been tested on substances with complex tastes as well as simple ones.[46] It abolished the sweet component of amino acids as would be expected but also altered the non-sweet components. Although this might seem to be evidence that the effects of *Gymnema sylvestre* are not specific to sweet, this is not the case. The mixture interactions discussed above would play a role in such an experiment. *Gymnema sylvestre* may have removed the interaction effects due to the sweetness of the amino acids when it removed the sweetness. A sucrose-adaptation control would help to resolve this issue.

Linda M. Bartoshuk

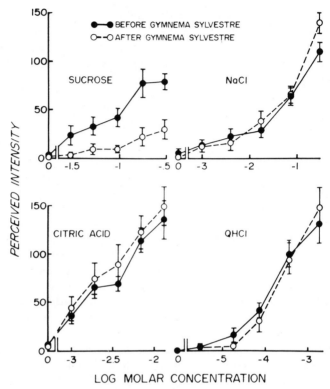

FIG. 8. Average perceived intensity ± 1 S.E.M. of sucrose, NaCl, citric acid and QHCl before and after exposure of the tongue to an extract of *Gymnema sylvestre* leaves. (From Bartoshuk.[47])

The effects of *Gymnema sylvestre* are species specific. It suppressed neural responses to sugars in the dog[48] and the hamster[49-52] but failed to do so in the squirrel monkey[53] and the African green monkey.[54] Although the specificity to sweet substances is unclear in non-human species, the hamster may show specificity much like that in Man.[52] *Gymnema sylvestre* suppresses neural responses to sugars and other substances in the rat[55,56] and housefly.[57]

The mechanism by which *Gymnema sylvestre* blocks the taste of sweet substances is not known although some form of site competition[58,59] seems most likely. Meiselman and Halpern[45] have shown that the effects take about 30 sec to reach maximum and may last longer than 50 min.

The exact structure of the active component of *Gymnema sylvestre* is not known. It is especially important to note that even the purified fractions used in the psychological research are not homogeneous.[60]

Synsepalum dulcificum (**miracle fruit**)

Synsepalum dulcificum is a densely-foliated bush, native to tropical west Africa, that produces deep red, oval berries about the size of Spanish peanuts. David Fairchild, an explorer for the US Department of Agriculture, sampled these berries on a trip to tropical west Africa and noted with astonishment that they caused his beer to taste sweet.[61] He suggested that the miracle fruit (as the berries have been commonly called for over 100 years[62]) worked by 'paralyzing' the sour receptors thus permitting the normal sweet tastes of beer and fruit to predominate. A more sophisticated version of this theory was later suggested by Dzendolet.[63] He suggested that miracle fruit blocked sour receptors and that acids subsequently tasted sweet because their anions tasted sweet (this was related to Dzondolet's proton-donor theory of sweetness[58]).

Figures 9 and 10 demonstrate the effects of miracle fruit on citric acid and HCl. Note that the perceived intensity of sourness is reduced and a sweet taste is added to both acids. If Dzendolet were correct, then treating the tongue with *Gymnema sylvestre* as well as miracle fruit should leave the acids tasting just slightly sour. Table 1 shows

TABLE 1
Sourness[a] of citric and hydrochloric acids

Experimental condition	0·014M Citric acid	0·013M HCl
Before miracle fruit	$100\cdot2 \pm 11\cdot7$	$108\cdot9 \pm 25\cdot8$
After miracle fruit	$16\cdot3 \pm 5\cdot6$	$45\cdot7 \pm 12\cdot2$
After miracle fruit and *Gymnema sylvestre*	$76\cdot9 \pm 19\cdot5$	$117\cdot6 \pm 14\cdot7$

[a] Sourness values are given $\pm$ S.E.M. (from Bartoshuk, Gentile, Moskowitz and Meiselman.[44])

that this does not happen. *Gymnema sylvestre* removes the sweetness induced by miracle fruit but the acids then taste about as sour as they normally do. This suggests that miracle fruit simply adds a sweet taste to substances that normally taste sour. The reduction in sourness appears to be an example of a mixture interaction. Figure 11 shows

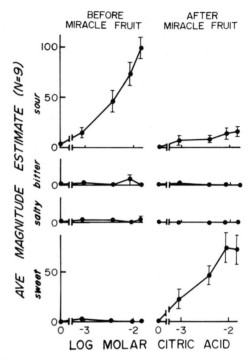

FIG. 9. Effects of miracle fruit on the taste of citric acid. Total taste is divided into sweet, salty, bitter, and sour components. (From Bartoshuk, Gentile, Moskowitz and Meiselman.[44])

additional evidence to support this conclusion. When either sucrose, L-arabinose, or D-xylose (the latter two sugars were chosen because of the role they play in the Kurihara–Beidler theory described below) were mixed with citric acid, the sourness of the acid decreased. Miracle fruit decreased the sourness of the citric acid to the extent that would be predicted by its sweetness.

The effects of miracle fruit, like *Gymnema sylvestre*, are species specific. Neural studies suggest that it may have effects similar to those in man in certain monkeys[64,54] but not in rats,[64] guinea pigs, pigs, rabbits,[54] or hamsters.[65]

The active component in miracle fruit is a glycoprotein.[66,67] Kurihara and Beidler[68] have suggested that the glycoprotein binds to the taste membrane near the sweet receptor site. Sugar groups attached to the glycoprotein (L-arabinose and D-xylose) are normally

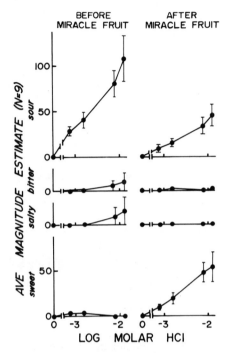

Fɪɢ. 10.   Similar to Fig. 9, but for HCl. (From Bartoshuk, Gentile, Moskowitz and Meiselman.[44])

unable to stimulate the sites. Acid produces a conformational change in the sweet receptor site such that the sugar groups can then stimulate the sweet receptor sites in the normal fashion. Although there is no direct experimental evidence for this view, it is consistent with the psychophysical observations described above.

Miracle fruit offers interesting potential as a non-nutritive sweetener. The US Food and Drug Administration has prohibited one company from marketing a miracle fruit based product in the United States on the grounds that it needed more tests. If miracle fruit is found to be safe, then it will be a very unconventional sugar substitute. Its use would be limited to only those situations where the addition of sweetness to sourness would be appropriate (e.g. fruit desserts) and it would be applied to the tongue not added to the food or beverage. The limitations on its use appear to this author to be an advantage. A variety of sweeteners each of use in only a limited

Linda M. Bartoshuk

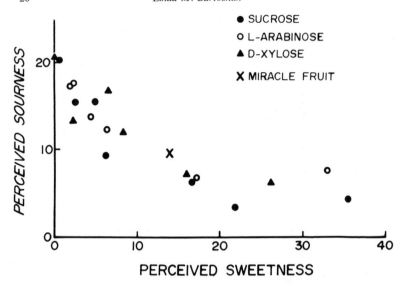

FIG. 11. Average perceived sweetness of different concentrations of sucrose, L-arabinose, and D-xylose added to 0·009M citric acid compared to the sweetness and sourness of 0·009M citric acid after miracle fruit. (From Bartoshuk.[47])

number of products would avoid dependence on one of them and also decrease the probability of over-ingesting a single sweetener.

Cynara scolymus (**globe artichoke**)

The globe artichoke is one of the oldest vegetables known to man. The Greek poet, Hesiod (700 BC), mentioned the artichoke in a pastoral poem on the seasons.[69]

> But when the artichoke is in flower,
> and the clamorous cricket
> sitting in his tree lets go his vociferous singing,
> that issues from the beating of his wings, in the exhausting
> season of summer;
> then is when goats are at their fattest,
> when the wine tastes best,
> women are most lascivious, but the men's strength fails them . . .

Eight hundred years later, the Roman scholar Pliny[70] apparently misunderstood Hesiod's poem and cited it as evidence that the artichoke was an aphrodisiac, an assertion viewed with some

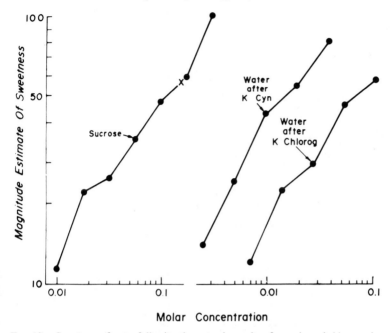

FIG. 12.   Sweetness of water following the potassium salts of cynarin and chlorogenic acid (artichoke constituents) compared to the sweetness of sucrose. (Modified from Bartoshuk *et al.*[73])

scepticism today. The artichoke was believed to have a variety of medicinal applications through the ages[71] but the earliest report of a taste modifying effect known to this author was that of Blakeslee.[72] Blakeslee described a banquet, designed to include taste tests, given for biologists at the 1934 meeting of the American Association for the Advancement of Science. The globe artichokes, eaten as the salad course, induced a taste (usually sweet) in water for 60% of the 250 people present.

Figure 12 shows a confirmation of the sweetness effect[73] and relates it to the potassium salts of cynarin and chlorogenic acid found in artichokes. The sweetness induced by artichokes correlates[74] with an effect described by Nagel[75] in 1896; exposure of the tongue to potassium chlorate induces a sweet taste in water.

The artichoke effect is a very dramatic example of an effect that has been under study in our laboratory for several years: the adaptation-induced water tastes. The taste of water is contingent on the nature of

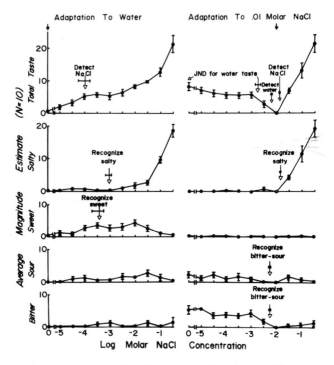

FIG. 13.   The taste of water and NaCl under two adaptation conditions: water and 0·01M NaCl (approximately equivalent to the Na^+ and Cl^- content of saliva). The top functions show the total taste intensity (± 1 S.E.M.). The lower functions show how the total is divided into salty, sweet, sour and bitter components. Appropriate threshold values (determined with the up–down procedure) are shown on each function. (From Bartoshuk.[78])

the substance that precedes it on the tongue.[33,76-78] For example, water tastes sweet when it follows a variety of acids, and bitter substances including caffeine and quinine. The sweet-water taste appears to be the easiest to produce.[76] Water tastes bitter when it follows sucrose and salty when it follows urea. Figure 13 shows one of the most behaviourally-important water tastes: the bitter–sour taste of water following NaCl.[78] Saliva contains NaCl in sufficient concentration in at least some individuals to produce a bitter–sour taste in water. This is apparently the origin of the bitter–sour taste believed by many to be intrinsic to distilled water (for example, see Brown[79]).

CONCLUSIONS

The phenomena described here are important because of the insight they provide into the sense of taste; however, they are of practical value as well. Foods from unconventional sources may become increasingly important as the world population grows. Taste research provides a description of the types of taste alterations that are possible through phenomena like mixture interactions as well as the more exotic modifiers like miracle fruit. Systematic study of taste modification will ensure that the necessary techniques to increase food palatability will be available when they are needed.

REFERENCES

1. Kiesow, F. (1894). *Phil. Stud.*, **10**, p. 523.
2. Öhrwall, H. (1901). *Skand. Archiv Physiol.*, **11**, p. 245.
3. Kiesow, F. (1894). *Phil. Stud.*, **10**, p. 329.
4. Kiesow, F. (1896). *Phil. Stud.*, **12**, p. 255.
5. McBurney, D. H. (1974). *Chem. Sen. Flav.*, **1**, p. 17.
6. Bartoshuk, L. M. (1975). In: *Appetite and Food Intake*, ed. T. Silverstone, Dahlem Konferenzen, Berlin.
7. Smith, D. V. and McBurney, D. H. (1969). *J. Exp. Psychol.*, **80**, p. 101.
8. McBurney, D. H., Smith, D. V. and Shick, T. R. (1972). *Percep. Psychophys.*, **11**, p. 228.
9. McBurney, D. H. (1972). *Percep. Psychophys.*, **11**, p. 225.
10. McBurney, D. H. and Bartoshuk, L. M. (1972). In: *Olfaction and Taste IV*, ed. D. Schneider, Wissenschaftliche Verlagsgesellschaft MBH, Stuttgart.
11. McBurney, D. H. and Bartoshuk, L. M. (1973). *Physiol. Behav.*, **10**, p. 1101.
12. Moskowitz, H. R. (1972). *Percep. Psychophys.*, **11**, p. 257.
13. Pangborn, R. M. (1960). *Food Res.*, **25**, p. 245.
14. Pangborn, R. M. (1961). *J. Food Sci.*, **26**, p. 648.
15. Beebe-Center, J. G., Rogers, M. S., Atkinson, W. H., and O'Connell, D. N. (1959). *J. Exp. Psychol.*, **57**, p. 231.
16. Fabian, F. W. and Blum, H. B. (1943). *Food Res.*, **8**, p. 179.
17. Kamen, J. M., Pilgrim, F. L., Gutman, N. J. and Kroll, B. J. (1961). *J. Exp. Psychol.*, **62**, p. 348.
18. Pangborn, R. M. (1962). *J. Food Sci.*, **27**, p. 495.
19. Pangborn, R. M. and Trabue, I. M. (1967). *Percep. Psychophys.*, **2**, p. 503.
20. Cameron, A. T. (1947). *The Taste Sense and the Relative Sweetness of Sugars and Other Sweet Substances*, Sugar Research Foundation, New York.

21. Stone, H. and Oliver, S. M. (1969). *J. Food Sci.*, **34**, p. 215.
22. Yamaguchi, S., Yoshikawa, T., Ideda, S. and Ninomiya, T. (1970). *Agricul. Biol. Chem.*, **34**, p. 187.
23. Paul, T. (1921). *Chem. Zeit.*, **45**, p. 38.
24. Moskowitz, H. R. (1973). *J. Exp. Psychol.*, **99**, p. 88.
25. Moskowitz, H. R. (1973). In: *Sensation and Measurement*, eds. H. R. Moskowitz, B. Sharf and J. C. Stevens, Reidel, Dordrecht, The Netherlands.
26. Yamaguchi, S. (1967). *J. Food Sci.*, **32**, p. 473.
27. Moskowitz, H. R. (1974). *J. Exp. Psychol.*, **4**, p. 640.
28. Bartoshuk, L. M. (1975). *Physiol. Behav.*, **14**, p. 643.
29. Bartoshuk, L. M. and Cleveland, C. T. (1977). *Sen. Proc.*, in press.
30. Meiselman, H. L. (1971). *Percep. Psychophys.*, **10**, p. 15.
31. Pfaffmann, C. (1959). In: *Handbook of Physiology*, Vol. I, Sect. 1, ed. J. Field, American Physiological Society, Washington, D.C.
32. Beidler, L. M. (1961). *Prog. Biophys. Biophys. Chem.*, **12**, p. 107.
33. Bartoshuk, L. M. (1968). *Percep. Psychophys.*, **3**, p. 69.
34. Bartoshuk, L. M. (1975). *Physiol. Behav.*, **14**, p. 643.
35. Bartoshuk, L. M., unpublished work.
36. Chopra, R. N. (1933). *Indigenous Drugs of India*, The Art Press, Calcutta.
37. Mhaskar, K. S. and Caius, J. F. (1930). *Ind. Med. Res. Mem.*, **16**, p. 1.
38. Anonymous. (1847). *Pharm. J.*, **7**, p. 351.
39. Hooper, D. (1889). *Chem. News*, **59**, p. 159.
40. Shore, L. E. (1892). *J. Physiol.*, **13**, p. 191.
41. Kiesow, F. (1894). *Phil. Stud.*, **9**, p. 510.
42. Warren, R. M. and Pfaffmann, C. (1959). *J. appl. Physiol.*, **14**, p. 40.
43. Bartoshuk, L. M., Dateo, G. P., Vandenbelt, D. J., Buttrick, R. L. and Long, L. (1969). In: *Olfaction and Taste III*, ed. C. Pfaffman, Rockefeller U. Press, New York.
44. Bartoshuk, L. M., Gentile, R. L., Moskowitz, H. R. and Meiselman, H. L. (1974). *Physiol. Behav.*, **12**, p. 449.
45. Meiselman, H. L. and Halpern, B. P. (1970). *Physiol. Behav.*, **5**, p. 945.
46. Meiselman, H. L. and Halpern, B. P. (1970). *Physiol. Behav.*, **5**, p. 1379.
47. Bartoshuk, L. M. (1974). *Ann. N.Y. Acad. Sci.*, **237**, p. 279.
48. Andersson, B., Langren, S., Olsson, L. and Zotterman, Y. (1950). *Acta Physiol. Scand.*, **21**, p. 105.
49. Pfaffmann, C. and Hagstrom, E. C. (1955). *Am. J. Physiol.*, **183**, p. 651.
50. Hagstrom, E. C. (1957). Ph.D. Thesis, Brown University.
51. Yackzan, K. S. (1969). *Alab. J. Med. Sci.*, **6**, p. 455.
52. Pfaffmann, C. (1969). In: *Reinforcement and Behaviour*, ed. J. T. Tapp, Academic Press, New York.
53. Snell, T. C. (1965). Master's Thesis, Brown University.
54. Hellekant, G., Hagstrom, E. C., Kasahara, Y. and Zotterman, Y. (1974). *Chem. Sens. Flav.*, **1**, p. 137.
55. Oakley, B. (1962). Ph.D. Thesis, Brown University.
56. Makous, W., Nord., W., Oakley, B. and Pfaffmann, C. (1963). In: *Olfaction and Taste I*, ed. Y. Zotterman, Macmillan, New York.

57. Kennedy, L. M., Sturckow, B. and Waller, F. J. (1975). *Physiol. Behav.*, **14**, p. 755.
58. Dzendolet, E. (1969). *Percep. Psychophys.*, **6**, p. 187.
59. Faull, J. R., Reilly, P. D. and Halpern, B. P. (1970). Paper presented at the Eastern Psychological Association, Atlantic City, N.J.
60. Dateo, G. P. and Long, L. (1973). *J. Agric. Food Chem.*, **21**, p. 899.
61. Fairchild, D. (1931). *Exploring for Plants*, Macmillan, New York.
62. Daniell, W. F. (1852). *Pharm. J.*, **11**, p. 445.
63. Dzendolet, E. (1969). *Percep. Psychophys.*, **6**, p. 187.
64. Diamant, H., Hellekant, G. and Zotterman, Y. (1972). In: *Olfaction and Taste IV*, ed. D. Schneider, Wissenschaftliche Verlagsgesellschaft MBH, Stuttgart.
65. Harvey, R. J. (1970). Ph.D. Thesis, Worcester Polytechnic Institute.
66. Kurihara, K. and Beidler, L. M. (1968). *Science*, **161**, p. 1241.
67. Brouwer, J. N., Well, H. V. D., Francke, A. and Henning, G. J. (1968). *Nature*, **220**, p. 373.
68. Kurihara, K. and Beidler, L. M. (1969). *Nature*, **222**, p. 1176.
69. Hesiod. *Works and Days*. (1959). Trans. R. Wilt, University of Michigan Press, Ann Arbor.
70. Pliny. *Natural History*. (1951). Trans. W. H. S. Jones, Harvard University Press, Cambridge.
71. Turner, W. (1569). *The Seconde Parte of William Turner's Herball*, Arnold Birkman, Collen.
72. Blakeslee, A. F. (1935). *Science*, **81**, p. 504.
73. Bartoshuk, L. M., Lee, C. H., and Scarpellino, R. (1972). *Science*, **178**, p. 988.
74. Bartoshuk, L. M., unpublished work.
75. Nagel, W. A. (1896). *Zeit. Psychol. Physiol. Sinn.*, **10**, p. 235.
76. McBurney, D. H. and Shick, T. R. (1971). *Percep. Psychophys.*, **10**, p. 249.
77. McBurney, D. H. (1969). In: *Olfaction and Taste III*, ed. C. Pfaffmann, Pergamon, New York.
78. Bartoshuk, L. M. (1974). *J. Comp. Physiol. Psychol.*, **87**, p. 310.
79. Brown, W. (1914). *U. Calif. Pub. Psychol.*, **1**, p. 199.

DISCUSSION

Shallenberger: (during presentation of paper) What happens to the intensity of sweetness at low concentrations?

Bartoshuk: At low concentrations they are definitely not sweet.

Questioner: How did you measure the perceived intensity?

Bartoshuk: Magnitude estimation.

Questioner: Were some samples mixtures?

Bartoshuk: Yes, but the panellists never knew that. They had either 3 or 2 attempts at each and ratios were then calculated based on the answers they gave.

Schallenberger: Diverse commercial compounds were used in the samples. You assume that this diminishes the response but it doesn't.

Bartoshuk: On the basis of information about the pure compounds, I can predict what is going to happen in the mixture.

Questioner: Does the suppression of sweet taste work with non-sweet sugars?

Bartoshuk: It works with everything we have tried.

Palmer: What are your views on Gregson's experiment in which tasters divided into two groups—'analytic' and 'gestalt'—were asked to say how sweet a sweet sherry was when, unknown to the tasters, citric acid was added.

Bartoshuk: I repeated this work using fruit acids: this causes masking of odour. Some people get enhancement and some inhibition but we must look at the normal distribution. It would be interesting to use controls. Sherry is a very complex substance to use.

Dirinck: When an apple ripens it turns from acid to sweet. Panel evaluations and chemical analyses indicated that this was due to changes in titratable acidity and not to changes in sugar content. Don't you have results from acid–sugar mixtures which could demonstrate this drastic change in sweet–acid ratio in a ripening apple?

Palmer: When you work in the food industry you have to use these complex products.

Bartoshuk: When doing research you have to use basic things.

Questioner: People take varying amounts of salt in their diet. Have you correlated this with the composition of their saliva?

Bartoshuk: What a lovely idea! Salt intake is complicated by many factors, e.g. hypertension lowers the salt threshold.

Questioner: But what about normal people?

Bartoshuk: Firstly, 10% of the population suffer from hypertension. We do try to use 'ordinary' people for measurements but it is very difficult with so few subjects.

Questioner: Has anyone looked at the active substances in glucose syrups?

Bartoshuk: Yes. It has been studied chemically since the nineteenth century. A variety of people have worked on this. A recent work by George Dadiel shows that glucose syrup is not homogeneous.

2

Colour and Appearance as Dominating Sensory Properties of Foods

F. J. FRANCIS

*Department of Food Science and Nutrition,
University of Massachusetts, USA*

ABSTRACT

Colour (and general appearance) is one of the most important visual attributes in food. Often, if the appearance is unattractive, a potential consumer may never experience the other two major attributes (flavour and texture).

Colour in a food may be measured by an analysis of the light reflected from a surface or transmitted through the food. The interpretation of pure reflection or transmission spectra in terms of how the human eye interprets colour is relatively straightforward and has been the subject of very intensive research over the past half-century. However, many foods are not completely opaque nor completely transparent; thus many of the rigorous colorimetric equations have had to be modified when applied to foods.

It is possible for an optical engineer to design a colorimeter to duplicate the response of the human eye with a relatively simple arrangement. The key elements are three filters which duplicate the red, green and blue response of the human eye, which when combined with a photocell in the appropriate geometry, comprise a simple colorimeter. Later refinements are merely in stability, closer adherence to the visual standard curves, convenience, etc. With the development of computers which minimised the labour input and increased the accuracy of calculation, spectrophotometric methods have become more feasible. A more recent introduction is the development of specialised colour scales to allow measurement of colour in a manner related to consumer acceptance of a particular product. Other recent developments are colour scales to allow measurement of both colour and pigment content of a given food.

INTRODUCTION

Colour is one of the three major quality attributes in food. The author admits to being biased but if the colour is unattractive a consumer may never get to judge the other two attributes (flavour and texture). This paper is addressed to the state of the art of food colorimetry.

The human eye is a very sensitive organ—it can detect up to 10 000 000 different colours. Some instrument makers have complained that this sensitivity is unfair competition, but in nature's realm, perhaps Man should be humble. Colour as seen by the human eye is an interpretation by the brain of the character of light coming from an object.[1] A number of complex mathematical and physical systems have been developed to illustrate the measurement of colour. Perhaps a description of this development of science would be appropriate.

THE CONCEPTS OF A COLORIMETER

A colorimeter is an instrument to reproduce optically and electronically the physiological sensation of the human eye. A colorimeter measures colour as such and is not to be confused with the earlier use of the word colorimeter in chemical analysis. Instruments used for estimating the amount of a chemical are called colour

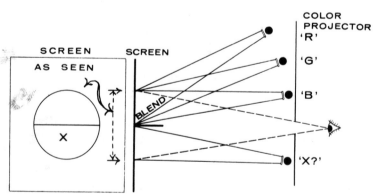

FIG. 1. Colour matching by the addition of lights. Screen is seen on edge and, to the left, in full view. Arrows indicate area on screen illuminated by lights used for matching (top half of circle) and light to be matched (bottom half, marked X). Blending is accomplished by varying the intensity of light from each projector of a primary colour; it occurs where the three beams overlap and the word 'BLEND' appears.

comparators and absorptiometers. Spectrophotometers can, of course, be used for both chemical analysis and calculation of colour coordinates.

The design of a modern colorimeter can best be understood by an analogy to the way the human eye sees colour. We have two anatomically distinct types of receptors in the human eye—the rods and cones. The rods are concerned with black and white vision in dim light and have no colour function. There are three types of cones in the human retina: one sensitive to red, one to blue and the other to green. They are anatomically indistinguishable and it was only eleven years ago that physical evidence was obtained that they were different even though Helmholtz had postulated 90 years ago that they had to be different. The human eye receives light reflected from an object to the retina and a signal from each type of cone is sent to the brain. The brain interprets the signals and assigns a 'colour' to the object.

A simple colorimeter can be designed to duplicate the response of the human eye.[2] In Fig. 1, three projectors with a red, green and blue filter, respectively, in front of the lens, shine a coloured beam on a screen. Another projector with a filter of unknown colour is projected

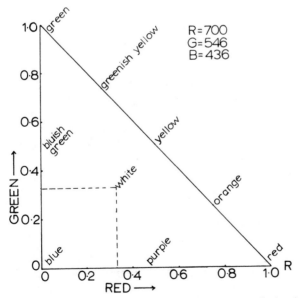

FIG. 2. A right-angled GRB chromaticity diagram (Maxwell triangle).

on the same screen. If the operator can vary the amount of red, green and blue light reaching the screen, he can match almost any colour. Then the unknown colour can be described by the amount of red, green and blue required to match it (Fig. 2). This principle has been used in several visual colorimeters to define the fundamental colour solid. The colorimeter itself is too crude for everyday use but the data can be used to define a much more appropriate colour solid. The

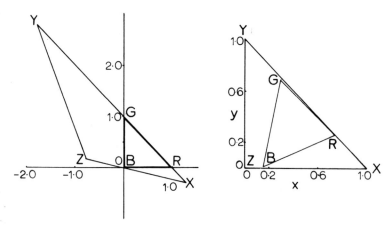

Fig. 3.   Transformation of the GRB to the XYZ chromaticity diagrams. The right diagram is the XYZ obtuse triangle transformed into a right-angled triangle.

triangle in Fig. 2 is shown in the left-hand portion of Fig. 3 and a new set of stimuli called XYZ are shown. The green-red-blue primaries are physically realisable in the laboratory whereas the XYZ primaries are not. The XYZ points were chosen for mathematical convenience and the fact that they cannot be made physically does not detract from their usefulness. Although it is not quite true, for ease of remembering, the X value may be considered as a degree of redness, Z blueness and Y greenness. The Y value also carries all the brightness factor. In the right-hand side of Fig. 3, the coordinate axes are shifted until the XYZ triangle is right-angled and of course the GRB is distorted. The XYZ diagram is accepted world wide as the fundamental colour solid. Every realisable colour will have three coordinates which locate the point within the colour solid. When one says 'measure the colour', one is asking for the three coordinates which locate a point in space.

THE DESIGN OF A COLORIMETER

The problem in designing a colorimeter to duplicate the response of the human eye can be appreciated with the set-up in Fig. 1. We can shine a spectral colour, say a blue of 400 nm, on the screen and ask the operator to match it with his red, green and blue controls. We can repeat the process for 410 nm and so on through the spectrum. The

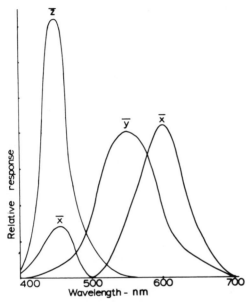

FIG. 4.   The CIE tristimulus values of the standard observer for the equal energy spectrum.

data obtained can be transformed from GRB units to XYZ units and plotted as in Fig. 4. The curves obtained will represent how the human eye sees the spectral colours. This information is all an optical engineer requires to design an instrument to duplicate the response of the human eye. A set of glass filters with transmission curves shaped like those in Fig. 4 are shown in Fig. 5 in a simple colorimeter. A photocell and meter can be used to take a reading of the light reflected from an object through each filter in turn and the readings are the XYZ values of the object. Every colorimeter uses this basic principle.

There are many types of colorimeters available which can be used to measure colour in a number of different mathematical systems. The

F. J. Francis

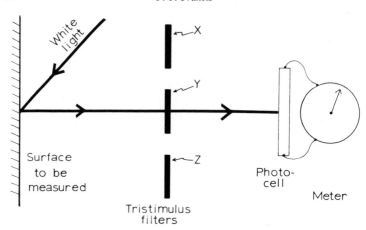

FIG. 5. A simple tristimulus colorimeter.

choice of instrument and colour solid and the interconversions of one system to another may be bewildering to a newcomer but they are all based on the same principle. One system, called the CIE (Commission Internationale d'Eclairage) has been adopted world wide as the universal system. Its units are X, Y, Z.

DEVELOPMENT OF INSTRUMENTATION

The measurement of colour from a visual approach was developed nearly a century ago. The Lovibond Tintometer is an example of its highest development in a commercially-available instrument. From an electronic and/or mechanical approach, the development of colorimetry is much more recent having started essentially about 50 years ago. Hardy set out to develop a spectrophotometer to measure colour in terms of a reflection or transmission curve integrated over the visual spectrum and modified by the type of illumination and the visual response curves of the standard observer (Fig. 6). He developed the Hardy recording spectrophotometer (later called the General Electric recording spectrophotometer and still later the Diano–Hardy recording spectrophotometer). It is remarkable that this instrument is still the reference instrument for colorimetry today. The Hardy instrument made it possible to obtain an accurate transmission or reflection spectrum, which could be used to calculate accurate XYZ

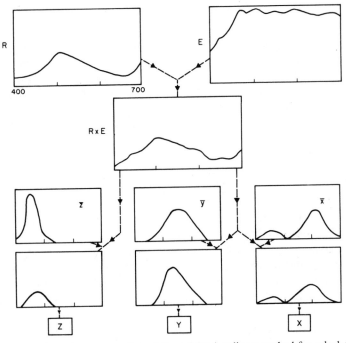

FIG. 6. Schematic representation of the weighted ordinate method for calculating tristimulus values.

values. However, the calculations were tedious requiring about a half-hour for each sample. Thus, cams were developed to integrate mechanically the areas under the curves and the XYZ values were obtained automatically. In later years, the mechanical cams were replaced by electronic integrators and automatic tristimulus integrators became generally available. One good example is the Davidson and Hemmendinger Tristimulus Integrator.

The combination of a spectrophotometer and an integrator worked very well. They were accurate, convenient and, unfortunately, expensive. A Diano–Hardy instrument with integrator today costs over $50 000. In past years, they were beyond the reach of a number of potential users. Consequently, makers of conventional chemical-type spectrophotometers made reflection attachments available. They worked well but were too tedious for most colorimetric work. This was the main reason for the development of the tristimulus colorimeters in the 1940s and 1950s. They removed the labour of

F. J. Francis

. calculation of colour data from spectra and enabled tristimulus data to be obtained in a matter of less than a minute per sample. This made it possible to use colorimeters as convenient tools for studying colorimetric changes and many more papers appeared in the literature. Empirical methods for measuring the colour of many foods were developed and this important quality control tool took its place alongside many others.

The colorimeters were convenient but some of them lacked flexibility and some were possibly less accurate than desired. Consequently, in the 1970s, another development appeared on the scene. It was the labour of calculation which contributed to the earlier demise of the spectrophotometric approach, and the development of digital computers has brought it back. Manual calculations could not cope for example, with a number of the very complicated formulae for calculating colour differences, but this factor was completely removed with access to a modern computer. It is just as easy to program a computer to solve a very complicated equation as a very simple one. Industrial and academic research laboratories either have their own computers or have telephone access to a computer service.

The development and ease of access to large computers and the possibility of building minicomputers into a colorimeter have led to a new concept of colorimetry. For example, one of the earliest was the development of a tomato colorimeter.[3] A great deal of research in the 1950s in the US was devoted to the development and interpretation of methods of measuring the colour of tomatoes and tomato products. The prime reason was that colour was associated with quality and processors wanted a method of paying growers for producing higher quality raw fruit. Also, purchasers of tomato products wanted more accurate quality specifications on the finished products. The research on the relationship of the colour of raw tomatoes to the USDA quality grades was developed using a Hunter Colour and Colour Difference meter. The equation relating colour and USDA grade turned out to be:

$$\text{Tomato colour} = \frac{2000 \cos \theta}{L}$$

θ is the angle that the point a, b in Hunter units makes with the origin, i.e. the angle with the horizontal axis. L is 'lightness' in the Hunter system.

$$\text{or in CIE terms} = \frac{21 \cdot 6}{(Y)^{1/2}} - \frac{3 \cdot 0}{(Y)^{1/2}} \left[\frac{Y - Z}{X - Y} \right]$$

An instrument, the tomato colorimeter, was developed to read out the above equation directly. It soon became obvious that a minicircuit could be incorporated into a regular Hunter colorimeter so today one can read the tomato colour with another switch on a regular instrument. A similar situation exists for the relationship between the colour of raw tomato juice and the processed juice. The equation in this case is bL/a which can be easily programmed in another minicircuit. The correlation of the bL/a score with visual judgements is only 0·902. Yeatman[4] suggested that the correlation could be improved by increasing the number of variables 'plugged-in' the equation. With modern microcircuits, this presents no difficulty.

DEVELOPMENT OF COLOUR SCALES

The availability of rapid calculation has been a boon to colorimetrists in many ways. One obvious way is to facilitate calculation of colour differences. They have always been important from an industrial point of view since the question as to whether a colour difference between two samples was below the 'Just Noticeable Difference' (JND) or not. Manufacturers making different portions of, say, a refrigerator in different factories wanted to know whether they would look different or not when they were assembled. Colour purchase specifications became very important and a number of complicated colour difference equations were developed to calculate JNDs. Unfortunately, the XYZ colour solid does not have visually-uniform differences in colour in all portions of the solid. Actually, when a modern computer was programmed to develop a colour solid which would have visually uniform colour differences in three dimensions over the whole solid, it was concluded that it was impossible. The earlier research workers, who were attempting to develop colour difference formulae sensed this and included in their formulae calibration factors for different portions of the colour solid. They developed graphical methods to solve their colour-difference formulae in view of the complexities of the calibrations. These graphical methods worked well but the built-in assumptions led to some inaccuracies. Later workers, who were not concerned with the degree of computational labour, developed more complicated equations, which necessitated the use of a computer. Today, nearly all

F. J. Francis

recommended methods for calculation of colour differences require a high-speed computer.

The development of more accurate equations for calculation of colour differences automatically led to the development of new colour solids and consequently new colour scales. In earlier years, the scales had to be relatively simple for practical use but this constraint has been removed. For example, there have been several modifications of the scales developed by Hunter for use with the early versions of the Hunter colour meter. One example can be taken from the measurement of colour in transparent liquids. The conventional L, a, b scales used in the Hunter colour meter were developed primarily for reflection purposes and adopted for transmission measurements. For dilute coloured solutions, they work fairly well but for more concentrated solutions, the application breaks down. Figure 7 shows a plot of colour parameters against concentration of pigments. An 'area of confusion' exists between 1 and 2 mg/ml of pigment in which the plot changes direction. A similar situation occurs with the b plot. Eagerman *et al.*[6] tested eleven common colour scales for their ability to rank a pigment dilution series. Only two were able to rank correctly solutions in the luminosity range of a number of dark fruit juices on

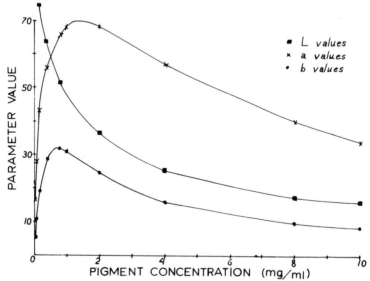

FIG. 7. Plot of Hunter L, a, b values versus pigment concentration for aqueous solutions of cyanidin-3-glucoside (the major pigment in blackberry juice).[5]

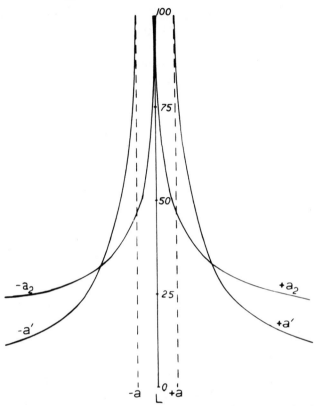

FIG. 8. Plot of the conventional 'a' scale and the expanded 'a''' and 'a_2' scales. L = luminosity.[2]

the market. None were satisfactory for the dark juices, when used with a 10 mm cell depth. Hunter attempted to improve this situation by developing a new set of scales (CR + CY) which expanded the readings at the lower luminosity levels.[7] These scales were incorporated into the citrus colorimeter. Hunter also developed another set of scales (L, a', b') which further expanded the readings at the low luminosity levels.[8] Employing the same logic, Eagerman *et al.*[9] introduced a simple modification to the L, a', b' scales to expand the lower end even more. The new scales were termed L, a_2, b_2 and the a_2 value was represented by the equation:

$$a_2 = \frac{170\,(1\cdot02\,X - Y)}{Y^2}$$

A plot showing the relative expansion of the a' and a_2 scales compared with a is shown in Fig. 8. Figure 9 shows a plot of a_2 for four colorant systems.[9] Obviously the areas of confusion have disappeared and the plots are relatively straight. It is a simple step to expand this reasoning to calculate the equations which would produce straight lines. A

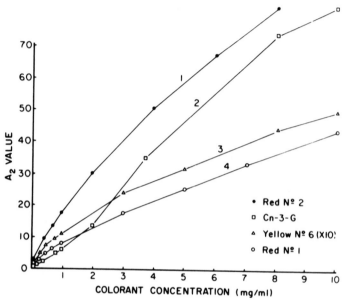

FIG. 9. Plot of the 'a_2' scale versus pigment concentration for four colorants.[9] Cn-3-G = cyanidin-3-glucoside.

computer was programmed to develop the line of best fit for each of the other pigments. An example for Red #2 is shown in Fig. 10. The equation turned out to be:

$$a^* = \frac{100\,X}{Y^{2\cdot30} - 0\cdot5}$$

Similarly, equations for a^* and b^* were calculated for five other colorants. Each pigment required its own equation for greatest accuracy in predicting pigment concentration.

The next step was to evaluate the ability of the new scales to correlate with visual responses. Johnson *et al.*[10] tested the relationship of scales:

$$a^* = \frac{170(1 \cdot 02\,X - Y)}{Y^{1 \cdot 60} + 200}$$

developed for cranberry juice cocktail and visual responses. The new scales correlated very highly for both anthocyanin concentration and visual rank. This makes it possible to use a colorimeter for quality

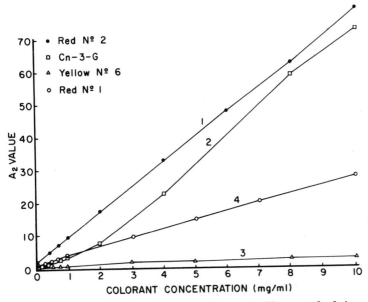

FIG. 10. Plot of the line of best fit for Red #2 (curve #1). The curves for 2–4 were plotted using the same equation. Cn-3-G = Cyanidin-3-glucoside.

control for both applications. One disadvantage is that the equations would have to be developed and then programmed for each application and this might make intercomparisons of data more difficult since mathematically one would have to deal with many more units. This may be the price one has to pay for increased accuracy.

The new scales are only necessary when the ratio of absorbance to transmittance is very high. Otherwise, i.e., in light coloured or dilute solutions, the conventional scales work very well. It would seem easier to use a thinner cell for measurement and raise the luminosity level. Unfortunately, we do not usually see beverages in such thin layers and the extrapolations are not reliable.

GENERAL APPLICATIONS

The exercise in scale development for particular applications may seem to be a complicated way of approaching specialised situations. It may well be and nearly all food applications might be considered special applications. The decision as to whether a generalised or a specialised approach is necessary may well depend on the end use of the data.

The conventional colour measurement approaches were developed for either completely reflecting or completely transmitting materials, and the equations for these applications are rigorous. Unfortunately, most foods are neither completely reflecting nor transmitting. They are a combination of the two, and in some cases the colour can be measured by either mode. The rigorous colour equations cannot hold in these intermediate cases and thus the measurement methods have a degree of empiricism in nearly every case. If the error involved in using conventional scales is small, then a sample can merely be placed on a colorimeter and colour readings obtained. Many factors will influence colorimeters in a different way. This has led to 'calibrations' of instruments in terms of visual responses. Two of the major factors affecting visual judgements are absorption and scattering. These have been termed the K and S coefficients in the Kubelka–Munk equations. They have been very useful in calculating amounts of pigments required to match a given colour in the paint, plastic and textile fields. Foods may be classified in terms of their K and S values and they may be useful in classifying foods as to the choice of colour measurement.[11-14] Again, the calculations are rather complicated for manual operations.

Colour measurement, by definition, refers to light coming from an object and reacting with the human eye. The eye and brain are capable of interpreting many object–light interactions in a manner meaningful to the eye. Some of these interactions are reflection, refraction transmission, diffusion, absorption, scattering, polarisation, fluorescence, and interference, and may be more or less important, but they all affect the colour to some degree. A detailed discussion of these aspects is beyond the scope of this paper and may be found elsewhere.[15]

It is difficult to predict the future course of development in methodology of colour measurement. However, it is likely that several fundamental systems of sample presentation combined with a conventional read-out will be standardised. These may be augmented by simple plug-in minicircuits to convert the read-out to specific scales designed for particular applications.

ACKNOWLEDGEMENTS

Contribution No. 2140 from the Univ. Mass. Agric. Expt. Station, Amherst. Appreciation is expressed to the Glass Container Manufacturers Inst., Washington, D.C. for financial support.

REFERENCES

1. Francis, F. J. and Clydesdale, F. M. (1975). *Food Colorimetry: Theory and Applications*, Avi Publ. Co., Westport, Conn. p. 61.
2. *ibid.*, p. 73.
3. Hunter, R. S. and Yeatman, J. N. (1961). *J. Opt. Soc. Amer.*, **51**, p. 552.
4. Yeatman, J. N. (1969). *Food Technol.*, **23**, p. 618.
5. Francis, F. J. and Clydesdale, F. M. (1975). *Food Colorimetry: Theory and Applications*, Avi Publ. Co., Westport, Conn., pp. 15, 46.
6. Eagerman, B. A., Clydesdale, F. M. and Francis, F. J. (1973). *J. Food Sci.*, **38**, p. 1051.
7. Hunter, R. S. (1967). *Food Technol.*, **21**, p. 906.
8. Hunter, R. S. (1969). Personal communication.
9. Eagerman, B. A., Clydesdale, F. M. and Francis, F. J. (1973). *J. Food Sci.*, **38**, p. 1056.
10. Johnson, L. E., Clydesdale, F. M. and Francis, F. J. (1976). *J. Food Sci.*, **41**, p. 74.
11. Gullett, E. A., Francis, F. J. and Clydesdale, F. M. (1971). *J. Food Sci.*, **37**, p. 389.
12. Huang, I. Lo, Francis, F. J. and Clydesdale, F. M. (1970). *J. Food Sci.*, **35**, p. 315.
13. *ibid.*, p. 771.
14. Little, A. C. and Mackinney, G. (1969). *Food Technol.*, **23**, p. 25.
15. Francis, F. J. and Clydesdale, F. M. (1975). *Food Colorimetry: Theory and Applications*, Avi Publ. Co., Westport, Conn., p. 170.

DISCUSSION

Harper: How would you handle heterogeneously-coloured surfaces?
Francis: Instruments work on a very small surface and there is therefore a sampling problem. This used to be done by rotating.

Now large area applicators are available, you can get a big surface. Most of the equipment does give at least adequate sample sizes. You must also take account of particle size, light, etc. You also have adaptation problems. The area is wide open in terms of point of view. Do not blend colours—it is misleading. Measure in the way the eye is going to see it. Be well aware of the concept of adaptation. This is a very fair question to pose.

Moskowitz: Researchers in psychophysics (e.g. Indow and Stevens) have shown that there is a non-linear relation between saturation and subjective saturation. (The function is empirically a power function.) Could you develop a computer programme that reads out both physical and sensory colour and saturation? And of course could you then develop an additional programme to read out acceptability (which can probably be related to a quadratic function of *subjective* saturation)? In all colour systems you can transform from one system to another via linear equations. Mathematically, you are on solid ground. On the other hand, suppose you map subjective saturation versus XYZ colour system, and you have psychological laws. Can you then transform these psychological laws *as easily* from laws based on the XYZ to laws based in CIE, etc. In short, therefore, can you have a parallel psychophysics of colour to complement your physics of colour, and will it have the same mathematical capabilities and properties?

Francis: You can read out CIE with any system. You can look at a point in space but what does it mean? With a simple system you can create a situation where it would be possible. As more work is done on the adaptation (relationship of eyes to background) it would be possible to programme it if you knew the laws relating to it. The laws are poorly defined.

Wiggall: To what extent can the gloss of a sample be assessed, as opposed to its colour, using the techniques described?

Francis: Most foods are between transparent and reflecting. We may plot a degree of scattering and a degree of absorption. If you calculate degree of scattering and absorption and put this on top of regular CIE read-out we can programme a function that gives a high degree of correlation. But the mathematics are not really worth it. The problem is developing the degree of gloss. We could try but there is not a simple way of measuring gloss quantitatively.

Land: Most foods are not uniform in colour or appearance. How can you instrumentally distinguish between differences in appearance due to non-uniformity?

Francis: You cannot! You may create two physical systems which are visually different but will give you an identical read-out. It is up to the ingenuity of the eye and the brain. The eye has a brain behind it and can tell you many things. It will make the judgement you want it to make. Instrumentally, you have to put more information into the system. How much science can you put into the measure of appearance? There is no reason why you cannot take a scan like a TV projector and get a read-out. This has never been put on the market but we think scanning can be electronically capable of that.

Jowitt: Would Professor Francis care to comment on the measurement of specular reflectance—an important appearance factor in foods in its own right—and of influence in the measurement of colour?

Francis: The consumer does not have a computer under her arm! Most people look at the product and this is the aim. There is no substitute for common sense. If I cannot see a colour difference there is no point in measuring it. I would look at it and rotate it and I could tell if there was a slight difference in colour.

3

The Importance of Visual Appearance of Foods to the Food Processor and the Consumer

J. B. HUTCHINGS

Unilever Research Laboratories, Sharnbrook, Bedford, England

ABSTRACT

Many individual factors contribute to the total perception of the appearance of a food product. This total perception is built up from all the visual sensations experienced when a product is viewed on the shelf, as it is being prepared and when it is presented on the plate, and all three situations are extremely important to the consumer and hence to the processor. The food technologist is now being asked to fabricate foods like steak from vegetable protein, yet at the same time is coming under increasing pressure to reduce the number and level of 'additives' in processed foods. These factors have forced us to consider objectively the whole philosophy of product appearance.

The paper begins by considering Kramer's views on sensory attributes and how these attributes are influenced by time and order of perception: the role of appearance is then discussed in relation to the total sensory experience of a product. The factors comprising appearance can be divided into three broad classes: the product's optical properties, its physical form and its mode of presentation, all of which combine at different times and in different ways to form the three images of any product, viz. on the shelf, in the pan, and on the plate. This formalisation of appearance science provides a framework against which both product technology and marketing can be discussed.

INTRODUCTION

The first impression of a food is usually visual, and a major part of our willingness to accept a food depends on its appearance. Appearance is

45

a compound of all the information about the product and its environment which reaches the eye.

Unfortunately the word 'colour' has superseded 'appearance' as the description of the total visual perception of foods. This was almost tolerable in the food industry as long as the food technologist was concerned with the changes accompanying relatively minor manipulations of natural foods, for example the effects due to storage or simple processing treatments. The change occurring was treated as a change in 'colour' even though, as is often the case in fish processing for example, the change could be entirely due to translucency effects. The technologist is now concerned with the fabrication of foods like steak made from vegetable protein, thus he is concerned even more with total appearance, including factors like size and shape, and not with colour alone. The food technologist is also under pressure to reduce the number of additives in processed foods, and so there is less opportunity to manipulate product attributes merely by the addition of colours.

The science of food colour has attracted consistent attention over the last twenty years[1] and an excellent survey has been published recently.[2] Hunter has long pioneered the physical specification of appearance[3] comprising colour, opacity and gloss. For the food industry this treatment can usefully be extended to include all the other factors which contribute to the total appearance of a product.

This paper contains an account of the place of appearance in the total human perception of food and then outlines the factors comprising it.

THE PLACE OF APPEARANCE IN TOTAL PERCEPTION

Kramer and Szczesniak[4] depict the sensory qualities of food in the form of a sensory circle. The perimeter of the circle is divided into three zones defined by the major senses: appearance as sensed by the eye, flavour as sensed by the papillae on the tongue and the olfactory epithelium of the nose, and kinesthetics, or texture, sensed by the muscle endings. Although these three senses may be regarded as separate and individual, the perceptions are not, that is, some properties overlap and can be perceived in different ways by more than one sense. Hence, the circle is a convenient way of visualising the total situation.

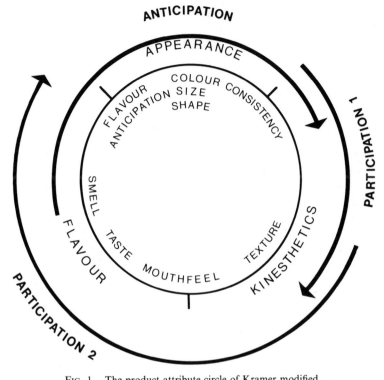

FIG. 1. The product attribute circle of Kramer modified.

The three zones merge into each other with consistency/visual
viscosity on the appearance/kinesthetics boundary, and mouthfeel on
the kinesthetics/flavour boundary. Kramer labelled the third region
of overlap 'defects' but the designation 'the anticipation of flavour
associated with appearance' or 'flavour expectation' is better suited to
our purpose. Product properties are thus regarded as a continuum
ordered according to perception and method of perception.

Product attributes using Kramer's view are not static but change
for each perceiver and for every different product perceived. (This of
course includes the same product in different forms. The model of
attributes when the product is on the shelf is different from that when
the product is on the plate.) When a product is perceived on the plate,
the product attributes can be divided according to time of perception
between those which are 'anticipatory' and those which are
'participatory'. This can be seen in Fig. 1. The anticipatory attributes

comprise Kramer's 'appearance' sector together with the overlapping regions of 'flavour expectation' and 'visual consistency'. There are two groups of participatory attributes. The first to be perceived consists of those product properties which are discovered by tactile peripheral cues, such as cutting with a knife (steak) or shaking while still in the pot (yoghurt). The second participatory attribute consists of all in-mouth perceived attributes. Again these three groupings of attribute are not isolated and individual, but as consumption progresses there is continual 'feed-back' of information giving a running total impression of the product. Whatever may be the comparative importance of these groupings they do occur in order, and those judgements formed during the 'anticipatory' stage will influence those which will be made during the 'participatory' stage.

This paper regards 'appearance' as those qualities of the material which are perceived by the eye. Thus besides the properties derived from the material itself, 'appearance' must also include the properties of the environment of the product.

APPEARANCE ITSELF

We can now examine the appearance zone of the attribute circle in more detail. Kramer was more concerned with the place of 'texture' in the circle and did not discuss the appearance zone further. Appearance can be divided under three headings as depicted in Fig. 2. As the major senses overlap in their perception of some properties so none of the following classes is entirely independent of the others.

1. *Optical Properties.* Those which depend on chromatic or geometric modification of the light which is incident upon the material under consideration. These properties are colour, gloss, translucency, the uniformity of these attributes over the surface of the product, and the appearance boundary condition 'visual flavour'.

2. *Physical Form.* This class comprises those properties which depend on the physical form and visual texture of the material. Included are shape, size, irregularity of surface (including the presence of fibres and granularity) and gross 'textural' or consistency properties (like fluidity, wobbliness).

3. *Mode of Presentation* (*both on the shelf and the table*). This

**Product
appearance image**

Product attribute classes

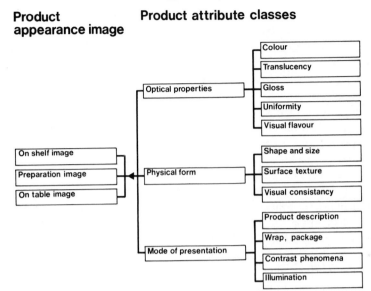

FIG. 2.   Product appearance attributes and images.

class includes those properties of the marketed product which
are due to the way the material is presented. This comprises
such variables as lighting of the material, contrast phenomena, product name, wrap and price.

These attribute classes, usually in combination, will comprise the
three product images: these are the 'on the shelf', the 'preparation' and
the 'on the table' images. These images lead directly to the key
decisions of 'buy or not to buy' and 'eat or not to eat'.

Where food products are concerned all three groups are vitally
important to the technological success in production and the
marketing success in selling. We shall now consider them in slightly
more detail but this further amplification will be kept in general terms
using non-mathematical terminology.

Class 1. Optical Properties
This class comprises *colour, gloss, translucency*, uniformity of
these three parameters and visual flavour.

Perception of colour (and of appearance generally) is a phenomenon unique to the individual and any attempt at standardisation or

even communication of colour must imply an agreement on the definition of the 'standard observer'. This is essential as about 8 % of the population have vision which is abnormal in an easily demonstrable way.[5] Similarly, because the colour of an object changes with illumination, standard light sources must be defined so that effective communication between observers can take place. Any sensory or instrumental work involving colour must take into account these important basic principles.

Gloss is the second optical property to be considered as playing an important part in object appearance. The perception of gloss suffers from none of the limitations applying to colour perception. Normally there are only geometrical considerations of angles of incident and reflected light beams to be taken into account, the effect being largely independent of the nature of the incident light and of the observer (human or electronic), as long as the radiation and the detector are compatible in terms of wavelength and intensity. The presence of a glossy surface affects the perceived colour by diluting it with the colour of the illuminating light. Thus the perceived colour of the surface changes with angles of illumination and viewing.

Translucency is the third optical property. Many materials are not opaque and possess a quality of translucency (which is somewhere along a transparent-opaque scale). In foods this quality is usually appreciated in those products which are almost transparent in their own right, like beer and table jelly, or in those which are usually viewed as a thin layer, like apple sauce, jam, or slices of bacon. Light which is not specularly reflected, as occurs in a mirror, penetrates into the surface and when light is passed through a translucent object absorption and/or scattering reduce the intensity.

All food materials contain colourants and scattering particles in different concentrations and the place of the material on the transparent to opaque scale is governed by the concentrations of both the colourant and the scatterer. A high concentration of either or both will lead to a material which looks opaque even when the sample is thin. The presence of absorbing and scattering material will of course determine the perceived *colour* as well as contribute to the perceived *translucency*. The additional factors normally necessary for the perception of translucency in translucent materials are either (1) the presence of a background which contains a contrast (viewing by reflected light) or (2) the known presence of a sufficient intensity of back lighting compared to surface lighting (viewing by transmitted light) (Fig. 3).

With foods the first mechanism (viewing by reflected light) is normally the most important; an exception is when a glass of wine or beer is held up to the light to examine its clarity.

In foods such as soup, tea, sauces and sliced meats, translucency is perceived because light enters the surface and is reflected from the vessel, and re-transmitted through the food. The contrasting

FIG. 3.   Conditions for translucency perception. Left: front illumination. Centre: no contrast. Right: back illumination.

background condition is obtained by patterns on the vessel or by varying depths of the food, as with tea in a cup. This is a most important class of attributes in the study of appearance as such attributes define major properties of the product itself.

Some foods, like fish, change appearance on storage not because of any degradation of colourant or pigment but because light scattering material is present. An example of the confusion which can exist concerns white coffee. A cup of brewed white coffee can contain a high concentration of light absorbing pigment or colorant (coffee solids) but appears to contain less if a significant amount of white, light scattering material (milk) is present.

Colour, gloss and translucency are capable of being specified using numbers which relate to the psychological response of the observer. With natural foods all three properties usually vary over the surface, therefore measurements have to be related to a particular area. These variations are very marked in ripening apples, for example, and an account of the distribution of optical properties must be included in a full description of a food product. This is because the very variation may be a fundamental character of the food. Hence uniformity of the foregoing three attributes is a class one attribute in its own right.

The optical properties, particularly colour, occur at the appearance/flavour interface where an anticipation of flavour is gained from the separate factors of appearance. An example of this is the green-coloured raspberry-flavoured jelly which was thought to taste of apple or gooseberry,[6] and it has also been shown that colour affects the threshold level at which different tastes are perceived.[7] The last Class 1 attribute is therefore visual flavour.

Class 2. Physical Form ·

The second class of product attribute can be described as physical form and this can be divided into three parts: *shape* and *size, surface texture* and *visual consistency.*

Product shape and size are obviously fundamental attributes which occur naturally with common products and difficulties only occur for the food technologist when he is attempting to fabricate natural-looking foods from more basic materials. Factors to be considered, for example, include the most desirable size and shape of fabricated apple pieces and whether fabricated beef steak will increase in acceptability if it is shaped like the genuine product.

Surface texture is an important quality of food appearance. Alignment of fibres in meat products, surface roughness of apple flesh, surface wrinkling of peas, and muscle structure of fish are all visual cues as to the quality and genuineness of the food.

FIG. 4.   Examples of visual consistency. Left: low viscosity. Centre: high viscosity. Right: gel.

Those products whose textural attributes can be suggested by their appearance can be said to have visual consistency and this forms the boundary region between appearance and kinesthetics. This can be a time-dependent phenomenon. The wobbliness of a jelly and the viscosity of syrup are properties which can be classed in this group. See, for example, Fig. 4.

Class 3. Mode of Presentation

This class of total product appearance, applicable both on the shelf and on the table, has four aspects:

1.   Product description, which includes the name and price.

2.   Wrap or package, which includes shape, design, colour, 'strikingness'.
3.   Contrast phenomenon of adjacent colours.
4.   Illumination.

All four aspects apply 'on the shelf' (the marketing mix), while the last two apply 'on the table'.

'The average housewife spends about twenty-seven minutes shopping in a supermarket and selects only fourteen items out of a possible 6300. More than 75 % of all purchases are made on impulse so the package must be able to catch the housewife's eye in less than one second.[8]

Stanley Sacharow[8] and Jane Wheatley[9] have outlined the principles, as they see them, of packaging design and the use and psychological significance of colour. Undoubtedly colours can have emotional and physical effects on people, e.g. in a red room a persons pulse and respiration rate increase and an increase in vivacity will be found in a normally apathetic child.

Colours can also have symbolic significance. Black, normally linked with death and disaster in Western countries, has been used with great success in the marketing of Alpen breakfast food, and black paper is used to upgrade certain brands of cigarettes. However, the use of black cartons significantly lowered sales of an ice cream product. Colour symbolism differs around the world; while green encourages British visions of wholesomeness and fresh fields, in Malaysia it is associated with jungle illness.

Examples can often be found where pack shape has been manipulated, for example, to increase handleability or, more subtly, to increase apparent product volume. The subject of package design and the use of colour and colour harmony[5] therein is not a straightforward subject but one clear lesson is that a new package design should never be used without being fully tested on the shelf in the store. Colours do not stand alone and inviolate but are changed by other colours and surfaces around them and by the light which shines upon them.

Adequate colour control must be employed on package batches. When two packs of the same product stand side by side, and one is of a lighter colour, the consumer tends to believe that the lighter of the packs is faded, therefore old, therefore containing a staler product. So belief about the package can influence belief about the product.

Colour contrast can be used to enhance this appearance of a food product, either the product itself or the picture on the package. The most common example is that of the presence of green enhancing the redness of raw meat or bacon. Colour-contrast techniques can be used effectively on the plate also, and even the perceived colour of milked tea can be markedly changed by presenting it in different coloured cups. 'I will paint the skin of Venus the colour of mud if you will allow me to choose the background colours', is a statement attributed to Rubens.[9]

The perceived colour of an object depends upon the light which illuminates it. Rather different considerations may be necessary for the 'on-shelf' and 'on-table' situations. The colour and design of a package must be tested in conjunction with the lighting used in stores to ensure that its full impact is not lost when in actual display. Although the colour-rendering properties of commercially available lamps is the subject of active research,[10] there is still no lamp which can attractively present all foods in any one store, and bad examples of lighting can still be seen. For example, raw beef is often found in refrigerated cabinets under blue-biased fluorescent tubes: this does not produce an attractive product.

It is reported[11] that different colours have different appetite appeal and hence the wrong lighting for a dinner table can ruin the most delicious meal. If the illumination contains too much blue, or has a very reduced spectral output (such as mercury or sodium vapour lamps) the colour of an appetising meal will be far from optimum. Having got the colour balance of the illumination correct so that the most desirable red–orange and orange foods are seen to advantage then almost any intensity of the illumination is tolerable to and can be adapted by the human system. Many large restaurants use versatile lighting installations, in which a bright flood of light can be used to encourage a brisk lunchtime trade, while a softer atmosphere of candle-like warmth is used for a longer and more relaxing evening meal.

PRODUCT IMAGE

The foregoing product attributes, either singly or in combination, will comprise three images which depend on the product situation. They are: the 'on-the-shelf', 'preparation' and 'on-the-plate' images. The latter two images will be reinforced by the additional anticipatory factor of smell or aroma. The decisions leading directly from these images are, respectively, 'to buy or not to buy', 'to serve or not to serve' and 'to eat or not to eat'. The latter two images will also probably form a significant part of the 'repeat buy?' decision.

The 'on-the-shelf' image must aim to *avoid*, *overcome* or *bypass* sales resistance or competition, which can vary in type from:

The cultural taboo: Sales resistance can be *avoided*, for example, by not attempting to sell horsemeat to the British.

To education: The Nescafé launching and the use of polyunsaturated fats in margarine are examples of using education to *overcome* sales resistance and competition.

To food or package presentation: The product is made 'irresistable' to the buyer by using say a free offer method or a re-usable container; this is the *bypass* technique.

'Mode of presentation' is the attribute mainly involved in the 'on-the-shelf' image of a wrapped product which must be designed to meet the financial constraints, likes, habits and basic psychology of the individual.

The total 'preparation' image includes aroma but is concerned a lot with changes in optical properties and physical form during preparation and with the differences between the actual product and the presentation mode properties (e.g. the picture on the pack) and with the individual's expectations. One point to be made regarding fabricated foods is that not only must the final cooked product be convincing but the housewife will be worried if the appearance behaviour 'in the pan' is atypical of the real thing.

The 'on-the-table' appearance image consists of a mixture of individual appearance attributes which must fulfil physical and emotional expectations. These include considerations like: what is on the plate should be stimulating; it should look sufficient to cope with the appetite of the moment; and it must live up to the advertising claims and the personal mental image of the product.

CONCLUSIONS

Consideration of the complex and interacting nature of all the above factors has led me to propose that the study of total appearance should be regarded as a science in its own right. This science can be applied to the food industry in the following ways:

1. The formalisation enables a logical view to be taken of all parameters which influence the appearance of a product whatever its situation and thus increase the awareness of the food technologist to potential and actual appearance problems as relevant to his product.

2. The boundary between the disciplines of technology and marketing is difficult to deal with, define and reconcile. The formalisation of appearance science provides a framework against which, for the subject of product appearance, the division and overlap of this disciplinary boundary can be discussed.

3. Appearance science should be applied to the development of a rational means of studying the factors which influence product appearance on the shelf; for example, highlighting the need for closer product or pack design and control.

Appearance science can be applied, of course, to a very wide range of industries other than those developing, producing and marketing foods.

REFERENCES

1. Mackinney, G. and Little, Angela C. (1962). *Color of Foods.* Avi Publishing Co., Westport, Connecticut.
2. Francis, F. J. and Clydesdale, F. M. (1975). *Food Colorimetry: Theory and Applications.* Avi Publishing Co., Westport, Connecticut.
3. Hunter, R. S. (1975). *The Measurement of Appearance.* John Wiley, New York.
4. Kramer, A. and Szczesniak, A. S. (1973). *Texture Measurements of Foods*, D. Reidel Publishing Co., Dordrecht/Boston, p. 5.
5. Judd, D. B. and Wyszecki, G. (1965). *Colour in Business, Science and Industry.* John Wiley, New York.
6. Scheide, J. (1976). *Ice Cream & Frozen Confectionery*, **28**, p. 228.
7. Maga, J. A. (1974). *Chemical Sense & Flavour*, **1**, p. 115.
8. Sacharow, S. (1970). *Color Engineering*, **9**, p. 25.
9. Wheatley, Jane (1975). *Dragoco Rpt.*, No. 3, p. 63.
10. Halstead, M. B., Bull, J. F. and Large, F. E. (1973). *Proc. 2nd Congress of the International Colour Association*, York, Adam Hilger, London, p. 357.
11. Birren, F. (1969). *Light, Color and Environment.* Van Nostrand Reinhold, New York/London, p. 94.

DISCUSSION

Dirinck: Don't you think the consumer's attitude about appearance attributes is changing? For example, people have a growing interest in old variety apples even if they have external defects.

Hutchings: This seems to be a problem of learning or the education of the consumer, allied to the example of margarine containing polyunsaturates being better for you. As an illustration of a similar effect, we had an experiment once in which a meat product was improved over a period of time without the realisation of the grader who had no reference stimulus with which to anchor his colour scale. His distribution of colour quality scores was constant. This whole area is psychophysics—the physics may not change but the psycho certainly can.

Francis: Should we maximise particle size and minimise proposed content for optimum appearance of formulated foods?

Hutchings: Without finding more natural or permitted colourants the only method the food technologist has left to improve the colour of his products is to use his ingenuity in the manipulation of his raw materials.

Williams: You mentioned one example of one colour influencing the usual appearance of another. Do you know of any other examples?

Hutchings: Red meat with green parsley is the most common example of the beneficial use of colour contrast. I must admit that I cannot think of any more common food examples in the heat of the moment, but the effect is very easy to demonstrate.

4

Colour in Meat

Douglas B. MacDougall

Meat Research Institute, Bristol, England

ABSTRACT

The pigment responsible for the colour of fresh meat is the purple ferrous haem pigment myoglobin. On exposure to oxygen it forms the covalent complex oxymyoglobin which is bright red. The cured pigment, nitric oxide myoglobin is also ferrous and pink. The colour of the oxidised pigment metmyoglobin is brown.

Oxidation of the attractive red pigments, oxymyoglobin and nitric oxide myoglobin to metmyoglobin during display is influenced by many factors the more important of which are oxygen availability, temperature and light. Post-slaughter history of the carcass and the reducing capacity of the meat also affect the rate of colour deterioration.

The lightness or darkness of meat is controlled by both pigment concentration and its light scattering properties. Pigment concentration is characteristic of species but varies with animal age, nutrition and muscle. Light scatter is important in the appearance of pale, soft exudative pork which is opaque and dark cutting beef which is translucent; both conditions result from stress at slaughter. The rate of chilling the carcass also affects light scatter.

Attractiveness of meat on display is affected by the illuminant. Differences in the spectra of fluorescent tubes used in commerce may shift the colour by more than the equivalent of 25 % oxidation.

INTRODUCTION

Meat is a particularly illustrative example of a foodstuff whose colour is influenced by a number of independent variables important in marketing, for example, animal age, pre- and post-slaughter handling and the display environment. Other appearance attributes besides colour are also important, for example, size and shape of joint or portion, fat level, presence of drip, neatness of butchery and presentation, but muscle colour is often the limiting factor in consumer acceptance.[1]

This paper deals with colour in meat under the following topics: pigmentation and colour change in fresh and cured meats, pigment concentration, muscle structure and lightness, and the effect of light and the illuminant on perceived colour.

PIGMENTS

The pigment responsible for the colour of fresh meat is predominantly the ferrous haem protein, myoglobin, along with small quantities of haemoglobin[2] which has similar colour properties to myoglobin. Haem pigments are characterised by an intense absorption band in the blue region of the spectrum between 410 and 430 nm (the Soret band).[3] At the concentrations found in beef (2–7 mg/g) myoglobin is purple; it has an absorption maximum at 555 nm in the green region of the spectrum. Exposed to oxygen it forms bright red oxymyoglobin whose spectrum has the double absorption peaks typical of covalent haem complexes. Oxymyoglobin, nitric oxide myoglobin and carboxymyoglobin are all examples of ferrous covalent complexes characterised by relatively-sharp maxima at 535–545 nm and 575–588 nm. The ferric form of the pigment metmyoglobin is brown with absorption bands with maxima at 505 and 630 nm which results in transmission (or reflectance) of more green and less red energy than either myoglobin or oxymyoglobin. A ferric pigment which is red is metmyoglobin nitrite. On heating the globin is denatured but the haematin nucleus remains intact, as in the more common brown globin myohaemichromogen and the less common red–pink globin myohaemochromogen. The cooked cured pigment nitric oxide myohaemochromogen is red.[3–5]

FRESH MEAT COLOUR SEQUENCE

The bright red surface of normal pH beef exposed to air is unstable and fades to the unattractive brown of metmyoglobin. This reaction, the limiting one in pre-packaged beef display is controlled by factors intrinsic to the meat and the environment.[6] Depth of oxygen penetration into a cut surface depends on the oxygen pressure,[7-9] the temperature (oxygen diffusion into meat is greater at low temperatures)[7,10,11] and the rate of oxygen consumption by residual enzyme activity.[12-17] The latter decreases with duration of ageing after slaughter; meat cut 2 days after slaughter and held at 1 °C will have a layer of oxymyoglobin about half as thick (2–4 mm) 24 h after exposure as that aged for 14 days before cutting.[6] The loss of reducing enzyme activity also means that aged meat will fade faster. Surviving respiratory activity varies with muscle; the oxygenated surface of beef *M. longissimus dorsi* is much more stable than that of *M. psoas major*; other muscles, for example the *M. gluteus medius, M. semimembranosus* and *M. semitendinosus* are intermediate in their rate of discolouration.[18,19] Metmyoglobin usually develops as a two-stage process because its formation is oxygen pressure dependent. The oxidation rate is maximal at about 4 mm oxygen pressure[10,20] and, when residual enzyme activity is low, metmyoglobin soon forms as a band at the limit of oxygen penetration several millimetres below the surface. Concurrent with this, the upper few millimetres oxidises more slowly at the higher oxygen pressure, and the brown layer extends towards the surface.[21]

The most important factors which can be controlled to attempt to maintain attractive shelf-life are temperature and oxygen pressure. Pre-packaged meat held in high oxygen concentration (60 to 100% oxygen) forms an oxymyoglobin layer > 10 mm thick resulting in much longer display life than meat with the normal oxymyoglobin layer of 3–5 mm in air.[19,21] Packaging techniques have been developed to extend attractive shelf-life in which high oxygen concentration is used to maintain redness and carbon dioxide to supress microbiological spoilage.[22,24] The effect of a low display cabinet temperature, so important in retarding fading, is not always recognised or monitored in commerce.[25] A decrease of 3–5 °C has been shown to halve the rate of metmyoglobin formation even if the meat had been held in an atmosphere of oxygen before display.[19]

The colour changes in fresh beef with time are illustrated in Fig. 1 by a sequential set of reflectance spectra of aged beef *M. semimembranosus*, (pH 5·5; 5·0 mg/g myoglobin) packed in polystyrene trays and overwrapped with film highly permeable to oxygen. The samples were held at 5 °C in 1000 lux fluorescent

Douglas B. MacDougall

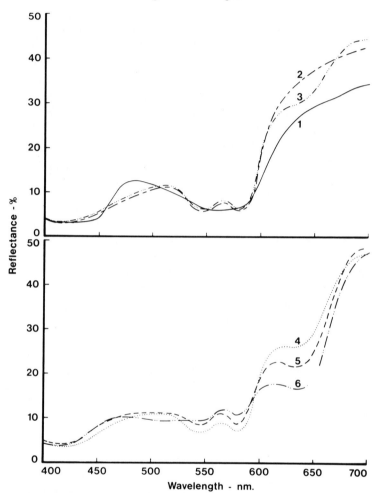

FIG. 1. Reflectance spectra of aged beef *M. semimembranosus* at various stages of pigment oxidation wrapped in oxygen-permeable film and stored at 5 °C under 1000 lux fluorescent illumination. Means of three samples. 1, Vacuum packed; 2, exposed for 1 h; 3, after 1 day; 4, after 2 days; 5, after 4 days; 6, after 7 days.

illumination which is typical of average but not best commercial display conditions. The speed of oxygenation is shown by the difference between the initial and the sample exposed to air for 1 h; the increase in reflectance at the red end of the spectrum is the result of the formation of an oxymyoglobin layer 2 mm thick which almost *oxidation*

Interpretation system[b]	Spectrum number					
	1 Vacuum	2 1 h	3 1 day	4 2 days	5 4 days	6 7 days
CIE						
Y	10·2	11·4	11·5	11·6	12·3	11·8
x	0·404	0·451	0·435	0·422	0·396	0·381
y	0·336	0·340	0·340	0·342	0·342	0·345
λ_d (nm)	598	601	599	597	594	590
P_e (%)	31	44	40	37	30	27
Hunter space						
L	31·9	33·8	33·8	34·1	35·0	34·3
a_L	12·5	21·0	18·1	15·4	11·3	7·5
b_L	7·7	11·3	10·4	9·9	8·6	7·9
H	31·7	28·4	29·9	32·7	38·5	46·2
S	14·7	23·8	20·8	18·3	14·2	10·9
Pigment form						
$K/S\ 507/573$	0·50	0·58	0·65	0·73	0·88	1·30
$K/S\ 473/597$	0·95	2·01	2·14	2·15	1·89	1·79
Metmyoglobin (%)	0	0	14	20	36	60
Myoglobin (%)	>95	25	21	19	32	37
Oxymyoglobin (%)	<5	75	65	61	32	3
$K/S\ 572/525$	1·55	1·54	1·32	1·22	1·06	0·78
Metmyoglobin (%)	0	0	8	20	43	73

[a] Commission Internationale d'Eclairage.[26]
[b] Storage at 5°C.

obliterates the underlying myoglobin. After 1 day's exposure there is clear indication of metmyoglobin formation by the loss of reflectance at 630 nm which loss continues until the 7th day when metmyoglobin is the predominant pigment in the surface layer.

Interpretation of the spectra in Commission Internationale d'Eclairage (CIE) colour terms[26] (luminous reflectance Y, chromaticity co-ordinates x, y, dominant wavelength λ_d, percent purity P_e) and Hunter uniform colour space (lightness L, redness a_L, yellowness b_L, hue H, saturation S) is shown in Table 1 with the proportions of the various pigments in the surface layer calculated by two methods,[27-28] using the K/S function of reflectance.[29]

Oxygenation of the surface is characterised by a change in dominant wavelength and hue towards red accompanied by increased purity and saturation. The hue then becomes more yellow and saturation more grey as metmyoglobin develops. Values of $S > 20$ are bright red, 18 is dull, 14 is distinctly brown and < 12 brown to grey-greenish brown.

COLOUR FORMATION IN CURED MEAT

Nitric oxide myoglobin is the red–pink pigment of uncooked cured meat. It is formed by the action of nitrite on myoglobin but the precise sequence of events whereby the pigment is formed is not yet fully understood.[30] Under anaerobic conditions in the absence of reducing compounds nitric oxide complexes are formed with both myoglobin and metmyoglobin.[31,32] An important step yet unelucidated is the reduction of metmyoglobin in the presence of nitrite when reducing systems are present. Reduction has been postulated to be carried out chemically by SH-groups, non-enzymatically by NADH in the presence of coenzymes or enzymatically by mitochondrial enzymes.[32-36]

Ascorbic acid is used as an aid to colour fixation especially when heat is an essential step in the process, for example in the manufacture of cooked ham;[30,37] it acts as a reducing agent to both the oxidised pigment and the nitrite ion. The quantity of sodium nitrite theoretically required for 50% conversion of myoglobin to nitric oxide myoglobin is at least 3 mg/kg[38] but considerably more is needed in practice because it is used up in other reactions.[39] Provided

25 mg/kg are present in the cured product, this is enough to ensure an adequately stable colour.[30]

LIGHT SCATTER AND PIGMENT CONCENTRATION

Muscle cut soon after an animal has been slaughtered is translucent and dark in appearance. During rigor mortis residual glycogen is converted anaerobically to lactic acid and the pH falls from 7 to about 5·5, the isoelectric point, provided sufficient glycogen was initially present.[4] Muscle at the latter pH is semi-opaque, scatters more light and is paler. If glycogen is depleted prior to slaughter,[40] for example, by stress from transportation to the abattoir, by mixing with strangers

TABLE 2

Effect of pigment concentration and muscle structure on muscle lightness. Means of 10 M. longissimus dorsi *in each group except the* M. semi-membranosus *sample in the chilling experiment*

Muscle type	pH_1	pH_F	Scatter S(mm)	Pigment		Lightness (L)
				Myoglobin (mg/g)	Haematin (µg/g)	
Beef						
normal		<5·7	0·14	3·6		33·1
dark cutting		>6·0	0·07	3·3		23·6
high pigment		<5·7		6·3		27·9
Veal						
normal		<5·6	0·23	1·1		46·0
high pigment		<5·6	0·19	2·3		37·5
Lamb						
2 months		<5·9		1·3		40·0
9 months		<5·7		2·9		35·5
2 years		<5·7		5·7		29·2
Pork						
normal	>5·9	<5·6	0·23		34	50·7
pale, soft, exudative	<5·9	<5·6	0·39		33	56·8
Beef chilling						
7 h to 10 °C		5·5	0·12	5·0		29·9
12 h to 10 °C		5·5	0·15	5·6		31·1
20 h to 10 °C		5·5	0·19	5·3		34·9

or by fatigue and shivering from sudden reduction in temperature, the final pH (pH_F) may not fall below 6·0 and the appearance of the meat will be similar to pre-rigor muscle. In beef this condition is known as 'dark cutting' and in pork the muscle is described as 'dark, firm and dry'. The severity of the darkening is directly related to pH_F.[41] The magnitude of the lightness difference between normal and dark cutting beef is twice that between normal levels of pigmentation and the high levels found in old animals (Table 2).

Another fault resulting from stress is 'pale, soft, exudative' muscle caused by extremely rapid pH fall immediately after slaughter. When this occurs in pork, the pH falls to < 5·9 in < 45 minutes while the carcass remains warm. The muscle becomes pale and opaque because denatured myofibrillar and sarcoplasmic proteins scatter light.[42-44] The value of the scatter coefficient S for the luminous reflectance Y is doubled[43] for the pale, soft, exudative condition and halved for the dark cutting condition. These conditions are the extremes of the effect of muscle translucency on appearance. However, variation in post-slaughter chilling also produces differences that are readily appreciated by eye. Muscles cool at different rates depending on how far they are from the surface, for example the *M. semimembranosus* when cooled in an intact hindquarter showed a much paler colour in the interior (Table 2). The 5 L unit difference between fastest and slowest cooling rate is the same as that resulting from a difference in pigment content of 2–3 mg/g. Hot de-boning techniques, where muscles are cooled more rapidly and evenly in smaller pieces virtually eliminate this cause of variability in appearance.

LIGHT AND ILLUMINATION

Attractive refrigerated display is usually achieved by incorporation of a separate illuminant in the cabinet in addition to the background lighting in the sales area. Radiation from the lamps heats the contents of packages on display resulting in actual product temperatures that can be several degrees higher than the air in the cabinet.[25] Light energy catalyses metmyoglobin formation in fresh, frozen and cured meats. Early work on the effect of light on fresh meat discolouration was contradictory[45] but more recently it has been shown to play a definite role in pigment oxidation.[45-47] The effect of light on wet meat is less severe than in either frozen or cured meats. Oxygenated meat, packed to avoid freezer-burn and frozen, will remain attractive for weeks at $-20\,°C$ in the dark, but illuminated at the level of commercial display fading occurs in less than 1 week.[48,49] The red–pink colour of cured meat is stable in the absence of oxygen both in the dark and in light, but if oxygen is available fading is rapid in the light.[2,33]

The customer in the self-service situation is influenced in her selection by the attractiveness and colour of the product. Spectral composition of the light source has special relevance to meat display. Fluorescent tubes include those with efficient light output but poor colour rendering properties (for example, 'white' tubes), those with high-fidelity colour-rendering properties simulating daylight and used for colour-matching purposes, and those with lower colour temperature and increased red energy used for domestic lighting and food display. Fresh and cured meats undergo visual colour shifts, the extent of which at different stages of pigment oxidation and under a variety of illuminants can be as large as that produced by several days' storage. For example, if the colour matching tube 'artificial daylight'[50] is used as reference, the visual difference between red–pink bacon (predominantly nitric oxide myoglobin) and brown bacon (predominantly metmyoglobin) can be defined as 100 units. If samples are viewed in 'white' fluorescent light and compared with the reference set they appear more brown by about 40–150 units depending on the amount of metmyoglobin. Similar samples viewed in 'de-luxe natural' are redder by 10 to > 100 units. Current work on intermediate stages of oxidation indicates that for tubes used in commerce the colour shift can be equivalent to about 25 % oxidation.

ACKNOWLEDGEMENT

The author thanks Mrs S. J. Jones for her assistance in the experimental work reported in this paper.

REFERENCES

1. Hood, D. E. and Riordan, E. B. (1973). *J. Fd. Technol.*, **8**, p. 333.
2. Fox, J. B. (1966). *J. agric. Fd. Chem.*, **14**, p. 207.
3. Lemberg, R. and Legge, J. W. (1949). In: *Hematin Compounds and Bile Pigments*, Interscience Publishers Ltd., London, p. 207.

4. Lawrie, R. A. (1974). In: *Meat Science*, Second Edition, Pergamon Press, Oxford, p. 286.
5. Francis, F. J. and Clydesdale, F. M. (1975). In: *Food Colorimetry: Theory and Applications*, Avi Publishing Co. Inc., Westport, Connecticut, pp. 279, 292.
6. MacDougall, D. B. (1972). In: *Proc. Symp. Meat Chilling*, Meat Research Institute, Bristol, p. 81.
7. Brooks, J. (1929). *Biochem. J.*, **23**, p. 1391.
8. Landrock, A. H. and Wallace, G. A. (1955). *Fd. Technol.*, **9**, p. 194.
9. Rikert, J. A., Bressler, L., Ball, C. O. and Stier, E. F. (1957). *Fd. Technol.*, **11**, p. 625.
10. Brooks, J. (1935). *Proc. Roy. Soc.*, **B118**, p. 560.
11. Urbin, M. C. and Wilson, G. D. (1958). In: *Proc. 10th Res. Conf.*, American Meat Institute Foundation, p. 13.
12. Bendall, J. R. and Taylor, A. A. (1972). *J. Sci. Fd. Agric.*, **23**, p. 707.
13. Giddings, G. G. (1974). In: *Critical Reviews in Food Technology*, ed. T. E. Furia, CRC Press Inc., Cleveland, Ohio, p. 143.
14. Ledward, D. A. (1972). *J. Fd. Sci.*, **37**, p. 634.
15. Saleh, B. and Watts, B. M. (1968). *J. Fd. Sci.*, **33**, p. 353.
16. Stewart, M. R., Hutchins, B. K., Zipser, M. W. and Watts, B. M. (1965). *J. Fd. Sci.*, **30**, p. 487.
17. Watts, B. M., Kendrick, J., Zipser, M. W., Hutchins, B. and Saleh, B. (1966). *J. Fd. Sci.*, **31**, p. 855.
18. Hood, D. E. (1971). In: *Proc. 17th European Meeting of Meat Research Workers*, Bristol, p. 677.
19. MacDougall, D. B. and Taylor, A. A. (1975). *J. Fd. Technol.*, **10**, p. 339.
20. George, P. and Stratmann, C. J. (1952). *Biochem. J.*, **51**, p. 418.
21. Taylor, A. A. and MacDougall, D. B. (1973). *J. Fd. Technol.*, **8**, p. 453.
22. Brody, A. L. (1970). *Mod. Packag.*, **43**, p. 81.
23. Georgala, D. L. and Davidson, C. M. (1970). Brit. patent No. 1 199 998.
24. Schweisfurth und Kalle Ag (1970). Brit. patent No. 1 186 978.
25. Malton, R. (1976). *Inst. Meat Bull.*, **91**, p. 17.
26. Wysecki, G. and Stiles, W. S. (1967). In: *Color Science, Concepts and Methods, Quantitative Data and Formulas*, John Wiley and Sons, New York, pp. 238, 321.
27. Dean, R. W. and Ball, C. O. (1960). *Fd. Technol.*, **14**, 271.
28. Stewart, M. R., Zipser, M. W. and Watts, B. W. (1965). *J. Fd. Sci.*, **30**, p. 464.
29. Judd, D. B. and Wyszecki, G. (1963). In: *Color in Business, Science and Industry*, John Wiley and Sons, New York, p. 387.
30. MacDougall, D. B., Mottram, D. S. and Rhodes, D. N. (1975). *J. Sci. Fd. Agric.*, **26**, p. 1743.
31. Brooks, J. (1937). *Proc. Roy. Soc.*, **123**, p. 368.
32. Koizumi, C. and Brown, W. D. (1971). *J. Fd. Sci.*, **36**, p. 1105.
33. Cheah, K. S. (1976). *J. Fd. Technol.*, **11**, p. 181.
34. Fox, J. B. and Ackerman, S. A. (1968). *J. Fd. Sci.*, **33**, p. 364.
35. Möhler, K. (1973). In: *Proc. Int. Symp. Nitrite Meat Prod.*, Zeist, Pudoc, Wageningen, p. 13.

36. Walters, C. L., Casselden, R. J. and Taylor, A. McM. (1967). *Biochim. Biophys. Acta*, **143**, p. 310.
37. Brown, C. L., Hedrick, H. B. and Bailey, M. E. (1974). *J. Fd. Sci.*, **39**, p. 977.
38. Ranken, M. D. (1972). In: *Proc. Meat Curing Symp.*, Institute of Food Science and Technology (UK), p. 52.
39. Fox, J. B. and Nicholas, R. A. (1974). *J. agric. Fd. Chem.*, **22**, p. 302.
40. Lawrie, R. (1977). *Meat Science*, **1**, p. 1.
41. MacDougall, D. B. and Rhodes, D. N. (1972). *J. Sci. Fd. Agric.*, **23**, p. 637.
42. Bendall, J. R. and Wismer-Pedersen, J. (1962). *J. Fd. Sci.*, **27**, p. 144.
43. MacDougall, D. B. (1970). *J. Sci. Fd. Agric.*, **21**, p. 568.
44. Scopes, R. K. (1964). *Biochem. J.*, **91**, p. 201.
45. Solberg, M. and Franke, W. C. (1971). *J. Fd. Sci.*, **36**, p. 990.
46. Setser, C. S., Harrison, D. L., Kropf, D. H. and Dayton, A. (1973). *J. Fd. Sci.*, **38**, p. 412.
47. Satterlee, L. D. and Hansmeyer, W. (1974). *J. Fd. Sci.*, **39**, p. 305.
48. Lentz, C. P. (1971). *J. Inst. Can. Technol. Aliment.*, **4**, p. 166.
49. Taylor, A. A. and MacDougall, D. B., unpublished data.
50. British Standard 950 Part 1. (1967). British Standards Institution, London.

5

Structural Aspects of Chemoreception

M. G. J. BEETS

*International Flavors and Fragrances, Europe, Hilversum,
The Netherlands*

ABSTRACT

*The chemoreceptory process starts with a reversible, physical
interaction between two molecular species, a population of structural
features of the sensory epithelium (receptor sites) and a population of
stimulant molecules. A few of the structural aspects of both are
discussed in this paper.*

*Since experimental approaches to the study of the former are still
rare, we depend for our knowledge of the receptor site largely on
reasoning and common sense, in combination with a few basic facts.
Two theoretical concepts of the nature of the receptor site, the
specialised and the generalised concept, are briefly considered.*

*The relationship between the molecular structure of the stimulant
and chemoreceptory response is illustrated by means of three
examples, representing widely different areas of chemoreception.*

*In the first place, the relationship of the structure of amino acids with
their taste as well as with the taste differences of their enantiomers is
discussed and certain structural aspects are indicated. In the second
place, a possible structural basis of the musk odours of two apparently
unrelated classes of aromatic compounds is demonstrated. Finally, a
possible relationship between certain structural details of carbohydrates and their effectiveness in bacterial chemotaxis, is pointed out.*

*The major purpose of this short discussion is to stress the importance
of systematic structural modifications on the basis of reasonable
postulates for research on structure–activity relationships in chemoreception.*

M. G. J. Beets

INTRODUCTION

Olfaction and gustation are probably the most complex and, at this stage of our knowledge, the least transparent of the five senses. I can only hope to say something meaningful in this short paper by avoiding most theoretical aspects and by selecting a few isolated topics.

Readers who are interested in the arguments and the theory behind the subject of this paper and, more specifically, in the structural and informational aspects of chemoreception, are referred to the book which is expected to appear not much later than the proceedings of this symposium.[1]

Since mechanisms involving the action of stimulant molecules at a distance or the chemical conversion of these molecules are no longer seriously considered, we may safely assume the initial step of any chemoreceptory process to be a reversible physical interaction between two molecular species, a population of stimulant molecules and a population of structural features of the chemoreceptory epithelium.

In the latter, we distinguish three levels, the macroscopic level of the epithelium, the microscopic level of the cell and the molecular level of those locations on the peripheral membrane of the receptor cell with which the stimulant molecules interact. The macroscopic and microscopic structures of the epithelia in vertebrates are well known.

The gustatory receptor system is organised on the basis of taste buds, barrel shaped aggregates of 30–50 cells belonging to various types. Although the identification of cell functions in the taste bud is not easy,[2] we have reasons to assume that the more slender cells with thin hair-like processes extending into the pore, are the receptor cells.

Figure 1 shows a scanning electron photomicrograph of the taste bud in the fungiform papillae of the rat, made in Professor Beidler's laboratory in Florida. We are looking into the pore giving access to the peripheral membranes of the cells. What we cannot see are the nerve fibres issuing from the connective tissue underneath, entering the taste bud and contacting all cell types.

In the olfactory epithelium, the scene of the interaction is the mosaic of the peripheral membranes of receptor cells and supporting cells. Each of the receptor cell membranes shows a small number of long, thin projections, the cilia, which are embedded in the thin layer of mucus covering the surface of the epithelium. Aspects of the receptor cell which may interest us here are, that there are

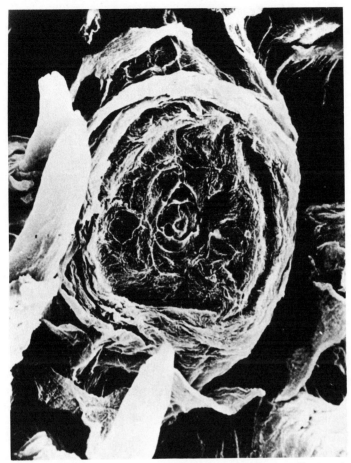

FIG. 1. Scanning electron photomicrograph of the rat fungiform papillae taste bud. (Courtesy Professor L. M. Beidler.)

approximately 10 million in the human epithelium and that each of them is connected directly, without branching, by means of its own axon, with a glomerulus in the olfactory bulb and, finally, that the structural features which interact with the stimulant molecules are believed to be located on the surface of the cilia.[3] The supporting cells carry a large number of very short projections, the microvilli.

The photomicrograph of the olfactory epithelium of the freshwater codfish, made by Professor Ottoson in Stockholm, gives

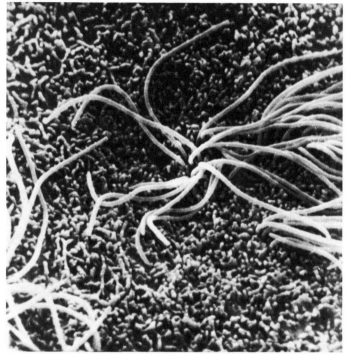

FIG. 2.   Photomicrograph of the olfactory epithelium of the freshwater codfish.
(Courtesy Professor D. Ottoson.)

an admirable impression of the cilia of a single-receptor cell,
surrounded by a dense network of microvilli (Fig. 2).

Let us consider this a little longer and realise that it takes us to the
extreme frontiers of the submicroscopic but also that it leaves us on
the brink of the abyss which separates us from the molecular events in
which we are interested and which remain, while we can see the scene
where they occur, as far beyond our reach as the boulders on the
surface of the planet Mars which are shown in such amazing detail on
the Viking pictures.

One of the obvious ways to learn about the peripheral events in
chemoreception is to start with the study of the two molecular species
involved—the stimulant molecules and the locations on the
epithelium with which they interact.

For the latter, experimental approaches are still rare and we depend
largely on the intelligent application of inductive reasoning to the few

basic facts regarding sensory epithelia and analogous structures which are available. For the study of stimulant structure on the other hand, many experimental pathways are open to us. The majority of all molecules with sufficient volatility or solubility in water, have either an odour or a taste or both. Our opportunities to study correlations between structural modifications and their effects on chemoreceptory response are nearly unlimited. In this paper we shall first pay some attention to the nature of the epithelial locations involved in chemoreceptory interaction and subsequently we shall discuss a few characteristic cases of structure–activity relationships.

THE RECEPTOR SITE

There is a tendency in the literature to consider the receptor site in olfaction and gustation as a highly-specialised piece of equipment on the membrane of a receptor cell with the ability to interact selectively with a narrow structural range of molecules and to generate an effect representing a specific type of odour or taste. In accordance with this specialised concept, receptor sites are often indicated by the response types with which they are presumably associated such as the musky site or the bitter site. These terms suggest that the generation of a specific type of response is entirely due to the interaction of suitable molecules with a collection of identical, highly-specialised sites. When, for any reason, this collection is absent or malfunctioning, a whole type of chemoreceptory response disappears, a whole category of stimulants becomes odourless, or tasteless and we have satisfactorily explained such well-known phenomena as specific anosmia and taste blindness.

There are several reasons to doubt the validity of this concept. In the first place, it can hardly be reconciled with the quasi-unlimited variety of stimulant structures and, more specifically, with the huge structural variety of stimulant molecules representing a single type of response such as camphoraceous or sweet. The requirement that a single type of membrane feature must be equipped to accommodate such a diversity of structures suggests a degree of technical sophistication which has never been encountered in nature. As far as we know there are no major structural differences between the peripheral membrane of a receptor cell and that of an unspecialised cell in similar tissues. The protein composition of the gustatory epithelium has been shown by Koyama and Kurihara[4] not to differ from that of the surrounding tissue.

Also, the informational complexity of odours and tastes and the wide range of enantiomeric response differences observed for chiral stimulants are hardly compatible with the expectations based upon the specialised concept.

The specialised concept does not help us to understand the informational structure of chemoreceptory response. Since the receptor cell has no known mechanism to label an energy effect generated by one of the structural features on its peripheral membrane, only that cell and not the receptor site can possibly have an informational identity except in the wildly improbable case that a cell membrane carries only one receptor site or a collection of identical ones.

An attractive alternative has been termed the generalised concept of the receptor site.[1,5] It is based upon the postulate that there are no receptor sites in the absolute sense but only potential receptor sites, i.e. normal structural features of presumably proteinaceous membrane components which may occur on the membrane of any cell. Such features are potential receptor sites because of their ability to complex reversibly with simulant molecules of suitable structures and because they happen to be located on the peripheral membrane of a cell which is equipped to generate information and to project it into the system to which it belongs.

According to the generalised concept, the peripheral membrane of each receptor cell contains a huge number of structural features in a wide structural and conformational variety, which may serve as receptor sites when suitable molecules happen to be presented to them. The energy effect generated by interaction with one of these features is informationally anonymous except for the collective criterion, shared with the energy effects of all other features on the same cell membrane, that it originates in the periphery of a specific cell. Consequently, the informational identity of the energy effect generated by interaction with a membrane feature is unrelated to the structural parameters of that feature and only related to the identity of the cell on which it originates.

In the framework of the generalised concept, the specificity of a receptor cell is due to the composition of the collection of structural features on its peripheral membrane which is assumed to differ between cells[6] and to the topology of its position on the sensory epithelium. This means that the initial product of the interaction between a population of stimulant molecules and the population of structural features on the sensory epithelium is a highly-complex peripheral information pattern consisting of the contributions of receptor cells rather than a simple collection of groups of identical signals produced by corresponding groups of specialised receptor sites.

The generalised concept of the receptor site has a better explanatory potential than the specialised one. It enables us, for instance, to explain the existence of unimodal and bimodal stimulants without the unattractive assumption, required by the specialised concept, that there are two different informational modalities, represented at the terminus by two indistinguishable but independent odour or taste components. The generalised concept also makes a rough prediction possible of the trends of enantiomeric response differences for chiral stimulants belonging to the various structural categories. One of its interesting consequences is that non-polar enantiomers can not be expected to have detectable odour or taste differences.

I realise that this subject is far too complex to be covered in so little space. I have mentioned a few of its aspects because the receptor site is one of the two partners involved in chemoreceptory interaction and as such deserves our interest. We shall now turn our attention to the second partner, the stimulant molecule.

AMINO ACIDS

Shallenberger[7] postulated that the basic unit of sweet taste is a pair of functional groups at a distance of approximately 3 Å, of which one can act as a proton donor and the second as a proton acceptor. During the interaction, these groups are assumed to combine reversibly by means of hydrogen bonds, with a complementary unit in the receptor site. This principle is illustrated schematically by Fig. 3a.

Kier[8] added a second postulate, i.e. that although Shallenberger's AH–B unit suffices to produce a sweet taste of fairly low intensity, similar to that of the carbohydrates, a third structural feature (X; Fig. 3b) in a specific configuration relative to the AH–B pair is required for intensive sweet taste.

How can we apply these postulates to amino acids? In order to find

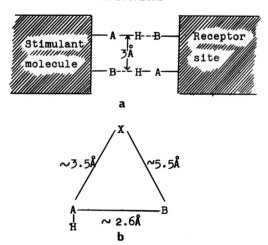

FIG. 3.   (a) The principle of stimulant–receptor interaction; (b) the X structural feature required for intensive sweet taste.

an answer to this question, we may have a look at the structures of a few representatives which, together with the intensities of their sweet tastes relative to that of sucrose, are shown in Fig. 4.

Shallenberger's AH–B unit is generally assumed to be represented in amino acids by the combination of the amino and the carboxylic functions which suffice to generate the fairly weak sweetness of glycine and D-leucine. The lack of taste in the straight-chain isomer of leucine may merely mean that its sweet taste is too weak to be observed. The taste intensity is enhanced when aromatic systems are present. The locations in D-phenylalanine and D-histidine which, according to Kier, may serve as the third feature in the interaction, are indicated by circles. Since the structures of D-tryptophan and D-histidine have much in common, Kier supposed the third features in both to be in analogous positions. Although this may be correct, it does not explain the five-fold increase of the taste intensity in D-tryptophan.

An interesting novel aspect appears when we compare the structure of D-tryptophan with that of glykergenic acid, described by Hofmann[9] to have 1000 times the sweet-taste intensity of sucrose. Clearly, glykergenic acid is a structural analogue and even a vinylogue of D-tryptophan but this does not help us to determine which functional groups may serve as the AH–B–X triplet. The methyl-amino group and the carboxylic group are too far apart to be

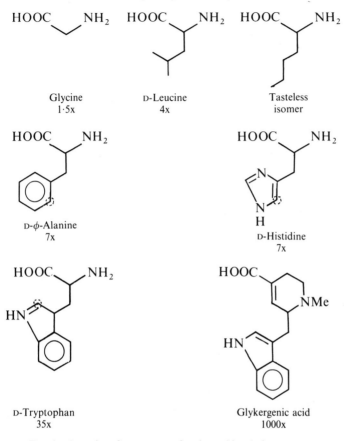

FIG. 4. Intensity of sweet taste of amino acids relative to sucrose.

identified as the AH–B unit in analogy to the NH_2–COOH pair in tryptophan.

An alternative explanation is suggested by the molecular models of both compounds which can easily assume a conformation, shown in Fig. 5, in which the carboxylic group and the indole nitrogen are in mutual positions enabling them to serve as the AH–B pair.

This would mean that the sweetness of tryptophan could have a structural basis which is different from that of the sweet taste of other amino acids.

The second problem is the identification of the third feature in both structures. This may or may not be the position (indicated by an

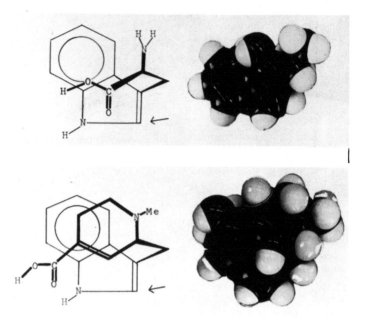

Fɪɢ. 5.   Conformation of ᴅ-tryptophan (top) and glykergenic acid (bottom) to enable AH–B pairing.

arrow), suggested by Kier for ᴅ-tryptophan. Also, the third feature may or may not be found in analogous positions in both compounds.

It seems fairly easy to design an experimental programme which may enable us to solve these problems. A few examples of analogous structures which, for obvious reasons, should be made and evaluated in the framework of such a programme, are shown in Fig. 6.

Since glykergenic acid has an asymmetric centre, also an evaluation of the taste of both enantiomers would be highly interesting.

Probably the best demonstration of the importance of the mutual configuration of the AH–B pair on the one hand and Kier's third feature on the other is presented by the taste differences between enantiomeric amino acids. The structures of amino acids possessing a potential third feature, can be represented by the general formula (Fig. 7) in which X⋯C symbolises a single or double bond or a bond forming part of an aromatic system between a carbon atom and any other suitable atom (C, O, S or N), i.e. the group of which the third feature is necessarily a part.

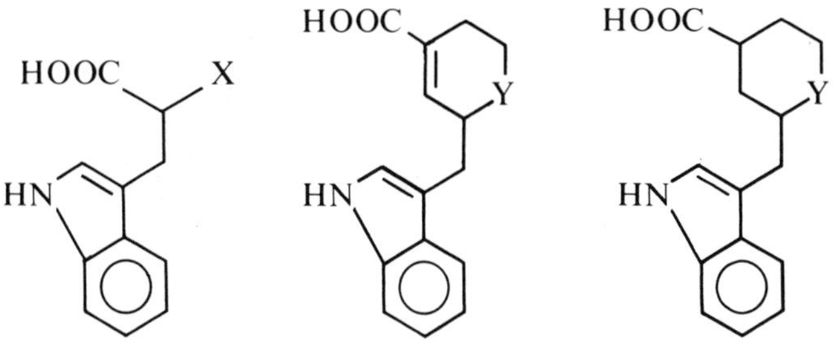

X = carbonyl,
sec-alcohol,
H/H or H/Cl

Y = —O— or $-CH_2-$

FIG. 6. Examples of structures which should be evaluated in experiments to solve problems of amino-acid sweetness.

If we arrange such amino acids in a sequence with increasing value of n, we find[1] that strong differences involving the taste quality of enantiomers, are only observed for $n = 1$.

We shall now turn our attention for a while to an example selected from the area of olfaction research.

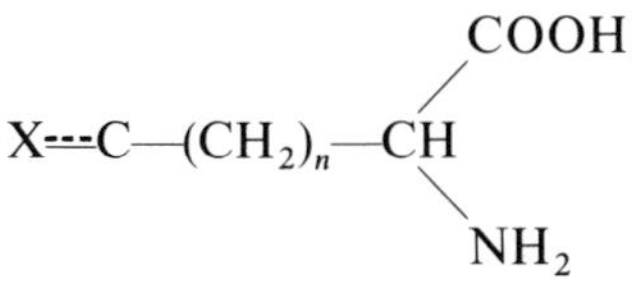

FIG. 7. The general formulae of amino acids possessing a potential third feature. --- = single, double or aromatic-system bond between a carbon atom and a suitable atom (C, O, S or N) in group X.

AROMATIC MUSKS

Before the Second World War only two structural classes of compounds with musk odours were known, the macrocyclic musks and the nitro musks. Figure 8 shows the structures of a few well-known representatives of the latter class.

Apart from these, numerous di- and trinitro compounds have been found to have musk odours.[1,10] The structural basis for the common odour character in this structurally-heterogeneous class and especially the function of the nitro group have remained a mystery since the discovery of the first nitro musk in 1888.

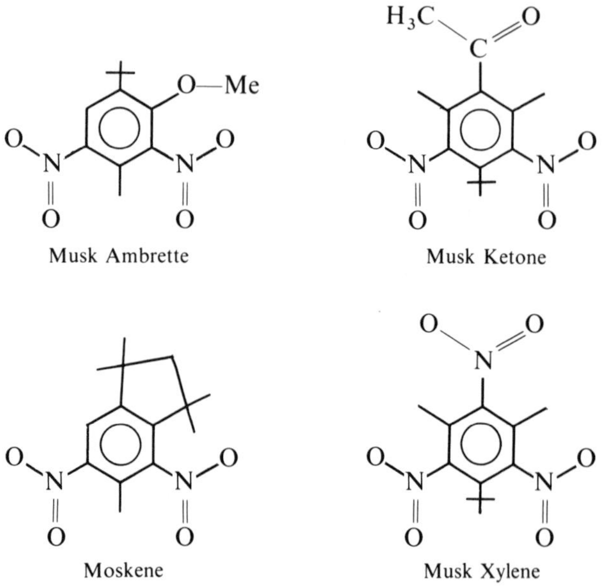

Fig. 8.   Examples of nitro aromatic musks.

Before we can discuss a possible solution to this problem, we must take a quick look at the more recent developments in the area of the musk odorants.

It has been demonstrated repeatedly that there are two general requirements for stimulants to have musk odours, i.e. a bulky molecular shape of which the dimensions must obey certain rules and a sterically-accessible functional group.

During the period 1950–1970 several novel types of aromatic musks were discovered of which the structures are based upon the simple principle that a bulky molecular profile of the desired dimensions can be obtained by the introduction into a benzene nucleus of two quaternary carbon substituents in *ortho* or *meta* positions. The resulting structures are represented schematically by Fig. 9, in which X is a sterically-unhindered polar group, usually but not necessarily a carbonyl group.

These two classes may be indicated as meta musks (Fig. 9a) and ortho musks (Fig. 9b).

In Fig. 10 a few of the most characteristic representatives of these types are shown.

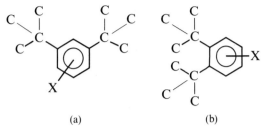

(a)   (b)

FIG. 9. Essential features of: (a) *meta* musks; (b) *ortho* musks. X = a sterically unhindered polar group.

The function of the tertiary alkyl groups in adjacent positions in the *ortho* musks and in 1,3 positions in the *meta* musks is clearly to contribute to the bulky profile required for musk odour. It is characteristic for such groups that two of the methyl groups are necessarily projecting out of the plane of the benzene nucleus.

With this in mind, and adopting the musk odour of *ortho* and *meta* musks as our axiom, we can easily interpret the structure of the nitro musks and the unique function of the nitro group by means of the simple postulate that the nitro group can play a double role. It can function as a polar group, analogous to that of the functional group in *ortho* and *meta* musks, when it is in a sterically-unhindered position of the benzene ring and its normal coplanarity with the ring is unimpeded.

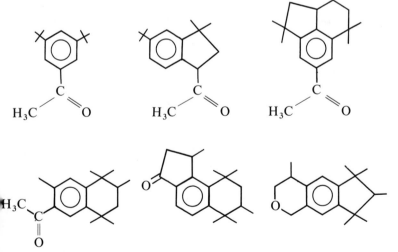

FIG. 10. Examples of *meta* musks (top) and *ortho* musks (bottom).

It can also act as a profile group, analogous to the quaternary carbon substituents in *ortho* and *meta* musks, when it is in a sterically-hindered position of the benzene ring in which its normal coplanarity with the ring is prevented and its two oxygen atoms, like the methyl groups in *ortho* and *meta* musks, are projecting out of the plane.

This steric hindrance may be realised in various ways which are shown schematically in Fig. 11.

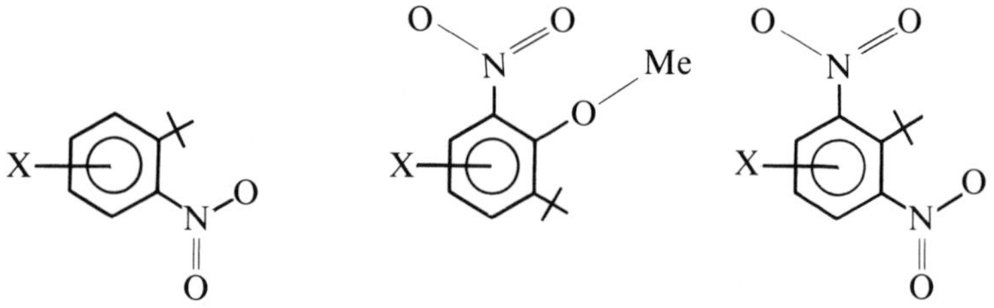

pseudo *ortho* musks   pseudo *meta* musks

Type I   Type II

FIG. 11.   Steric hindrance.

Coplanarity between a nitro group and the benzene ring may be prevented simply by means of a tertiary alkyl group in the adjacent position. It will be understood that this combination mimics the two adjacent quarternary carbon groups in ortho musks and, consequently, nitro musks of which the structures are based upon this principle, will be termed *pseudo ortho* musks.[1]

The profile of the two quaternary carbon groups in *meta* musks may be mimicked by the nitro group in different ways. In the first place we may put a suitable substituent in the position between a tertiary butyl group and a nitro group. This group should relay the steric hindrance caused by the former to the latter. A characteristic example is the methoxy group of which the methyl is pushed by the tertiary butyl group into a position in which it hinders the coplanarity of the nitro function with the ring (Fig. 11, type I). A second way to achieve the same effect is to place nitro groups on both sides of a tertiary alkyl group (Fig. 11, type II). In this case the profile of both quaternary carbon groups in *meta* musks is mimicked by nitro groups. All nitro musks in which one or two nitro groups mimic the steric pretensions of quaternary carbon groups in *meta* musks will be called *pseudo meta* musks.[1]

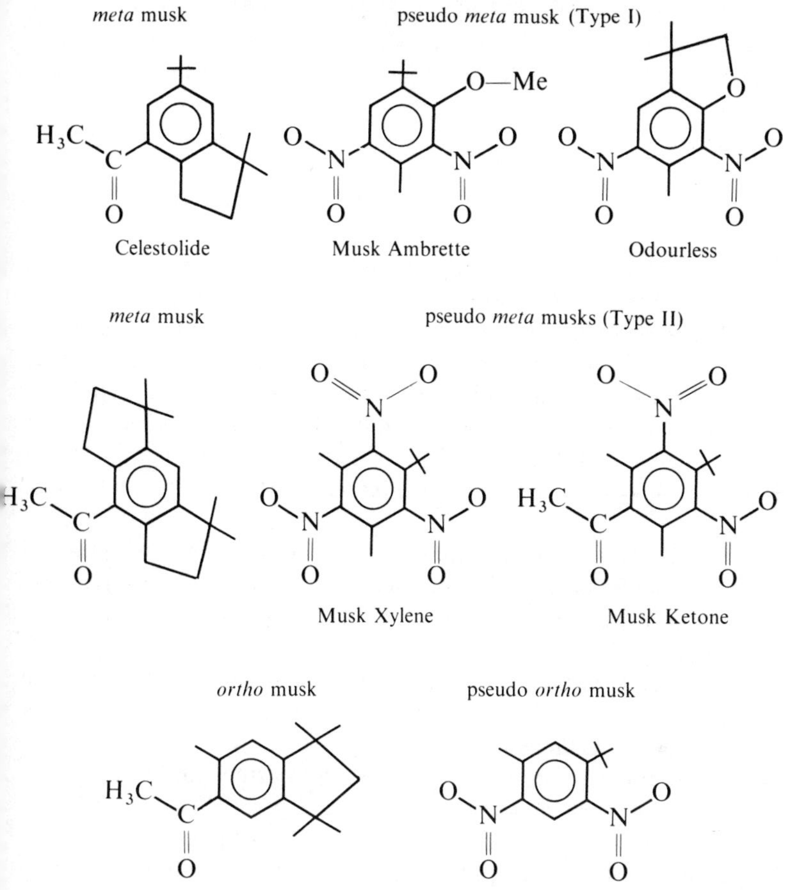

FIG. 12. Examples of *ortho* musks, pseudo *ortho* musks, *meta* musks, and pseudo *meta* musks.

A few characteristic examples may illustrate these principles and conclude our discussion of this subject (Fig. 12).

Musk ambrette is clearly a pseudo-analogue of the strong *meta* musk celestolide. A structural analogue of musk ambrette, in which the intervening methoxy group forms a ring with the tertiary butyl group, is odourless, in spite of its close structural similarity with musk ambrette.[11] This is not surprising since, owing to the ring closure, the coplanarity of the nitro group is no longer prevented and it cannot mimic the profile of a quaternary carbon group.

The second type is illustrated by a fairly weak *meta* musk and by two of its pseudo analogues, musk xylene and musk ketone. Finally, an example of an *ortho* musk and one of its pseudo analogues is shown.

CARBOHYDRATES IN CHEMOTAXIS

As the last example of this paper we select a small detail from a totally different area of chemoreception, bacterial chemotaxis.

The presence of chemical agents in the medium of microorganisms may cause attraction or repulsion. This phenomenon, which is called chemotaxis, is being studied extensively by several groups. It offers unique, and as yet insufficiently explored opportunities for research on structure–activity relationships in chemoreception, since it uses a technically-simple system which cannot influence its data subjectively.

Our example is found in the excellent work of Adler[12] who studied chemotaxis for carbohydrates, using *Escherichia coli* as his system. By studying attraction and mutual inhibition for a large number of carbohydrates, Adler could identify 8 different chemoreceptors in his system, each with its own specificity. I shall only mention a detail involving two of these receptors. Figure 13 shows a schematic presentation of the results.

Chemotaxis toward D-fucose was completely inhibited by the presence of D-galactose. In the reciprocal experiment nearly complete inhibition was observed. Adler concluded that fucose and galactose use the same chemoreceptor. Influenced by the generalised concept of the receptor site mentioned in the first section of this paper, we prefer to express the same principle somewhat differently, by saying that fucose and galactose interact with largely overlapping collections of membrane locations which may be labelled as the galactose group of sites.

The attraction to galactose was also completely inhibited by the presence of D-glucose but in the reciprocal experiment the inhibition was only 60–70 %, no matter how high the galactose concentration was. In this case, Adler's conclusion, translated again into the terminology of the generalised concept, was that the large majority of the galactose as well as of the glucose molecules interact with the galactose group but that a second group of membrane locations,

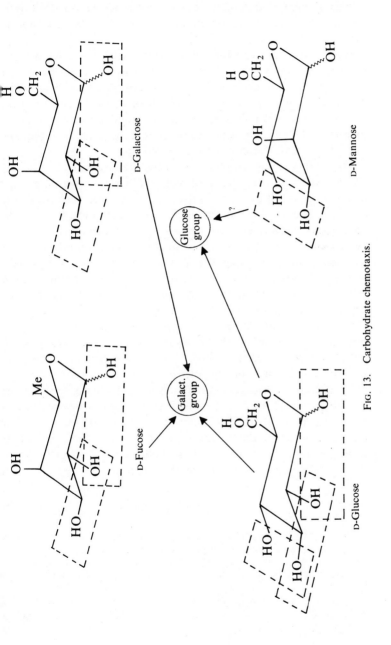

Fig. 13. Carbohydrate chemotaxis.

which may be termed the glucose group and which has very little or no overlap with the galactose group, binds to glucose but not to galactose.

What can be the structural basis of this selectivity? We see that these three sugars have potential AH–B units consisting of the hydroxyls in positions 1 and 2 as well as in positions 2 and 3 but that only glucose has also a diequatorial pair of hydroxyl groups in the positions 3 and 4. An obvious explanation could be that either the 1,2 pair or the 2,3 pair interacts with the sites of the galactose group and the 3,4 pair with those of the glucose group.

The validity of this postulate can, of course, be checked by studying chemotaxis for a larger group of monosaccharides possessing either of the two AH–B pairs or both and for suitable derivatives and analogues such as deoxy sugars, methyl glycosides and cyclic polyols, analogous to the strategies shown in the elegant research of Birch and his group[13] for sweetness and bitterness in the same stimulant classes.

As an arbitrary example, Fig. 13 shows D-mannose which, since it has only the 3,4 pair of hydroxyls in suitable conformation, can be expected to interact with the glucose group of receptor sites and not with the galactose group.

In chemotaxis as well as in all other areas of chemoreception, two partners are involved—the organism and the stimulant. It is insufficiently realised that not only the former but both have structures and that both are potential sources of information.

I hope that the three widely-different cases mentioned in this paper have illustrated, however sketchily, that stimulant structure deserves more attention than it usually gets and that its systematic modification under the guidance of *ad hoc* postulates, derived by extrapolation from the known facts, offers attractive opportunities to improve our understanding of chemoreception.

REFERENCES

1. Beets, M. G. J. (1978). *Structure–Activity Relationships in Human Chemoreception*, Applied Science Publishers Ltd, Barking.
2. Murray, R. G. and Murray, A. (1970). In: *Taste and Smell in Vertebrates*, eds. G. E. W. Wolstenholme and J. Knight, J. & A. Churchill, London, p. 3.
3. Reese, T. S. and Brightman, M. W. (1970). In: *Taste and Smell in Vertebrates*, eds. G. E. W. Wolstenholme and J. Knight, J. & A. Churchill, London, p. 115.

4. Koyama, N. and Kurihara, K. (1971). *J. Gen. Physiol.*, **57**, p. 297.
5. Beets, M. G. J. (1974). In: *Transduction Mechanisms in Chemoreception*, ed. T. M. Poynder, Inform. Retr. Ltd, London, p. 129.
6. Gesteland, R. C., Lettvin, J. Y., Pitts, W. H. and Rojas, A. (1963). In: *Olfaction and Taste I*, ed. Y. Zotterman, Pergamon Press, Oxford, p. 19.
7. Shallenberger, R. S. (1963). *J. Food Sci.*, **28**, p. 584.
8. Kier, L. B. (1972). *J. Pharm. Sci.*, **61**, p. 1394.
9. Hofmann, A. (1972). *Helv. Chim. Acta*, **55**, p. 2934.
10. Beets, M. G. J. (1957). In: *Molecular Structure and Organoleptic Quality*, Society of Chemical Industry, London, p. 54.
11. Beets, M. G. J. (1967). *La France et ses parfums*, **1967**, p. 113.
12. Adler, J. (1972). In: *Olfaction and Taste IV*, ed. D. Schneider, Wissensch. Verlagsgesellsch., Stuttgart, p. 70.
13. Birch, G. G. (1976). *Critical Reviews in Food Science and Nutrition*, **8**, p. 57.

DISCUSSION

Hough: Would you care to comment on the sweetness of 6-D-chlorotryptophan within the context of your discussion on the sweetness of tryptophan and glykergenic acid?

Beets: A very difficult question without starting wild speculation. We have learned that chlorine atoms are very effective. There is a possibility that chlorine modifies the profile of the aromatic ring. It is a problem for structural modifications. What happens when a chlorine atom is replaced by another group? It is very easy to design an experimental programme.

Land: Can you reconcile the configuration of the macro-cyclic and other musks to the configuration requirements shown for the nitro musks?

Beets: Yes, it is rather remarkable that if you look at molecular models of musks the profiles are similar. You would not expect it but it is true. They are all bulky molecules. With experience you arrive at a situation in which you can almost predict when a molecule will have a musk odour.

6

Chemical Clues to the Perception of Sweetness

R. S. SHALLENBERGER

*New York State Agricultural Experiment Station,
Cornell University, New York, USA*

ABSTRACT

*Studies of the stereochemistry of compounds that elicit the sweet taste
response have advanced to the point that the initial chemical
interactions with the receptor site can be described as bipartite (a
concerted AH–B interaction) or tripartite (a concerted AH–B–γ
interaction). The bipartite interaction is associated with the quality
(sweetness) of the interaction whilst the tripartite interaction is
associated with the intensity of the response.*

*One consequence of a tripartite receptor site is that principles of
symmetry can now be applied to further understanding of sweetness. In
essence, the sweetness attributes of compounds, particularly those of
enantiomers, is now explainable on the basis that the receptor site is
dissymmetric in that it exhibits bilateral asymmetry. Moreover, the
tripartite saporous unit of a compound, in order to react with the
receptor site, is usually but not necessarily diastereoisomeric with it.
The D-amino acids are an example of the first case, the sugars are an
example of the latter case.*

INTRODUCTION

The AH–B thesis for sweet taste was first proposed in 1967.[1] In
essence, that thesis suggested the chemical identity, in general terms,
for the saporous unit common to all compounds regardless of
chemical class that is responsible for the demonstrable and
fundamental proposition of sweetness. Perhaps because the thesis has

a molecular basis, it has been utilised in various fields of chemistry, physiology, pharmacology and psychology. Moreover, since much of the continued development of the thesis is directly due to discussions held at the Weybridge Symposia, I am pleased to be able to present the latest developments on chemical clues to the perception of sweetness.

FUNDAMENTALS OF THE AH–B CONCEPT

The saporous unit of all compounds that taste sweet was initially viewed as being a covalently bound hydrogen-bonding proton and also an electronegative orbital positioned at a distance of about 3 Å from the proton, or A-H-B,[1] and constitutes a first chemical clue to the perception of sweetness. While this description of the sweet saporous unit seems to be original with us, and brought a certain degree of order to seemingly anomalous relations between structure, functional groupings, and sweet taste, it also neatly embraced earlier thoughts on the subject.[2] Moreover, since the sweetness of a compound, especially the sugars, seemed to vary inversely with hypothetical potential for intramolecular hydrogen bonding, the corollary that followed was that the initial chemistry of

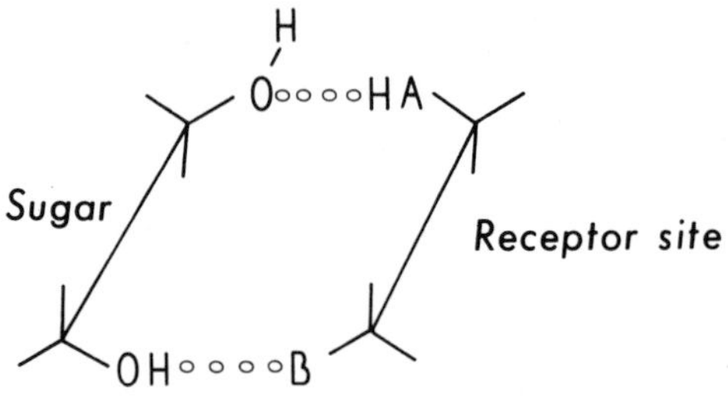

FIG. 1.   Interaction of vicinal sugar hydroxyl groups (AH–B) and a geometrically commensurate AH–B unit at the receptor site.

the sweet taste response must be a concerted intermolecular hydrogen bonding phenomenon, such as is shown using vicinal sugar hydroxyl groups as a compound's AH–B unit and interacting them with a geometrically commensurate AH–B unit at the receptor site (Fig. 1).

To our way of thinking, the concerted hydrogen bond interaction accounts for the importance of the Hammet sigma constant in the revised Deutsch[3] and Hansch equation[4] for sweetness since this constant correlates with a compound's dipole moment.

$$\log RS = 1\cdot434\,\pi - 1\cdot026\,\sigma + 1\cdot584$$

FUNDAMENTALS OF THE AH–B–γ CONCEPT

The correlation of the π constant shown in the equation for relative sweetness (RS) seems to be due to a compound's hydrophobic bonding potential and also to its lipophilic character. Which of the latter two parameters is the more important in special cases is difficult to sort out, but we are presently making an attempt to do this using certain sugar analogues.

A possible interaction of the hydrophobic bonding potential of π with the saporous unit AH–B of a compound has recently been proposed,[5] and I would like to spend some time developing the consequences of this added bit of insight.

To explain the varying sweetness of amino acids and the Blanksma–Hoegen series of 2-amino-4-nitrobenzene compounds,[6] Kier[7] called attention to the stereodisposition of a 'dispersion' function in these compounds in relation to the AH–B unit. Briefly, the tripartite grouping of the three functional groups describes a scalene triangular plane skewed to the 'left'.

We define the proposed third component of the saporous unit as γ, and based upon the findings of the Weybridge School[8] to the effect that there is probably a primary AH–B unit for each sugar, examined the sugars for probable γ sites. The key compounds, as before, turned out to be glucose, fructose, and galactose. For glucose[9] and fructose,[10] the primary AH–B function is shown in Fig. 2.

With the primary AH–B of both glucose and fructose thus located, it was quite exciting to discover that the only plausible choice for a γ

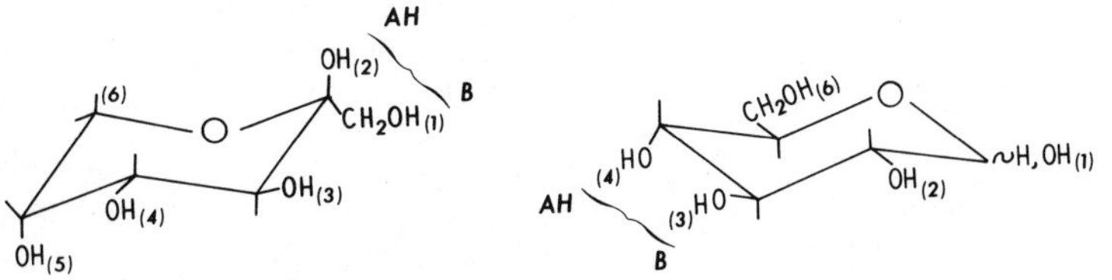

FIG. 2.   Location of the primary AH–B unit for sweetness in β-D-fructopyranose and D-glucopyranose.

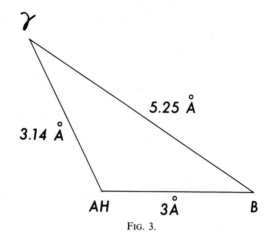

FIG. 3.

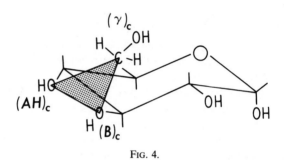

FIG. 4.

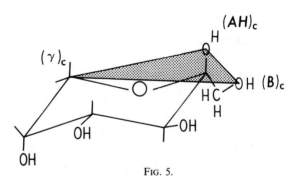

FIG. 5.

FIGS. 3 to 5. The relationship between AH–B and γ superposed on glucose and fructose.

entity for these two compounds (the external methylene C-6 carbon atom for glucose and the ring methylene C-6 carbon atom for fructose) was sterically located at the same position with respect to AH–B. Moreover, the relation between AH–B and γ as the saporous unit for these compounds bore a striking relation to that described by Kier[11] for the amino acids and the aminonitrobenzene compounds. Its structure is shown in Figs. 3–5 alone and superposed on glucose and fructose.

The Significance of γ

The question of the chemical significance or role of γ as a *second chemical clue* to the perception of sweetness poses several intriguing possibilities. The first of these, as previously mentioned, is the partitioning of γ between a chemical role as a simple lipophilic attribute and as a hydrophobic bonding parameter. If it functions primarily as a hydrophobic bonding site, is it related to sweetness intensity, as has been proposed,[5,11] and how does it do this? Is it simply that a tripartite fit is a 'stronger' interaction or does a concerted 'γ-interaction' activate an otherwise inert or relatively inert AH–B unit on the compound? I believe that we now have examples to answer each of these questions.

It seems certain that an element of lipid solubility is related to a short 'impact time' whenever a compound elicits the sweet sensation. The rapid but short-lived sweet sensation evoked by chloroform seems to be a good example as is the rapidity with which the sweetness of fructose is experienced.

To elaborate upon the 'activation' of AH–B by γ (or alternatively on the idea that the steric location of γ directs which sugar OH groups will function as AH and B), reference is made to the recent results of Lemieux and Brewer[12] on the rotamer population arising from rotation about the CH_2OH–C bond of hexopyranoid structures. According to these investigators, a hexopyranoid C-6 hy-droxymethylene group in a hydrophobic environment will position itself in space so that the OH group strongly bonds the oxygen atom of the OH group at carbon atom number 4 (Fig. 6). The net result is that the OH_4 group becomes a better proton donor, and the OH_3 oxygen atom becomes a better proton acceptor for hydrogen bonding systems. This more sophisticated insight into the chemistry of those very OH groups identified as the sweet AH–B unit led us to examine again some of our original tenets, particularly the idea that sugar

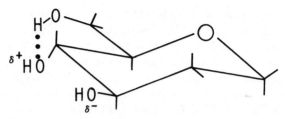

FIG. 6. Orientation of a hexopyranoid C-6 hydroxymethylene group in a hydrophobic environment.

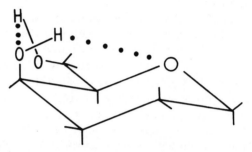

FIG. 7. Primary AH unit disposed to hydrogen bond intramolecularly resulting in decreased sugar sweetness.

sweetness varies inversely with the potential for intramolecular hydrogen bonding. It now seems apparent that intramolecular hydrogen bonding will decrease sugar sweetness especially when the primary AH unit is disposed to hydrogen bond intramolecularly. This is shown in Fig. 7 for a key compound, D-galactose. Analogous behaviour for D-fructopyranose serves to accentuate the proton

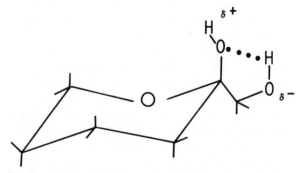

FIG. 8. Analogous behaviour as in Fig. 7 for D-fructopyranose.

donating capacity of OH_2 and fixes the position of OH_1 in space so that the AH–B distance is nearly ideal for action as the saporous unit for sweet taste (Fig. 8).

SYMMETRY IMPLICATIONS OF A TRIPARTITE SAPOROUS UNIT AH–B–γ

If the sweet-eliciting saporous unit of compounds is indeed tripartite, (but does not necessarily need to be tripartite in all cases) some problems encountered in explaining the relations observed between structure and sweet taste can be approached by application of symmetry principles. In this respect the major problem to be resolved is: 'What is the element of dissymmetry exhibited by the receptor site to account for the fact that the enantiomeric amino acids differ in their ability to elicit sweet taste whereas the mirror-image structured sugars do not'? The answer to this symmetry question is attractive, and may have rather general application to problems of the relation between structure and the biological activity of chemicals. It does not, however, necessarily eliminate the 'spatial barrier' explanation for the varying sweetness of enantiomeric amino acids proposed earlier.[13, 14]

In current symmetry language the expression of the problem stated above becomes: 'Why is the sweet-taste receptor site a chiral-recognising site for the amino acids, but not for the sugars?'

If the saporous unit of sweet-tasting compounds possesses the stereogeometry previously described, then the tripartite receptor site is either I or II, shown in Fig. 9.

The choice between I and II is directed by the fact that the tripartite saporous unit is in itself chiral. The element of dissymmetry leading to

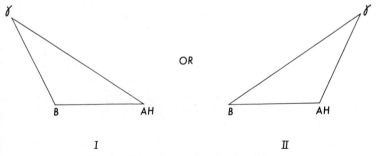

I   II

FIG. 9.   Tripartite receptor sites I and II.

this handedness is that the scalene-triangular tripartite structure does
not possess bilateral symmetry (or, it does not possess two-
dimensional point symmetry). Thus, to account for the difference in
ability between the D- and L-amino acids to elicit sweet taste, the
tripartite receptor site need only be diastereoisomeric with the
saporous unit. Receptor I meets this minimum criterion (No. II is

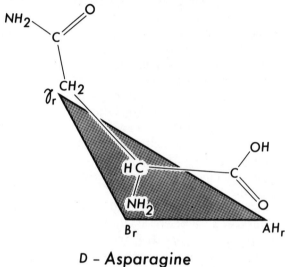

D – Asparagine

Fig. 10.   Tripartite positioning of D-asparagine (sweet) upon the tripartite receptor
for sweet taste.

enantiomeric with the saporous unit), and as shown in Fig. 10, D-
asparagine, which tastes sweet, neatly fits the tripartite receptor
whereas L-asparagine, which is tasteless, is capable of only a bipartite
fit (Fig. 11).

The diastereoisomeric receptor site I can also account for the fact
that D- and L-glucose are *equally* sweet. This is because the formation of the D-sugar ring from an L-sugar ring, or *vice versa*, has
generated an automorphism with respect to the tripartite saporous
unit! Put another way, the tripartite saporous units of the
enantiomeric sugars are congruent, i.e. superposable on themselves,
and equally diastereoisomeric with the receptor. This relation is
shown in Fig. 12.

To explain the 'anomalous' chiral-recognising ability of the sweet
receptor in symmetry terms, therefore, only requires reference to the

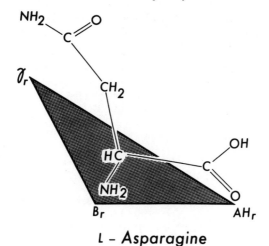

L - Asparagine

FIG. 11. Bipartite positioning of L-asparagine (tasteless) upon the tripartite receptor for sweet taste.

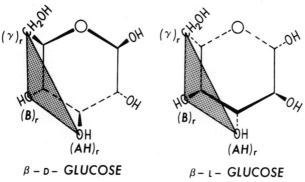

β – D – GLUCOSE β – L – GLUCOSE

FIG. 12. Tripartite superpositioning of D- and L-glucose (equally sweet) upon the tripartite receptor for sweet taste.

simplest possible case of a dissymmetric arrangement of three different functional groups in two dimensions, i.e., that of a scalene-triangular structure.

REFERENCES

1. Shallenberger, R. S. and Acree, T. E. (1967). *Nature* (London), **216,** p. 480.

2. Birch, G. G. (1976). In: *Critical Reviews in Food Science and Nutrition*, Vol. 8, No. 1, ed. T. E. Furia, CRC Press, Cleveland, p. 57.
3. Hansch, C. (1970). *J. Med. Chem.*, **13**, p. 964.
4. Deutsch, E. W. and Hansch, C. (1966). *Nature* (London), **211**, p. 75.
5. Shallenberger, R. S. and Lindley, M. G. (1977) *Fd. Chem.*, in press.
6. Blanksma, J. J. and Hoegen, D. (1946). *Rec. Trav. Chim.*, **65**, p. 333.
7. Kier, L. B. (1972). *J. Pharm. Sci.*, **61**, p. 1394.
8. Birch, G. G., Cowell, N. D. and Eyton, D. (1970). *J. Fd. Technol.*, **5**, p. 277.
9. Birch, G. G., Lee, C. K. and Rolfe, E. (1970). *J. Sci. Fd. Agric.*, **21**, p. 650.
10. Lindley, M. G. and Birch, G. G. (1975). *J. Sci. Fd. Agric.*, **26**, p. 117.
11. Kier, L. B. (1972), personal communication.
12. Lemieux, R. U. and Brewer, J. T. (1973). In: *Carbohydrates in Solution.*, ed. H. S. Isbell, *Adv. Chem. Series*, **117**, Amer. Chem. Soc., Washington, D.C., p. 121.
13. Shallenberger, R. S., Acree, T. E. and Lee, C. Y. (1969). *Nature* (London), **221**, p. 555.
14. Lelj, F., Tancredi, T., Temussi, P. A. and Toniolo, C. (1976). *J. Am. Chem. Soc.*, **98**, p. 6669.

DISCUSSION

Land: How do you account for differences in intensity of sweetness of different molecules by this theory?

Shallenberger: I can account for the difference in intensity of sweetness between sugars on the basis of AH and B. For intense sweetness we must invoke a concept of a greasy function. Perhaps sugars have no greasy function. They are poor sweetening compounds.

7

The Chemical Basis of Bitterness in Sugar Derivatives

G. G. Birch, C. K. Lee and A. Ray

National College of Food Technology,
University of Reading, Weybridge, Surrey, England

ABSTRACT

When sugar molecules are chemically modified the resulting derivatives are almost always bitter, sweet or bitter/sweet. The two basic tastes are therefore intimately associated in this class (as well as other classes) of compound. Bitterness is elicited by steric, polar and hydrophobic character in modified sugar molecules, and evidence, so far available, implicates the anomeric centre, ring oxygen atom and hydroxyl substituents at C-2 and C-6 in the response. In bitter/sweet glucopyranose types of structure these features represent those parts of the molecule not directly involved as sweet-eliciting AH–B systems. Hence the molecules may be 'polarised' on taste receptors, one 'end' eliciting sweetness and the other bitterness. Evidence for the proximity of both types of receptor site is now available.

INTRODUCTION

Unlike saltiness and sourness, bitterness resembles sweetness in that it results from the stereochemistry of stimulus molecules. The sensation is evoked by carbohydrates, amino acids and more complicated types of compound, all of which may exhibit intrinsic asymmetry, and size as well as shape of the stimulus molecule may govern the response. Definitive structure–response studies with conformationally understood compounds may therefore be expected to yield information about the nature of the bitter receptor site, as well as to produce novel bitter substances potentially useful in the food industry.

FEATURES OF BITTER SUGARS

The chemical modification of sugars often results in a transition of taste from sweet to bitter, partial modification (e.g. by glycoside formation or synthesis of monodeoxy or monomethyl compounds) often resulting in bitter/sweet types. Complete esterification of sugars (e.g. by formation of peracetates) can change a very sweet sugar into a very bitter one, sucrose octaacetate for instance having a threshold bitterness similar to that of quinine sulphate.[1] Although the exact nature of the bitter pharmacophore is still unknown it is clear that certain structural features are associated with bitterness, and in sugar molecules these are as follows: First the β-anomers seem more likely to be bitter than their α- counterparts, as exemplified by D-mannose, in which the α-form is sweet and the β-form is bitter, and α,α-trehalose which is purely sweet whereas β,β-trehalose is fairly bitter. The anomeric centre must therefore be involved in the bitter response since these pairs of analogues differ only in the configuration of the hemiacetal carbon atom. If an aglycone is lipophilic, increase in its chain length is accompanied by increasing bitterness, and any such aglycone with more than two carbon atoms will contribute a distinct bitterness to its glycoside. For instance (Fig. 1) methyl and ethyl glycosides tend to be sweet or bitter/sweet, while propyl glycosides are very bitter. Again, aglycones of this type substituted in the β-configuration are more likely to be bitter than those substituted in the α-position. The anomeric oxygen atom itself is another important feature of bitter compounds as its removal leads to loss of bitterness.

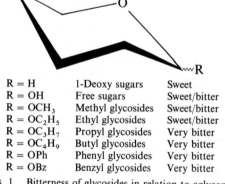

R = H	1-Deoxy sugars	Sweet
R = OH	Free sugars	Sweet/bitter
R = OCH_3	Methyl glycosides	Sweet/bitter
R = OC_2H_5	Ethyl glycosides	Sweet/bitter
R = OC_3H_7	Propyl glycosides	Very bitter
R = OC_4H_9	Butyl glycosides	Very bitter
R = OPh	Phenyl glycosides	Very bitter
R = OBz	Benzyl glycosides	Very bitter

Fig. 1.   Bitterness of glycosides in relation to aglycones.

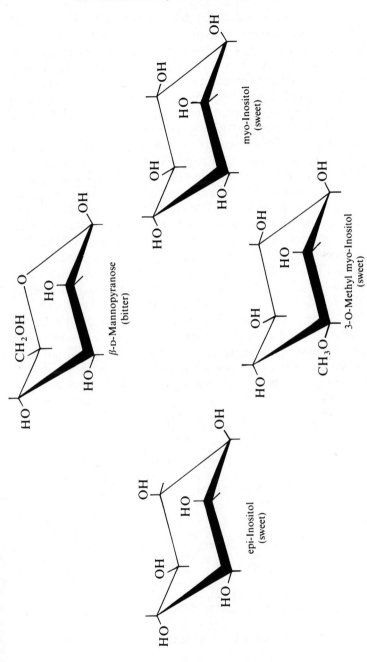

FIG. 2. Analogy of β-D-mannose and epicyclitols.

This is clearly illustrated with 1-deoxy β-D-mannose in which the bitterness of β-D-mannose is completely removed and indeed, unlike other monodeoxy sugars, the 1-deoxy sugars do not in any case exhibit even trace bitterness. Second, the ring oxygen atom of sugar molecules, as well as the primary alcohol group in the adjacent carbon atom seem to be involved in bitterness. Thus, whereas β-D-mannose is bitter, its analogue epiinositol is sweet, the cyclitol differing from the sugar only in the absence of the ring oxygen atom and primary alcohol group[2] (Fig. 2). The involvement of both the ring oxygen atom and the anomeric oxygen atom in bitterness is consistent with chemical structure in that the latter cannot exist without the former. A good example of this is provided by a recent study of coumarin analogues,[3] two of which are shown in Fig. 3. Many members of this class are now known and their stereostructure allows them to be tasteless or sweet. All are devoid of an anomeric centre and all are devoid of bitterness. The importance of the primary alcohol group of sugars in evoking bitterness is clear from an examination of β-D-lyxose which differs from β-D-mannose only in the absence of this function, and which, unlike β-D-mannose, is devoid of bitterness.

The configuration and chemical modification of the second hydroxyl group of aldopyranose types of structure also seems to be involved in the bitter response. Thus β-D-mannose with an axial hydroxyl group in this position is bitter whereas β-D-glucose, with an equatorial one, is not. Furthermore, mono 2-deoxy derivatives are

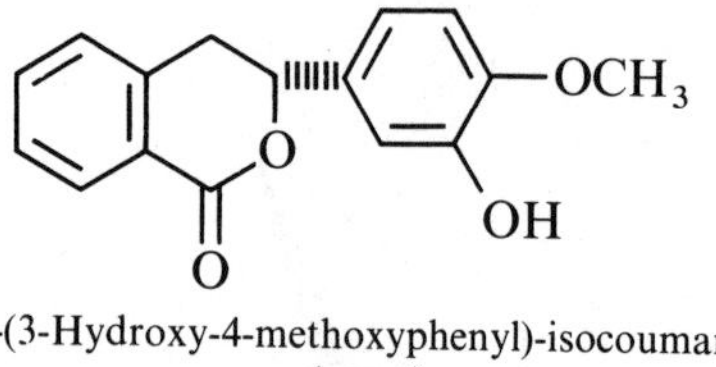

3-(3-Hydroxy-4-methoxyphenyl)-isocoumarin
(sweet)

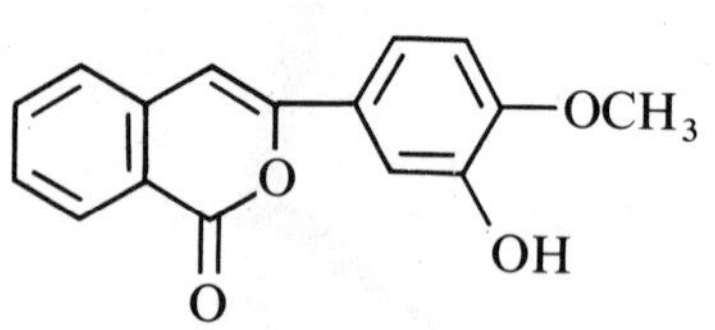

3-(3-Hydroxy-4-methoxyphenyl)-3,4-dihydroisocoumarin
(tasteless)

FIG. 3.   Taste and chemical structure in isocoumarin analogues.

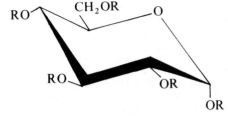

Ether (less bitter)

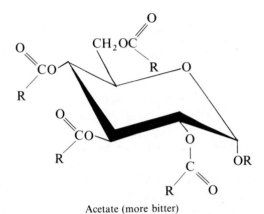

Acetate (more bitter)

FIG. 4. Acetates, ethers and taste.

distinctly bitter while the 3- and 4-deoxy analogues are not. A relationship between bitterness and lipophilicity also appears to exist because increase in lipophilic character by esterification, etherification, increase in methylene functions (as in deoxy sugar formation) or lengthening of the carbon chain of an aglycone, results in a concomitant increase of bitterness. Acetates are particularly bitter (Fig. 4) and this illustrates that polarity, as well as lipophilicity, is involved in the bitter response. However, the threshold differences in bitterness among different acetates emphasise the fine interplay of structural factors which may be involved.

In attempting to correlate bitterness with structure of carbohydrates, the sugar α,α-trehalose again seems to be an ideal model.[4] Its unique character as a disaccharide facilitates the synthesis of symmetrically-substituted analogues by which the influence of each chiral centre on total gustatory response may be assessed. Asymmetric derivatives of trehalose may also be prepared and an interesting

TABLE 1
Threshold bitterness of some sucrose and trehalose acetates

Sugar acetate	Threshold concentration
Sucrose octaacetate	7.6×10^{-6} M
Sucrose heptaacetate (6' OH)	8.6×10^{-6} M
Sucrose hexaacetate (4,6' OH)	13.2×10^{-6} M
Sucrose hexaacetate (6,6' OH)	13.1×10^{-6} M
Sucrose hexaacetate (1',6' OH)	22.0×10^{-6} M
α,α-Trehalose octaacetate	12.9×10^{-6} M
β,β-Trehalose octaacetate	22.1×10^{-6} M
α,α-Trehalose hexaacetate (6,6' OH)	22.0×10^{-6} M
α,α-Trehalose hexaacetate (4,6 OH)	41.0×10^{-6} M

comparison is the asymmetric (4,6 OH) hexaacetate with the symmetric (6,6^1 OH) hexaacetate. The former is less bitter than the latter and less bitter than sucrose octaacetate. Therefore the glucose residue with the greater number of free hydroxyl groups seems to determine the bitterness. It is probable that in an oligosaccharide derivative only one residue binds to the bitter receptor. Evidence in support of this idea has already been accrued from trehalose derivatives. This accords with the previous analogous observation with sweet compounds. In sucrose acetates it seems that the fructofuranosyl residue is involved in the bitter response, and here the C-1^1 primary alcohol group contributes whereas the C-6^1 primary alcohol group does not.[5] In summary, carbon atoms 1, 2, and 6, and the ring oxygen atom are positively implicated in the bitter response, and overall polarity and lipophilicity of the molecule each play an important part.

SIMILARITIES IN NON-CARBOHYDRATE MOLECULES

Following an early observation by Shallenberger[6] that intramolecular hydrogen bonding inhibits sweetness but is associated with bitterness, Kubota and Kubo[7] claimed that an A–B interorbital spacing of 1.6 Å gave rise to bitterness, but this generalisation does not seem applicable to other classes of compound.[4]

Although a general rule applicable to the amino acids is that the D-forms are sweet and the L-forms are bitter, Ariyoshi[8] has recently pointed out that certain conditions such as size, shape and hydrophobicity of substituents must be satisfied for the taste response to occur. Generally, the amino acids with a single asymmetric carbon atom are easier to categorise in this way than the sugars, which exhibit multiple chirality. However, the lack of conformational definition in acyclic compounds means that their orientation on receptor sites is less easily understood.

It is interesting that a recent study by Wieser and Belitz[9] of about 60 amino acids and related compounds has concluded that hydrophobic, polar and steric factors are all required for bitterness in these molecules. This work, which was conducted completely independently of the Weybridge work on bitterness in sugars, suggests that a spacing of about 3 Å between the polar and lipophilic regions of a molecule is a criterion of bitterness.[10,11] In a related study on the sweet taste of dipeptide esters Brussel *et al.*[12] have examined the shape of sapid molecules and discussed two space filling maxima in the extended chain, about 3 Å from each other, and also (for the first) about 3 Å from the asymmetric carbon atom. This is reminiscent of Shallenberger's[6] original AH–B interorbital spacing of 2·9 Å and the coincident conclusion of these independent approaches is striking. Molecular distances of the order of 3 Å are of course the span of simple cyclic molecules like sugars, and this point is possibly fundamentally significant in the known association between sweet and bitter tastes.

RECEPTOR SITES AND BINDING MODALITIES

Dastoli and co-workers[13] reported the isolation of a protein fraction from bovine epithelia which complexed with bitter molecules. Other workers,[14–16] however, favour the idea of interaction of the bitter molecule with the lipid layer of the gustatory membrane. Whichever is the case, evidence in support of the separateness of sweet and bitter receptor sites is provided by the action of gymnemic acid.[17] This substance has the ability to block sweetness without affecting the bitter response. Although some taste cells are undoubtedly specific others are not[18] and this being so, the location of sweet and bitter receptor sites on non-specific cells is relevant to the effectiveness of sapid molecules. The possible overlap of the two basic tastes may be represented diagrammatically as in Fig. 5.

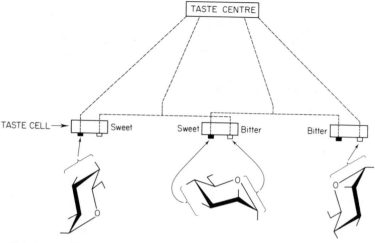

FIG. 5.   Possible overlap of sweet and bitter taste information via receptor sites.

Chemical modification of sugars[19] has revealed that one 'end' of the molecule (the third and fourth OH groups of glucopyranoside types of structure) elicits sweetness and the other 'end' (the first and second hydroxyl groups, ring oxygen atom and primary alcohol group of glucopyranoside types of structure) elicits bitterness. How then do bitter/sweet types of sugar exert their effect? Do such molecules distribute themselves, some on sweet receptor sites, and some on bitter? Or is it possible that a single molecule could span both receptor sites simultaneously, possibly by a chelating mechanism? Evidence in support of the latter hypothesis[20] has been obtained from an experiment in which subjects were asked to taste the bitter/sweet sugar methyl α-D-mannopyranoside after pre-saturating their tongues with sucrose. Under such conditions the bitter taste of the glycoside was significantly diminished, while a control test with quinine sulphate showed no significant effect on the bitter response. When the entire experiment was repeated the other way round (i.e. pre-saturation of the tongues with quinine sulphate and tasting for sweetness) again the taste of the glycoside was diminished but not that of a sucrose control. These results can be interpreted to mean that impairment of one binding modality of the bitter/sweet sugar (i.e. by pre-saturation of receptor sites) inhibits total gustatory response. Hence such molecules need to span both types of receptor simultaneously.

The known association of sweetness and bitterness now seems to be emphasised with studies of taste response to conformationally defined molecules. Bitterness, like sweetness, is a truly molecular effect,[21] depending on stereochemical, hydrophobic and polar structural features, and some at least of the bitter receptor sites may be located within 3–4 Å of the sweet receptor sites. These results offer a fascinating clue to the molecular patterns ultimately responsible for both basic tastes.

ACKNOWLEDGEMENT

We thank Cadbury–Schweppes Ltd. for a generous grant supporting bitterness research at this College.

REFERENCES

1. Lee, C. K. (1976). Paper presented at the VIII *IUPAC International Carbohydrate Symposium* Kyoto, Japan.
2. Birch, G. G. and Lee, C. K. (1976). *J. Fd. Sci.*, **41**, p. 1403.
3. Yamamoto, M., Hashigaki, K., Uenishi, J., Yamakawa, I., Sato, N. and Koyama, T. (1975). *Chem. Pharm. Bull.*, **23**, p. 3101.
4. Birch, G. G. (1976). *Crit. Rev. Fd. Sci. and Nutr.*, **8**, p. 57.
5. Birch, G. G., Lee, C. K. and Ray, A. (1976). *Paper presented at the 2nd ECRO Congress, Reading.*
6. Shallenberger, R. S. (1963). *J. Fd. Sci.*, **28**, p. 584.
7. Kubota, T. and Kubo, I. (1969). *Nature*, **223**, p. 97.
8. Ariyoshi, Y. (1976). *Agr. Biol. Chem.*, **40**, p. 983.
9. Wieser, H. and Belitz, H-D. (1975) *Z. Lebensmit. Unters-Forsch.*, **159**, p. 65.
10. Wieser, H. and Belitz, H-D. (1976). *Z. Lebensmit. Unters-Forsch.*, **160**, p. 383.
11. Wieser, H. and Belitz, H-D. (1976). *Z. Lebensmit. Unters-Forsch.*, **160**, p. 251.
12. Brussel, L. B. P., Peer, H. G. and A. van der Heijden (1975). *Z. Lebensmit. Unters-Forsch.*, **159**, p. 337.
13. Dastoli, F. R., Lopiekes, D. V. and Price, S. (1968). *Nature*, **217**, p. 884.
14. Faull, J. B. and Halpern, B. P. (1969). *Fed. Proc.*, **28**, p. 275.
15. Kurihara, Y. (1973). *Biochim. Biophys. Acta*, **306**, p. 478.
16. Koyama, N. and Kurihara, K. (1972). *Biochim. Biophys. Acta*, **288**, p. 22.
17. Bartoshuk, L. (1977). In: *Sensory Properties of Foods*, eds. G. G. Birch, J. G. Brennan and K. J. Parker, Appl. Sci. Publishers, London.
18. Beidler, L. M. (1971). In: *Sweetness and Sweeteners*, eds. G. G. Birch, L. F. Green and C. B. Coulson, Appl. Sci. Publishers, London.

19. Birch, G. G. (1976). In: *Structure–Activity Relationships in Chemoreception*, ed. in chief G. Benz, IRL, London.
20. Birch, G. G. and Mylvaganam, A. R. (1976). *Nature*, **260**, p. 632.
21. Beets, M. G. J. (1978). *Structure–Activity Relationships in Human Chemoreception*, Appl. Sci. Publishers, London.

DISCUSSION

Harries: May we learn a little more, please, about the sensory methods used in determining the flavour characteristics of the compounds? In this paper threshold concentrations have been quoted and one would like to know which threshold. In much of the published literature on flavour chemistry is seems to me that too little attention sometimes is paid to the biological and psychological variability inherent in the sensory tests on which many of the conclusions are based.

Ray: Taste panel experiments are done and values are obtained for bitterness or sweetness. Dr Lee can furnish the details.

Lee: We used the method of Gregson (R. A. M. Gregson, 1962, *J. Food Sci.*, **27**, 376) for threshold determination. The values quoted are recognition thresholds and not detection thresholds.

Shallenberger: I should like to pose the question—how do you define sweetness? It is a sensory response, a fundamental proposition and that is all. We then move into the area of detection and recognition of the threshold. I am now abandoning the concept of detection threshold.

Palmer: As regards the limitations of threshold values, we must know the procedure for threshold tests. There is no absolute value for a threshold—merely a value for a particular population.

Lee: We fully agree with your comments. The values we reported were all carried out under the same conditions and by the same panellists and as such these are comparable. We do not claim these to be absolute threshold values.

Shallenberger: Sucrose is bitter at very low levels. But does sucrose really have a bitter taste?

Bartoshuk: It is important to distinguish between detection and recognition thresholds. For example, one 'detects' the presence of quinine hydrochloride, or one 'recognises' the quality bitterness. In order to prevent confusion between water taste thresholds and solute taste thresholds, the tongue should be rinsed before *each* stimulus is tasted.

Lee: We fully realise the importance of mouth rinse and in all our determinations the panellists were asked to do this with a water sample before and in between each tasting, though we must admit that the rinsing procedure was not as elaborate as that described by Dr Bartoshuk. Though the problems of cross-adaptation may arise, this should not affect our result, since all the sugars should be affected similarly. In any case, at the particular moment, we are interested mainly in scanning to see which analogues are worth studying in greater detail.

8

Correlating Instrumental and Sensory Flavour Data

E. VON SYDOW and C. ÅKESSON

SIK—The Swedish Food Institute, Göteborg, Sweden

ABSTRACT

Perceived odour and taste as well as flavour preference originate from stimulation of the sensory cells with compounds present in the food and having proper stimulation properties. With few exceptions it is a matter of several or many compounds taking part in the stimulation. The compounds responsible can be characterised in terms of identity and quantity, using well-known analytical techniques. Perceived flavour is not so straightforward in analytical terms. However, it can be dealt with using profiling techniques and in principle one can arrive at a set of qualitative sensory data corresponding to the set of chemical data. The intensity of a sensory attribute is sometimes a parametric function but often the relations are non-parametric, i.e., the sensory attribute can only be classified into a specified number of classes such as high, medium and low.

There are theoretical and practical reasons for investigating how the relations are between these sets of data. If one can derive mathematical models which adequately describe these relations in qualitative and quantitative terms, these models will help explain the mechanisms of stimulation and perception and thus be of help in physiological and psychophysical research. From a practical point of view the models may be used in such a way that panel work can be complemented or supplemented with instrumental methods in routine quality control or in product and process development work, e.g. the optimisation of product quality.

One perceived property may originate from several stimulants and, vice versa, one chemical compound may stimulate so that several distinguishable attributes are perceived. Flavour preference is usually guided by several sensory attributes.

One general, parametric equation for response–stimuli relation is

$$R = F[f_1(X_1) + f_2(X_2) + \cdots + f_k(X_k)] + \varepsilon$$

Difference in preference values between two samples P_K and P_L can be expressed as:

$$P(P_K, P_L) = F\left[\sum_{i=1}^{N} f_i(|X_{i_K} - X_{i_L}|)\right] + \varepsilon$$

where X_i is the concentration of compound i.

The advantages and limitations with these types of approach for predicting sensory data from instrumental is discussed in relation to data on heat sterilised beef products. A comparison between a parametric and a non-parametric treatment of data is also made. The impact of the accuracy of the instrumental data used is demonstrated using Monte-Carlo simulation procedures.

INTRODUCTION

We judge flavour of foods with our chemical senses, olfaction and taste. The perceived odour and taste and also flavour preferences are generated by stimulation of the sensory cells by specific compounds present in the food and having proper stimulation properties. With few exceptions it is a matter of several or many compounds taking part in the stimulation. The compounds responsible can be characterised in terms of identity and quantity, using well-known physico-chemical techniques. Perceived flavour is not so straightforward in analytical terms. However, it can be dealt with using profiling techniques and in principle we can arrive at a set of sensory data.

There are theoretical as well as practical reasons for investigating how the relations are between these sets of data. If we can derive mathematical models which adequately describe these relations in qualitative and quantitative terms, these models will help explain the mechanisms of flavour stimulation and perception and thus be useful in physiological and psychophysical research. From a practical point of view such equations may be used in such a way that panel work can be complemented or supplemented with instrumental methods in routine quality control or in product and process development work, e.g., the optimisation of product quality.

If one can specify the stimulants causing a desired flavour perceived by the consumer, it is possible in theory to produce a food product containing these stimulants. This is, in principle, how the flavour industry works. For finished food products the situation is, however, very complicated as there are limitations in how much the formulation and processing can be changed and also because of interactions between various properties. There is also lack of sufficient characterisation of 'desired flavour' in words and figures. In practice, therefore, successful applications of flavour steering by formulation or processing have, so far, more often been concerned with removal of off-flavours than with the development of desirable flavour. One example concerned with canned beef will be used here to demonstrate techniques for relating sensory and instrumental data. A comparison between a parametric and non-parametric treatment of sensory data will be made and the impact of the accuracy of the instrumental data used will be demonstrated using Monte-Carlo simulation procedures.

BACKGROUND EXPERIMENTS

The heat necessary for sterilisation of foods sometimes causes an off-flavour, particularly in canned protein foods. This effect limits the usage of this excellent method of preservation and distribution. Limitation or removal of this off-flavour is thus highly desirable from the marketing point of view. In a series of experiments over 40 combinations of formulation, processing, packaging and storage parameters of canned beef were investigated from the flavour point of view, by instrumental and sensory methods.[1-6]

Some 100 volatile compounds were identified and many of them quantified using gas chromatography (GC) and mass spectrometry. The off-odour and its formation and changes were evaluated sensorially by an odour quality assessment technique originally developed by Harper *et al.*[7,8] and further developed in our laboratories.[2]

RELATIONS

Models for relating instrumental and sensory data may be classified into the following levels of validity:[3]

 (i)   Accidental (*ad hoc*) models being valid only for a given, finite set of data obtained at a certain occasion and thus having no general validity.
 (ii)   Predictive models providing generally valid predictor variables for certain types of data, i.e. predictive models satisfying some predetermined statistical criterion of accuracy for every data set under consideration.
 (iii) Causative models indicating genuine stimulus–response patterns in a psychophysical sense and not merely statistical regularities.

Most models, hitherto reported, belong to the categories (i) or (ii).

The main purpose of our investigations was to find out whether the sensory properties of aroma and flavour could be predicted by using only GC measurements and, in particular, whether the predictions obtained were sufficiently accurate to be useful in practical applications. Another important and related objective was to investigate the possibility of using GC data to predict preference judgements of aroma and flavour.

In order to develop not only predictive models but also potentially causative ones, a psychophysical approach rather than a pure statistical one must be attempted. This has, so far, not been done by us due to lack of sufficient information on how odour stimulants interact on the physiological and the perceptual levels (for a review and discussion, cf. Cain[9]). From another point of view, one stimulant can lead to several perceived odours and it is not well known how the intensities of these different perceived odours vary with concentration of the stimulant, although it is generally accepted that the total odour intensity follows Stevens' law, $R = c \cdot S^n$. However, correct predictive models can help develop causative ones and they have thus a double value.

MODELS

Parametric/Non-parametric Approaches to Sensory Data

A parametric analysis of sensory data is, in principle, based on the following assumptions:

(a)   the sensory attributes (qualities) to be evaluated are perceived
      as 'continua' with respect to magnitudes of intensity;
(b)   the subjects are able to estimate, in a consistent way, the
      perceived magnitudes of intensity in terms of numbers (or
      some equivalent scale categories);
(c)   the distribution of the (numerical) response data obtained
      follows some parametric distribution function (notably, the
      normal or the log–normal distribution function).

Assumptions (a) and (b) imply that sensory data are considered as
interval-scaled data.

A number of so-called psychometric methods have been developed
for deriving sensory intensity scales on the basis of numerical
response data. Such well-known methods are, for example, the
magnitude and ratio estimation techniques. In spite of the simplicity
of these techniques, it seems that many intricate methodological
problems may arise in practical applications, due to e.g. 'idio-
syncratic' handling of numbers, interactions between the stimuli
involved, etc. Therefore, one may argue that the meaning and the
interpretability of sensory scales, derived from numerical response
data, are only incompletely understood.

The non-parametric approach to sensory data involves less
stringent assumptions:

(d)   the sensory attributes may or may not be perceived as
      'perceptual continua';
(e)   the subjects are only able to rank or classify the stimuli
      (samples) into a set of discrete categories (specified by
      numbers or otherwise);
(f)   parametric specifications of the underlying distribution of the
      response data obtained cannot be made.

The non-parametric approach implies that, from a metric point of
view, sensory data are considered as ordinal or nominal data,
necessitating the use of e.g. discriminant analysis for determining the
relations between instrumental and sensory data.

Discriminant analysis of GC data has successfully been used for
classifying several food and drink products. It has, however, been
used mostly to classify samples in groups according to geographical
origin, brand, blending, product quality, etc. Qvist *et al.*[10] use stepwise
discriminant analysis for identifying chemical predictors of sensory

qualities in meat products containing unconventional protein raw materials.

A quantitative analysis of 'non-parametric' sensory data (ordinal or nominal data) may in some cases be extremely difficult to perform. However, from a psychological point of view, we believe that a non-parametric approach is more justified than a parametric one.

Functional Regression Models

The basis of the models tested is that sensory intensity is assumed to be generated by some additive combination of a number of compounds. The most general formula is given by (1):

$$R = F[f_1(X_1) + f_2(X_2) + \cdots + f_k(X_k)] + \varepsilon \qquad (1)$$

where R is the sensory intensity of one attribute expressed in terms of numerical judgements and X_k is the concentration of compound k.

Specialised cases of (1) are (2) and (3):

$$R = a[w_1 X_1 + w_2 X_2 + \cdots + w_k X_k]^n + \varepsilon \qquad (2)$$

$$R = F[a_1 X_1{}^{n1} + a_2 X_2{}^{n2} + \cdots + a_k X_k{}^{nk}] + \varepsilon \qquad (3)$$

For preference judgements the following functional model (4) was applied:

$$P(\text{sample}_K, \text{sample}_L) = F\left[\sum_{i=1}^{N} f_i(|X_{i_K} - X_{i_L}|)\right] + \varepsilon \qquad (4)$$

where P is the difference in preference values between the two samples K and L.

Of several f_i-functions tested the following (5) gave satisfactory results in most cases:

$$f_i = a[(Z + 1)e^{-bZ} - 1] \qquad (5)$$

The necessary algorithms have been developed by Åkesson.[11] The concentrations were normalised before calculation.

Classification Models

Stepwise discriminant analysis is a well-known technique.[12] A linear discriminant function was used to separate the samples into the predetermined classes or categories.

When dealing with preference there is a need for transformation of the observed differences in instrumental data before carrying out the linear discriminant analysis. The reason for this is that several chemical predictors are not monotonically related to preference value. The transformation is done so that small differences within one class are made smaller and large differences between classes made larger.[13]

RESULTS

Functional Regression Models

For most odour qualities investigated, the judgements of intensity were related to the gas chromatographic values in a parametric and monotonic way. Additive combinations of up to six different compounds gave highly significant and accurate results when using functional models of type (3). For the odour attribute 'canned beef off-flavour' the following equation is a good example:

$$Y = 0.56X_1^{0.64} + 0.27X_2^{0.33} + 0.17X_3^{0.14} + \varepsilon \qquad (6)$$

X_1, X_2 and X_3 are the concentrations of 2-methylbutanal, hydrogen sulphide and dimethylsulphide, respectively. Y is the perceived intensity (observed and calculated or predicted) of the attribute 'canned-beef off-flavour'. The parameter estimators in eqn. (6) were calculated from 18 samples. The correlation coefficient for calculated

TABLE 1

Correlation coefficients and mean difference (on a 10-point scale) relating observed and predicted 'canned-beef off-flavour' and preference using functional regression models (6) and (7)

	Random error (%)	Correlation coefficient	Mean difference (absolute value)
'Canned-beef	0	0.96	0.09
off-flavour'	5	0.93	0.23
	10	0.85	0.29
	20	0.72	0.43
	40	0.51	0.79
Preference	0	0.95	0.12
	5	0.93	0.26
	10	0.84	0.31
	20	0.73	0.49
	40	0.40	0.84

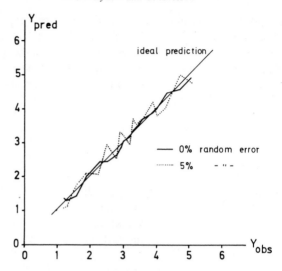

FIG. 1. Predicted intensity of 'canned-beef off-flavour' as a function of observed intensity. Regression model (6); 18 samples; 10 judges; 4 replicates. ————, Based on instrumental data; ·····, 5% random error applied to instrumental data.

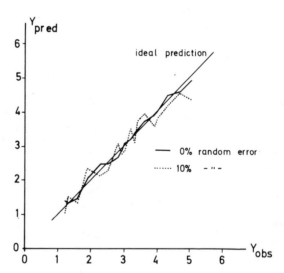

FIG. 2. As for Fig. 1. ·····, 10% random error applied to instrumental data.

and observed intensities for these samples was 0·96. The equation was used to predict odour intensities for the same 18 samples (Fig. 1). The importance of the accuracy of the instrumental data is demonstrated with the dotted curves in Figs. 1–3. These curves represent simulated, predicted intensities when the instrumental data are subjected to a 5,

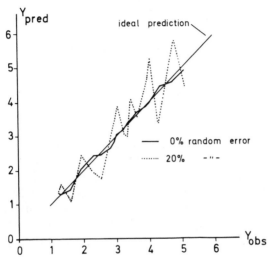

FIG. 3. As for Fig. 1. ······, 20% random error applied to instrumental data.

10 and 20% random error using Monte-Carlo simulation techniques.[14,15] Correlation coefficients and mean difference values (on a 10-point scale) are given in Table 1.

Preference values can be accurately predicted by adopting models according to (4) and (5). As can be expected, preference value is not necessarily a monotonic function of the concentration of all odour stimulants. For example, the preference value of canned beef has a maximum value at a concentration of ~ 2000 ppb of methanethiol and ~ 30 ppb of 2-methyl butanal.[6]

The following turned out to be one of several good equations to predict preference value:

$$P(\text{sample}_K, \text{sample}_L) = 1 \cdot 67\{0 \cdot 79[(Z_1 + 1)e^{-0 \cdot 21 Z_1} - 1]$$
$$+ 0 \cdot 63[(Z_2 + 1)e^{-0 \cdot 19 Z_2} - 1] + 0 \cdot 33[(Z_3 + 1)e^{-0 \cdot 11 Z_3} - 1]\} \quad (7)$$

P is the difference in preference value between samples K and L. $Z_i = |X_{i_K} - X_{i_L}|$ where X_i is the concentration of compound i in samples K

TABLE 2

Correlation coefficients and mean differences on a 10-point scale (absolute values) for 'canned-beef off-flavour' and preference

	Correlation coefficient[a]	Correlation coefficient[b]	Mean difference when predicting unknowns[c]
'Canned-beef off-flavour'	0·96	0·91	0·22
Preference	0·96	0·92	0·17

[a] 35 reference samples.
[b] 12 'unknown' samples.
[c] 10-point scale, absolute values.

and L, respectively. Compounds 1, 2 and 3 were 2-methylbutanal, methanethiol and pentanal, respectively. The parameter estimators in eqn. (7) were calculated from the same 18 samples mentioned above. The correlation coefficient for calculated and observed preference values for these samples was 0·95. The equation was used to predict preference values for the same 18 samples (Fig. 4).

The effect of applying 5, 10 or 20% random error on the chemical data is shown in Figs. 4–6. Correlation coefficients and mean

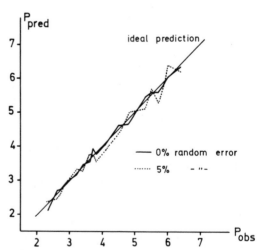

FIG. 4. Predicted preference value as a function of observed preference value. Regression model (7); 18 samples; 10 judges; 4 replicates. ———, based on instrumental data; ······, 5% random error applied to instrumental data.

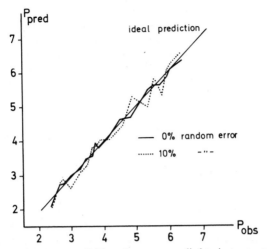

FIG. 5. As for Fig. 4. ······, 10% random error applied to instrumental data.

difference values (on a 10-point scale) are given in Table 1. In another experiment functional models similar to eqns. (6) and (7) were developed based on 35 reference samples of canned beef.[6] These models were applied to 12 other samples regarded as unknown. The correlation coefficients and mean differences obtained (on a 10-point scale, absolute values) are given in Table 2.

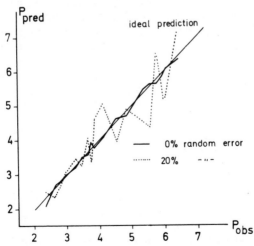

FIG. 6. As for Fig. 4. ······, 20% random error applied to instrumental data.

TABLE 3

Compounds resulting from stepwise discriminant analysis of 22 compounds in 18 samples of canned beef (in order of importance as predictors)

'Canned-beef off-flavour'	Preference
2-methylbutanal	2-methylbutanal
hydrogen sulphide	methanethiol
dimethyl sulphide	pentanal
methanethiol	hexanal
2-methylpropanal	2-pentylfurane

Classification Models

It was assumed that the canned-beef samples could be grouped in a number of distinct classes according to odour intensity of specific attributes or preference value. It was further assumed that it is possible to describe unambiguously the classified samples chemically, e.g. with GC data. Relations between odour qualities or preference on one hand and corresponding GC data on the other can then be estimated by stepwise discriminant analysis, resulting in linear combinations of concentrations of compounds which 'correlate' with the samples classified according to odour intensity or preference value.

Twenty-two chemical compounds present in 18 different samples of canned beef were subjected to discriminant analysis with the purpose of developing classification models. The intensity of 'canned beef off-flavour' and preference values was divided into three classes: low,

TABLE 4

Classification of 'canned-beef off-flavour', based on discriminant analysis of 22 GC-components. 18 samples

		Random error 0%, 5%, 10% or 20%					*Random error* 40%		
		predicted						predicted	
		l	m	h			l	m	h
	l	4	0	0		l	2	2	0
observed	m	0	5	0	*observed*	m	1	3	1
	h	0	0	9		h	1	2	6

[a] l = low intensity 'canned-beef off-flavour' = 1·00–1·99.
 m = medium intensity 'canned-beef off-flavour' = 2·00–2·99.
 h = high intensity 'canned-beef off-flavour' ≥ 3·00.

TABLE 5

Classification of preference based on discriminant analysis of 22 GC-components. 18 samples

		Random error 0%, 5% or 10%						Random error 20%		
		predicted						predicted		
		l	m	h				l	m	h
	l	6	0	0			l	3	3	0
observed	m	0	5	0		*observed*	m	2	3	0
	h	0	0	7			h	2	2	3

[a] l = low preference = 2·00–3·49.
  m = medium preference = 3·50–4·49.
  h = high preference ≥ 4·50.

medium and high. Predicted classification was carried out for the 18 samples using 5 chemical compounds for 'canned-beef off-flavour' and 5 for preference (Table 3).

The results are shown in Tables 4 and 5 (0% random error). The actual test of this model is carried out when random error is applied to the chemical data. The effect of applying 5, 10, 20 or 40% random error is shown in Tables 4 and 5. As can be seen, the model for preference is more easily ruptured than the one for 'canned-beef off-flavour', which can withstand up to at least 20% random error without collapsing. The classification models developed seem to work well for the material investigated.

Comparing these results with those described above concerning functional regression models, good agreement can be found. Predictors for 'canned-beef off-flavour' and preference, respectively, are more or less the same compounds in the two situations. In the case of 'canned-beef off-flavour' the common compounds are 2-methylbutanal, hydrogen sulphide and dimethylsulphide in order of importance. For preference value the common compounds are in order 2-methylbutanal, methanethiol and pentanal. The advantage of using classification models is, however, that there is no demand on continuity of intensity of the perceived properties.

APPLICATIONS

Models developed in the way described here are at the most predictive and the choice is based entirely on the statistical decision rules applied. The identification of causative models necessitates more information on how stimulants interact, the odour profile of individual stimulants, etc. Accurate predictive models can, however, be very useful in developing causative models, thus helping to explain true stimulus–response relations on the physiological and psychophysical level.

The predictive models can be applied in essentially two ways. One is in quality control, the other in product and process development. In quality control a limited number of compounds can be identified and used as predictors of specific sensory properties and preference values. In this way tedious panel work can be supplemented with instrumental techniques such as gas chromatography. In product and process development work the results can be used in optimising sensory and other properties. Possible parameters are formulation, component composition and time–temperature–pressure relationships during processing. They can be applied not only to improvements of established products and processes but also to more novel developments. An example is the application of unconventional protein raw materials and products in the development of conventional or semi-conventional food products with high-quality properties such as good flavour. A prerequisite is that one knows which way to steer the flavour properties. For this more knowledge about the consumer is needed.

REFERENCES

1. Persson, T. and von Sydow, E. (1973). *J. Fd. Sci.*, **38,** p. 377.
2. Persson, T., von Sydow, E. and Åkesson, C. (1973). *J. Fd. Sci.*, **38,** p. 386.
3. Persson, T., von Sydow, E. and Åkesson, C. (1973). *J. Fd. Sci.*, **38,** p. 682.
4. Persson, T. and von Sydow, E. (1974). *J. Fd. Sci.*, **39,** p. 406.
5. Persson, T. and von Sydow, E. (1974). *J. Fd. Sci.*, **39,** p. 537.
6. Åkesson, C., Persson, T. and von Sydow, E. (1975). *Proc. IVth Int. Congress Food Sci. Technol.*, 1974, Vol. 2, p. 183.
7. Harper, R., Bate-Smith, E. C., Land, D. G. and Griffiths, N. M. (1968). *Perf. Essent. Oil Rec.*, **59,** p. 22.
8. Harper, R., Land, D. G., Griffiths, N. M. and Bate-Smith, E. C. (1968). *Br. J. Psychol.*, **59,** p. 231.
9. Cain, W. S. (1975). *Chemical Senses and Flavor*, **1,** p. 339.
10. Qvist, I., von Sydow, E. and Åkesson, C. (1976). *Lebensm.-Wiss. u. Technol.*, **9,** p. 311.
11. Åkesson, C., unpublished data.
12. Morrison, D. (1969). *J. Marketing Res.*, **6,** p. 156.

13. Koontz, W. and Fukunaga, K. (1972). *IEEE Transactions on Computers*, **C21**, p. 56.
14. Knuth, D. E. (1969). *The Art of Computer Programming*, **2**, p. 1.
15. Kuki, H. A fast normal random number generator, Computation Center, The University of Chicago, Chicago, Illinois, USA.

DISCUSSION

Lee: You added errors at different percentage values to your data. Were these errors percentages of the concentrations of volatile compounds determined instrumentally? Do your results therefore indicate the degree of experimental error in the chemical analytical method allowable for 'meaningful' results?

Von Sydow: Yes, correct. It was the instrumental data which were systematically made worse by the Monte-Carlo simulation technique. In answer to your second point, that is one of the reasons we increased the level of error here to find out how much the models could withstand before they collapsed. For the preference model it was 20% and for the off-flavour attribute it was closer to 40%, which in a way was expected, I think.

9

Useful Taste Properties of Amino Acids and Proteins

J. D. HIGGINBOTHAM and C. A. M. HOUGH

Tate & Lyle, Ltd, Philip Lyle Memorial Research Laboratory, Reading, England

ABSTRACT

The removal of cyclamate from the sweetener market in 1969 has led to an intensive search for new sweetening agents. The poor taste quality of saccharin combined with toxicological doubt has intensified the quest for the ideal sucrose replacement and much attention has been focused on amino acid based and natural protein sweeteners.

Although certain amino acids had been known to be sweet, when the dipeptide L-aspartyl–L-phenylalanyl methyl ester was found to be intensely sweet, a new era of sweetener research started. The synthesis of a wide range of dipeptides has led to further speculation on the molecular basis of sweetness.

The discovery of the protein sweeteners was unprecedented for no large molecular weight taste stimulator had even been predicted. The fruits of two W. African plants, Thaumatococcus daniellii *and* Dioscoreophyllum cumminsii *contain sweet-tasting proteins of molecular weight 21 000 and 10 800, respectively. The physical and hedonic properties of the protein sweeteners are reviewed and parameters affected by the presence of salts are described. The wide range of sweetness intensity found in the amino acids, peptides and protein sweeteners provides useful models for studying sweetness mechanisms. Present hypotheses are discussed and extended in the light of recent findings.*

INTRODUCTION

Examination of the title of this presentation would perhaps lead to the exclusion of the word 'useful' and inclusion of 'interesting', since 'useful' in commercial terms implies that profit could be made. It is unlikely that the characteristic flavours of many of these compounds will ever be of commercial value, for economic, practical or toxicological reasons. The flavour properties of amino acids and proteins that occur naturally in foods will not be discussed in detail since this discourse will concentrate on the sweetening properties of these compounds.

The primary function of taste is to stimulate eating and consequently is an essential part of the survival process. It can be shown in a variety of species that there is an innate response to specific chemical substances, for example, an isolated garter snake with no previous eating experience of its normal diet, the earthworm, will exhibit a complex consumptive response when presented with the washings of earthworm mucus.[1]

It has long been recognised that, from the foetus onward, sweet taste is a pleasurable sensation and that the taste function can also be used for reward.[2,3] This phenomenon has even worked its way into the dictionaries with sweetness being defined as 'pleasurable', 'melodious' and 'lovable'. However, it is not strictly true that the taste of an essential food is correlated to a positive physiological response. Electrophysiological behavioural tests on domestic rats have shown that certain non-essential amino acids exert a greater electro-physiological response than essential ones and are also preferred.[4] Man's response to the synthetic sweeteners also contradicts any hypothesis concerning taste appeal and nutritive value.

Research into new sweeteners has received much attention recently and, although the taste qualities of amino acids have been known for some time, the discoveries that showed certain dipeptide esters and even proteins to be sweet have resulted in an avalanche of publications concerning amino acid-based sweeteners. These discoveries have led to potentially commercial sweeteners on the one hand and stimulating research tools on the other. There is increasing interest in the molecular basis for sweetness and these new compounds are assisting the comprehension of the 'sweetness phenomenon'.

AMINO ACIDS

It is possible to group the amino acids by virtue of their taste qualities (Table 1): amino acids with bitter or sweet taste; amino acids with varying taste; amino acids without taste.[5,6]

TABLE 1

Taste of amino acids in 0·3 % aqueous solutions (pH adjusted to 6·0)[a]

Name	L-Enantiomorphs	D-Enantiomorphs
Group 1 *Amino acids without taste*		
arginine	flat	slightly sweet (D,L)
aspartic acid	flat	flat
isoleucine	flat	flat
lysine	flat	flat
proline	flat, slightly sweet	flat (D,L)
serine	flat	flat
threonine	flat	flat
valine	flat	flat
Group 2 *Amino acids with varying taste*		
cysteine	sulphurous	sulphurous (D,L)
glutamic acid	unique glutamate	flat
methionine	sulphurous, meaty slightly sweet	sulphurous, meaty slightly sweet
Group 3 *Amino acids with bitter or sweet tastes*		
alanine	sweet	flat
histidine	flat	sweet
leucine	bitter	sweet
phenylalanine	bitter	sweet
tryptophan	bitter	sweet
tyrosine	bitter	sweet
glycine	sweet	

[a] Solms *et al.*[5]

The variation experienced in the intensity of sweetness is marked, where D-tryptophan is 35 times sweeter than sucrose, and glycine is 1·5 times sweeter than sucrose, compared to 0·3 % sucrose solutions. There are also marked differences in quality of taste and intensity of sweetness when isomeric forms of the amino acids are compared.

In five cases from group 3, the D-isomer is sweet and the L-isomer bitter but alanine is the exception to this particular rule, where the L-isomer is sweet and the D-isomer is flat.

The taste intensities of the aromatic amino acids is noteworthy, for in the 'bitter/sweet' group, L-tryptophan is approximately half as bitter as caffeine and D-tryptophan is 35 times sweeter than sucrose. The L and D isomers of phenylalanine and tyrosine have similar though less intense qualities. The substitution of a halogen atom into the 5 and/or 6 position of the D-tryptophan aromatic ring yields a

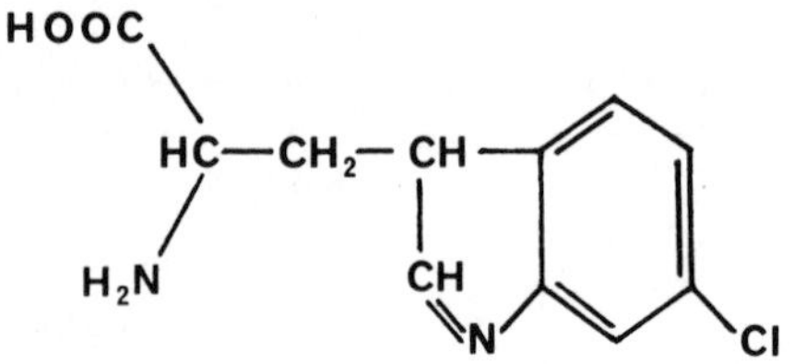

FIG. 1.   6-chloro-D-tryptophan. Sweetness: 600–1000 × sucrose.

sweetener of even greater intensity, which is reported as being 1300 times sucrose for 6-Cl-D-tryptophan[7] (Fig. 1).

PEPTIDES

The taste of peptides is complex, but a classification system for dipeptides has been drawn up by Kirimura.[8] Three groups are defined as (Tables 2 and 3):

     (1)   compounds having sour taste qualities
     (2)   compounds having bitter taste qualities
     (3)   compounds having little or no taste qualities.

It may be noticed that there are no sweet dipeptides among these groups and none has ever been identified. The discovery that the methyl ester of L-aspartyl–L-phenylalanine[9] was intensely sweet has led to extensive research in this field.

L-aspartyl–L-phenylalanine methyl ester is a white, crystalline powder and is estimated as being 150–200 times sweeter than sugar (Fig. 2).

The taste of the component amino acids is no indication of the compound's flavour, since L-aspartic acid is tasteless and L-phenylalanine is bitter. The methyl ester is essential for sweetness and

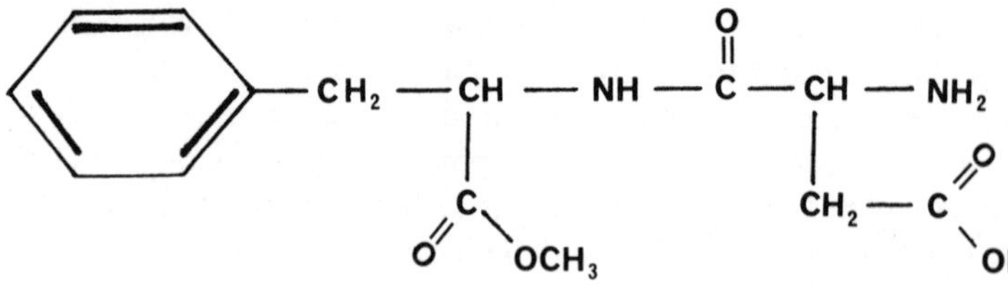

FIG. 2.   L-aspartyl–L-phenylalanyl methyl ester (aspartame). Sweetness: 150–200 × sucrose.

TABLE 2
Taste of peptides in 0·2% aqueous solution

Group 1. *Sourness*
  Gly–L-Asp, Gly–L-Glu
  L-Ala–L-Asp, L-Ala–L-Glu
  L-Ser–L-Asp, L-Ser–L-Glu
  L-Val–L-Asp, L-Val–L-Glu
  L-Asp–L-Ala, L-Asp–L-Asp
  L-Glu–L-Ala, L-Glu–L-Asp, L-Glu–L-Glu
  L-Glu–L-Phe,[a] L-Glu–L-Tyr[a]
  γ-L-Glu–Gly,[b] γ-L-Glu–L-Ala,[b] γ-L-Glu–L-Asp[b]
  γ-L-Glu–L-Glu[b]
  L-Phe–L-Asp, L-Phe–L-Glu
  L-Trp–L-Asp, L-Trp–L-Glu
  Gly–L-Asp–L-Ser–Gly
  L-Pro–Gly–Gly–L-Glu
  L-Val–L-Val–L-Glu
Group 2. *Bitterness*
  Gly–L-Ile, Gly–L-Met, Gly–L-Phe, Gly–L-Tyr
  L-Ala–L-Phe
  L-Val–L-Ala, L-Val–L-Val, L-Val–L-Leu
  L-Leu–Gly, L-Leu–L-Leu, L-Leu–L-Tyr
  L-Lys–Gly, L-Lys–L-Ala
  L-His–L-His
  L-Val–L-Val–L-Val
  L-Arg–L-Pro
Group 3. *Having Little or No Taste*
  Gly-Gly, Gly–L-Ala, Gly–L-Ser, Gly–L-Thr
  Gly–L-Asp(NH$_2$), Gly–L-Pro
  L-Ala–Gly, L-Ala–L-Ala
  L-Val–Gly
  L-Lys–L-Glu
  L-Phe–L-Phe[c]
  L-Pro–Gly, L-Pro–L-Ala
  Gly-Gly-Gly-Gly

---

[a] Accompanied by bitterness and astringency.
[b] Accompanied by astringency.
[c] Taste in solid state.

the size of the ester is also important, for the ethyl ester of the dipeptide is 10 times sweeter than sucrose[10] and the isopropyl and butyl esters are isosweet with sucrose.

Early studies on the structure–taste relationships of dipeptide esters indicated L-aspartic acid to be essential for sweetness, but that

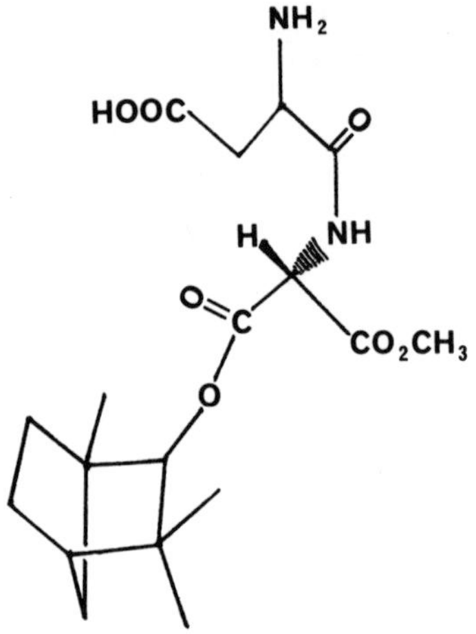

FIG. 3. α-L-aspartylaminomalonic acid fenchyl methyl ester. Sweetness: 22 000–33 000 × sucrose.

the phenylalanine portion could undergo considerable modification. This variability allowed large numbers of patent applications as new sweet derivatives were discovered.[9,11] However, replacement of L-aspartic acid by aminomalonic acid does not reduce the sweetness of the molecule.[12] Also the free amino group of the aspartyl portion was considered to be essential for sweetness, but N-terminal protection of the molecule gave the N-trifluoroacetyl–L-aspartyl–L-phenylalanine methyl ester, which is 120 times sweeter than sucrose.[13]

The sweetest dipeptides reported are the L-aspartylaminomalonic acid alkyl fenchyl diesters, where the methyl fenchyl diester is estimated as being 30 000 times sucrose[14] (Fig. 3).

STRUCTURE–TASTE RELATIONSHIPS

There is a great deal of interest in structure–taste relationships of sweet compounds, and several laboratories are involved with work on the dipeptide-based sweeteners. Although the perfect experiment has not yet been conducted,[15,16] i.e. formulating a model for a sweetener of predicted potency and then making it, there has been much interesting and stimulating work in this field.

A recent paper[15] on the preferred conformation of L-aspartyl–L-phenylalanyl methyl ester in solution, describes the stereochemistry

TABLE 3

Taste of dipeptides

N = N-terminal amino acid; C = C-terminal amino acid

N \ C	SWEET AMINO ACIDS					BITTER AMINO ACIDS								SOUR AMINO ACIDS	
	GLY	ALA	SER	THR	PRO	VAL	LEU	ILE	TRP	TYR	PHE	LYS	ARG	ASP	GLU
GLY															
ALA															
SER															
THR															
PRO															
VAL															
LEU															
ILE															
TRP															
TYR															
PHE															
LYS															
ARG															
ASP															
GLU															
γ-GLU															

BITTERNESS   SOURNESS   ASTRINGENCY

of the compound giving the best fit into a hypothetical receptor molecule, and this may provide a useful model for further studies.

Belitz and Wieser[16] relate the steric arrangement of polar and hydrophobic groups in dipeptides to the occurrence of sweet and bitter taste, stating that a bipolar/hydrophobic contact elicits sweet taste whereas a monopolar/hydrophobic contact represents bitterness.

The bitterness of peptides has been known for a long time and the bitterness of Gouda cheese results from a peptide that was first isolated by Raadsveld.[17] A variety of bitter peptides have been isolated from hydrolysates of casein[18] and the results of Matoba and Hata[19] suggest that the bitterness of peptides is not so rigorously dependent on specific three-dimensional configurations as the sweet dipeptide esters.

It is evident from studies on amino acids and dipeptides that sweet and bitter taste qualities are closely linked in terms of their stereochemistry, and evidence for this is available from work on carbohydrates[20] and flavanones also.[21]

If a lock-and-key hypothesis for sweetness/bitterness is accepted, this implies that the receptor molecules designated as proteins, are also very similar at the receptor site. The efficient evolution of such receptor proteins would not account for the separate development of two molecules that have to undergo the complex series of manoeuvres known as taste. It is possible that one receptor evolved from the other, leading to a discriminatory taste function.

PROTEINS

Perhaps one of the most extraordinary developments in sweetener research has been the discovery of macromolecular sweeteners, in the form of proteins extracted from the West African plants, *Thaumatococcus daniellii* and *Dioscoreophyllum cumminsii*, colloquially known as Katemfe and the Serendipity berry respectively.[22,23] These plants are found in the tropical regions of West Africa and it was in 1855 that Dr W. F. Daniell first reported the existence of the

TABLE 4
Some characteristics of the sweet-tasting proteins[26–36]

Criteria		Thaumatin I	Thaumatin II	Monellin
Isoelectric point		12	12	9·03
Mol wt		21 000 ± 600	20 400 ± 600	11 500
$A_{1\,cm}^{1\%}$ (pH 5·6, 278 nm)		7·69	7·53	16·2
Sweetness intensity (times sweeter than sucrose)				
on a molar basis		1×10^5	1×10^5	$8·4 \times 10^4$
on a weight basis		1 600	1 600	2 500
Temperature (°C) above which sweetness disappears				
at pH	3·2	55	55	50
	5·0	75	75	65
	7·2	65	65	55

'miraculous fruit of Soudan'.[24] This is not to be confused with the 'miraculous berry' (*Synsepalum dulcificum*) which contains a glycoprotein, miraculin, that has unusual sweetening properties.[25]

MIRACULIN

Miraculin is not sweet on its own but if the tongue is treated with a solution of miraculin, both mineral and organic acids are perceived as being sweet. Isolation of the active glycoprotein has revealed the molecular weight to be in the range of 42 000–44 000 and the carbohydrate content has been reported to be only L-arabinose and D-xylose in one case,[37] and to be a combination of arabinose, glucose, ribose, rhamnose and galactose units in another.[38]

A mechanism of action for miraculin suggested by Beidler involves the binding of the protein portion of the molecule to an appropriate location on the taste cell membrane, adjacent to a receptor site.[39] Exposure to acid is believed to result in a conformational change of the protein portion so that the carbohydrate portion is brought into contact with a 'sweet' receptor site. However, considering the rather specific action of gymnemic acid which can block sweet taste altogether but not sour or bitter tastes, it is quite possible that miraculin binds to a particular site on the receptor molecule, rather than an apparently random position on the taste cell membrane. This would imply that there are two sites that can be occupied on the 'sweet' receptor, one having a non-stimulatory function, but important for binding, the other being responsible for the recognition of sweetness.

MONELLIN

The sweet protein from the Serendipity berry (*Dioscoreophyllum cumminsii*) is present in its mucilage and is characterised by its intensely sweet and persistent taste, along with a liquorice-like after-taste[23,26] (Fig. 4).

The first biochemical report identified the active ingredient as a carbohydrate,[27] but Morris and Cagan of the Monell Chemical Senses Center reported the sweetener to be a protein, having a molecular weight of 10 800 and named it monellin. At the same time, van der Wel also purified monellin and several papers were published describing purification and characterisation techniques[26,28-30] (Table 4).

Monellin[31-39] is composed of two polypeptide chains that are free of any intermolecular covalent links and is estimated as being 2000 times sucrose's sweetness. Separation of the chains, designated A and B, eliminates sweetness and neither separate chain displays any

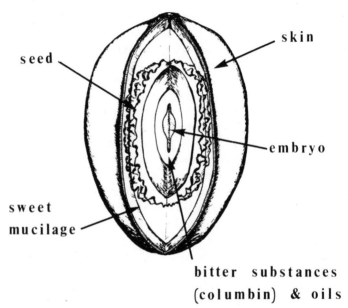

skin

seed

embryo

sweet mucilage

bitter substances (columbin) & oils

FIG. 4.   *Dioscoreophyllum cumminsii* fruit.

chemostimulatory properties. Aqueous recombination of the A chain (44 amino acids) with the B chain (50 amino acids) results in the slow reappearance of sweetness, although never to the original level experienced (Tables 5 and 6).

However, the conditions used to achieve this separation are sufficient to cause other conformational changes and hence alter sweetness. Similarly, blockage or oxidation of the single sulphydryl group of chain B abolishes sweetness,[31] as does CNBr cleavage at the adjacent single methionine residue. This cleavage liberates an octapeptide,[32] Lys-Lys-Thr-Ile-Tyr-Glu-Asn-Glu, which would alter not only the shape of the residual molecule but also reduce its basicity.

Blockage of the sulphydryl group is only achieved in alkaline or

TABLE 5
Amino acid composition of monellin

Amino acid	Chain A	Chain B	Native monellin
Aspartic acid	4	6	10
Glutamic acid	4	8	12
Serine	2	—	2
Threonine	1	3	4
Proline	4	2	6
Glycine	3	5	8
Alanine	2	1	3
Valine	2	2	4
Leucine	4	2	6
Isoleucine	2	6	8
Methionine	—	1	1
Phenylalanine	2 (3)	3	5
Tyrosine	5	2	7
Half-cystine	—	1	1
Histidine	—	—	—
Lysine	4	5	9
Arginine	5	2	7
Tryptophan	—	1	1
Total	44	50	94

TABLE 6
Monellin A and B amino acid sequences

The amino acid sequence of monellin A chain:

$\overset{0}{Phe}$-Arg-Glu-Ile-$\overset{5}{Lys}$-Gly-Tyr-Glu-Tyr-$\overset{10}{Gln}$-Tyr-Leu-Tyr-Val-$\overset{15}{Tyr}$-Ala-Ser-
$\overset{20}{Asp}$-Lys-Leu-Phe-Arg-$\overset{25}{Ala}$-Asp-Ile-Ser-Glu-$\overset{30}{Asp}$-Tyr-Lys-Thr-Arg-Gly-
$\overset{35}{Arg}$-Lys-Leu-Leu-Arg-$\overset{40}{Phe}$-Asn-Gly-Pro-Val-$\overset{44}{Pro}$-Pro-Pro

Asp:Asn 3:1	Glu:Gln 3:1
Arg 5, Lys 4	Basic:acidic 11:6

The amino acid sequence of monellin B Chain

$\overset{0}{Gly}$-Glu-Trp-Glu-$\overset{5}{Ile}$-Ile-Asp-Ile-Gly-$\overset{10}{Pro}$-Phe-Thr-Gln-Asn-$\overset{15}{Leu}$-Gly-
Lys-Phe-Ala-$\overset{20}{Val}$-Asp-Glu-Glu-Asn-$\overset{25}{Lys}$-Ile-Gly-Gln-Tyr-$\overset{30}{Gly}$-Arg-Leu-
$\overset{35}{Thr}$-Phe-Asn-Lys-Val-$\overset{40}{Ile}$-Arg-Pro-Cys-Met-$\overset{45}{Lys}$-Lys-Thr-Ile-Tyr-Glu-
$\overset{50}{Asn}$-Glu

Asp:Asn 5:5	Glu:Gln 9:3
Arg 7, Lys 9	Basic:acidic 24:14

dissociating media and because of the sensitivity of monellin it is unlikely to be involved in the sweet taste of the native molecule.

The search for a small fragment of monellin that retains the sweetening properties of the entirety has been unsuccessful and the evidence gathered suggests that the tertiary structure of the molecule is essential for sweetness,[33,34] although slight conformational changes can be tolerated without loss of sweetness. Now that the sequence of monellin is known, and X-ray diffraction data are being collected,[36] it is hoped that building of the three-dimensional model will lead to the determination of the physiological mode of action of this protein.

THAUMATIN

The sweetening agent from *Thamatococcus daniellii*[40−49] is isolated from a membranous sac, known as the aril, attached to the seed of the fruit. A high percentage of the protein content of the aril is made up of the proteins identified as thaumatin which were first reported in 1972.[40] After aqueous extraction of the aril and ion-exchange

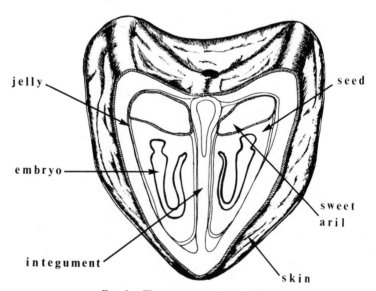

FIG. 5. *Thaumatococcus daniellii* fruit.

separation, van der Wel reported the presence of two sweet-tasting proteins: thaumatin$_1$ (T_1) and thaumatin$_{11}$ (T_2). We have shown by ion-exchange chromatography that there are at least three other sweet proteins, all eluted before T_1 and designated as being Ta, Tb and Tc[49] (Figs. 5 and 6). The amino acid composition of the thaumatins is known (Table 7).

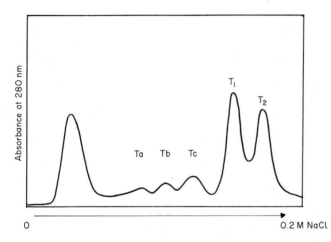

FIG. 6.   Gradient elution of sweet thaumatins from Whatman CM32 (Na$^+$) (column size 30 × 1·5 cm) using 0–0·2M NaCl gradient in phosphate buffer, pH 7·4 at 4 °C.

The thaumatins have extremely similar molecular weights, isoelectric points and sweetening properties (Table 4). The sweetness is described as being slow to develop and persistent. It is also characterised by a liquorice-like after-taste.

Effects of Salts on the Extraction of Thaumatin

Analysis of the metal ion content of an aqueous aril extract shows a surprisingly high level of Al^{3+}, up to 6 residues per molecule of thaumatin. This was brought to light after an earlier observation showing that aluminium salts should be used preferentially for the extraction of sweet protein from the aril. The yield of sweet protein is much increased when compared with extractions involving other trivalent or mono- or divalent ions. The molarity and ionic strength of the aluminium salts required for optimal extraction is low[45] (Table 8).

Evidence to show that aluminium ions are capable of binding to the thaumatin is given by its increased stability, solubility and sweetness and the difficulty in removing aluminium from the protein.

There are reports[40] in the literature stating that aqueous extractions of thaumatin have a *threshold* sweetening power of 1600 times sucrose, or 10^5 times sucrose when compared on a molar basis.

TABLE 7
Amino acid composition (residues/mol) of the thaumatins

Amino acid	Thaumatin I	Thaumatin II
Aspartic acid	21	19
Glutamic acid	10	10
Serine	12	10
Threonine	19	17
Proline	12	12
Glycine	23	22
Alanine	15	14
Valine	9	8
Leucine	9	9
Isoleucine	7	7
Methionine	1	1
Phenylalanine	10	10
Tyrosine	7	8
Half-cystine	14	13
Histidine	—	—
Lysine	10	11
Arginine	11	12
Tryptophan	3	3

A conservative estimate for aluminium-extracted thaumatin is 2000–3600 times sucrose (when compared to 10 % sucrose solutions) and $\sim 100\,000$ at threshold, which is 6×10^6 on a molar basis.

The sweetness of Thaumatin 1 and 11 (T_1 and T_2) is estimated at one-third to one-half of that of an unseparated preparation, weight for weight. Recombination increases sweetness, demonstrating synergy.

T_1 and T_2 have an almost identical molecular weight and amino acid profile. It could be argued that they are the same molecule differing only in charge. Elution of a thaumatin solution from a cation exchange resin can reveal small amounts of three other sweet proteins.

and these are eluted prior to T_1 and T_2.[49] All have a similar molecular weight and amino acid composition but are less sweet than T_1. These are either natural aril constituents or from their elution position they may have originated from T_1 or T_2 but have lost some of their amide groups during isolation. In ripe fruit, T_1 is present in amounts 1·2–1·5

TABLE 8

Effect of ions on extraction of thaumatin

Salt	Molarity at 1 % solution	Yield from 10 seeds/arils (mg)		
		Concn of salts: 0·1 %	0·5 %	1 %
H_2O	—	—	(19·7)	—
NaCl	0·171	—	—	84
$AlCl_3 \cdot 6H_2O$	0·041	—	—	89
$AlK(SO_4)_2 \cdot 12H_2O$	0·021	10·5	63	110
$AlNH_4(SO_4)_2 \cdot 12H_2O$	0·021	31·5	73·5	105
$Al_2(SO_4)_3 \cdot 16H_2O$	0·016	52·5	147	199

× T_2, T_1 having a slightly higher molecular weight but being slightly less sweet than T_2. The increased mobility of T_2 towards the cathode, during electrophoresis, indicates greater basicity and a recent publication[46] stressed the importance of basicity to the sweetness of T_1 which demonstrated that, unlike acetylation, methylation of one or more of the lysine residues has no effect. Hence T_2, having a higher isoelectric point and thus higher basicity, should have higher sweetness.

Enzymatic and chemical cleavage experiments at our laboratory have shown no evidence for the separation of sub-units, after electrophoresis in dissociating and reducing systems, although T_1 and T_2 contain cystine residues. Similarly, performic acid oxidation gave no smaller chains and only 1 N-terminal unit, namely alanine, has been identified.[40]

As with monellin, the tertiary structure of the protein seems to be important for sweetness,[30] and preliminary results of X-ray studies on crystalline thaumatin 1 have been published.[48] It is hoped that details from these studies will give further insight as to the mode of action of the protein sweeteners.

Effect of Salts on the Taste of Thaumatin

It has been well documented that many salts affect the three-dimensional structure of proteins,[41] and simple experiments on the effects of a variety of salts on the taste of thaumatin have shown that profound differences can be obtained.

For example, the juice of an aril from a fresh fruit is extremely sweet but the sweetness experienced is less than that from a solution containing an equivalent amount of purified thaumatin. Dialysis of the aril extract produces a material of greater sweetness intensity than that experienced in the original form and cation analysis has shown that Na^+ and K^+ are present in the arils at concentrations of up to 2%.

If weak salt solutions are added to a standard thaumatin solution, sweetness is extensively suppressed. 0.1% NaCl (aq) will greatly reduce the sweetness of a 0.005% thaumatin solution, and 0.025% $CaCl_2$ (aq) reproduces the effect. Both salts display this phenomenon in concentrations below their own taste threshold values. At an equivalent Na^+ ion concentration, Na_2SO_4 is 3 times more effective than NaCl, whereas both CH_3COONa and $(CH_3COO)_2$ Ca are 10 times more effective.

By comparing the suppressive effect per amino acid (aa) unit at equivalent Na^+ concentration, there are 16 ions/aa for NaCl, 4 for Na_2SO_4 and 1 for CH_3COO Na. Comparison of Ca^{2+} on the same scale reveals 3 ions/aa for $CaCl_2$ and 1 ion/aa for $(CH_3COO)_2$ Ca.

Obviously, both cationic and anionic effects are important in sweetness suppression, and by ranking effectiveness, $Ca^{2+} > Na^+$ and $CH_3COO^- > SO_4^{2-} > Cl^-$ (Table 9).

The salt effect was limited to the mono and divalent ionic species, for the trivalent aluminium salts, $AlCl_3$ and $Al_2(SO_4)_3$ displayed no suppressive effect, even at levels above their own taste threshold values. Indeed as we have stated there is some evidence to show that the aluminium salts increase the sweetness of thaumatin. However, these acidic salts reduce the pH of a solution of thaumatin in water to 3.5, which introduces the consideration of acidity. HCl at this pH does not affect sweetness whereas citric acid slightly increases the levels of sweetness perception as it does with sucrose.

In 1963, Anderson et al.[42] reported that the response of the dog chorda tympani to sucrose was suppressed by $0.2M$ or $0.5M$ NaCl and Miyake et al. recently reported the suppressive effects of salts on the sugar response of the frog.[43] They have been able to rank other anions

and cations in order of suppressive effect from their electrophysiological studies, finding $KCl = NaCl > MgCl_2 > K_4Fe(CN)_6$ for the
suppression of the sweetness of 0·5M D-galactose.

We compared the taste of solutions of 9% sucrose and 0·005%
thaumatin, in the presence and absence of 0·05% or 0·1% NaCl.
There was no significant difference in the sweetness level in the sucrose
solutions whereas even 0·02% NaCl suppressed the sweetness of
thaumatin.

TABLE 9
Salt levels required to suppress taste of thaumatin

Salt	Effective molarity	Relative molarity to thaumatin	Cation concentration ratio to thaumatin	Number of ions per amino acid
NaCl	$1·9 \times 10^{-2}$	$7\,800 \times$	$3\,100 \times$	16
Na_2SO_4	$5·6 \times 10^{-3}$	$2\,300 \times$	$760 \times$	4
CH_3COONa	$1·8 \times 10^{-3}$	$750 \times$	$210 \times$	1
$CaCl_2$	$4·6 \times 10^{-3}$	$1\,800 \times$	$670 \times$	3
$(CH_3COO)_2Ca$	$1·6 \times 10^{-3}$	$670 \times$	$170 \times$	1

Ozeki and Sato[44] stated that the receptor potential of the rat taste
cell in response to sucrose was diminished by 0·04M NaCl(0·2% NaCl).
The suppressive effect of the salts has been explained as being a result
of induced changes in the phase boundary potential of taste cell
membranes, the phase boundary potential being a function both of the
charge density at the membrane surface and of the ionic strength in
solution.[43] According to Miyake *et al.*, increasing the ionic strength
lowers the phase boundary potential (or the taste receptor potential)
and hence the magnitude of the sugar response is lowered, if the
surface charge density stays constant in a given concentration of
sugar. Since the sugars are not electrolytes, changes observed in
surface charge density could be attributed to conformational changes
in the receptor membrane.[43]

Thaumatin is a polyelectrolyte and the suppressive effects of salts
are not so easily explained. As with the experiments of Miyake *et al.*[43]
it is evident that both anions and cations affect the sweet response.

The sweetness of thaumatin is more sensitive to selected salts than sucrose, at isosweet concentrations. The lingering, persistently-sweet quality of thaumatin has also been shown to be affected by salts. Salt solutions tasted immediately after thaumatin suppress the sweetness experience, but, interestingly, sweetness returns with time or on rinsing the mouth with water.

It would appear, therefore, that salts do not interfere with the binding of thaumatin to the taste receptor but affect the sweet stimulating site of the protein. This may be compared with the action of miraculin and gymnemic acid and suggests that thaumatin is capable of binding strongly to a sweet receptor, without necessarily stimulating a sweet response. This could also account for the persistence of the sweet taste of thaumatin. The action of these salts may be either to block an essential chemical portion of the sweet stimulating site or to induce a conformational change in the three-dimensional structure, rendering this site unavailable to the receptor.

REFERENCES

1. Kare, M. R. (1969). *J. Agr. Food Chem.*, **17**, p. 677.
2. Desnoo, K. (1937). *Monat Geburt.*, **105**, p. 88.
3. Desor, J. A., Meller, O. and Turner, R. E. (1973). *J. Comp. Physiol. Biochem.*, **84**, p. 496.
4. Halpern, B. P., Bernard, R. A. and Kare, M. R. (1962). *J. Gen. Physiol.*, **45**, p. 681.
5. Solms, J., Vutaz, L. and Egli, R. H. (1965). *Experientia*, **21**, p. 692.
6. Solms, J. (1969). *J. Agr. Food. Chem.*, **17**, p. 686.
7. Kornfeld, E. C. (1974). Abstracts of papers, *Am. Chem. Soc.*, **16**, p. 41.
8. Kirimura, J., Shimizu, A., Kimizuka, A. N., Ninomiya, T. and Katsuya, N. (1969). *J. Agr. Food Chem.*, **17**, p. 689.
9. Mazur, R. H., Schlatter, J. M. and Goldkamp, A. M. (1969). *J. Am. Chem. Soc.*, **91**, p. 2684.
10. Ariyoshi, Y., Yasuda, N. and Yamatani, T. (1974). *Bull. Chem. Soc. Jap.*, **47**, p. 326.
11. Mazur, R. H., Goldkamp, A. H., James, P. A. and Schlatter, J. M. (1970). *J. Med. Chem.*, **13**, p. 1217.
12. Briggs, M. T. and Morley, J. S. (1972). *Brit. Pat.* 1 299 265.
13. Lapidus, M. and Sweeney, M. (1973). *J. Med. Chem.*, **16**, p. 163.
14. Fujino, M., Wakimasu, M., Tanaka, K., Aoki, H. and Nakajuma, N. (1973). *Naturwissenschaften*, **60**, p. 351.
15. Lelj, M., Tancredi, T., Temussi, P. A. and Toniolo, C. (1976). *J. Am. Chem. Soc.*, **98**, p. 6669.

16. Belitz, H. and Wieser, H. (1976). *Z. Lebensm. Unters-Forsch*, **160**, p. 251.
17. Raadsveld, W. (1953). *Intern. Dairy. Congr. Proc.* 13 (*Hague*), **2**, p. 679.
18. Matoba, T., Hayashi, R. and Hata, T. (1970). *Agric. Biol. Chem.*, **34**, p. 1235.
19. Matoba, T. and Hata, T. (1972). *Agric. Biol. Chem.*, **36**, p. 1423.
20. Birch, G. G. (1976). *Crit. Rev. Food Sci. Nut.*, **8**, p. 57.
21. Horowitz, R. and Gentili, B. (1974). In: *Symposium: Sweeteners* Ch. 16, ed. G. E. Inglett, Avi Publishing, Westport, Conn.
22. Irvine, F. R. (1961). In: *Woody Plants of Ghana*, Oxford University Press, London, Ch. 32, p. 596.
23. Inglett, G. E. and May, J. F. (1968). *Econ. Bot.*, **22**, p. 326.
24. Daniell, W. F. (1855). *Pharmacol. J.*, **14**, p. 158.
25. Daniell, W. F. (1852). *Pharmacol. J.*, **11**, p. 445.
26. Morris, J. A. and Cagan, R. H. (1972). *Biochim. Biophys. Acta.*, **261**, p. 114.
27. Inglett, G. E. and May, J. F. (1969). *J. Food Sci.*, **34**, p. 408.
28. van der Wel, H. (1972). *Febs Lett.*, **21**, p. 88.
29. Morris, J. A., Martenson, R., Deibler, G. and Cagan, R. H. (1973). *J. Biol. Chem.*, **248**, p. 534.
30. van der Wel, H. and Loeve, K. (1973). *Febs Lett.*, **29**, p. 181.
31. Bohak, Z. and Li, S.-L. (1972). *Eur. J. Biochem.*, **31**, p. 221.
32. Frank, G. and Zuber, H. (1976). *Hoppe-Seylers Z. Physiol. Chem.*, **357**, p. 585.
33. Morris, J. A. and Cagan, R. H. (1976). *J. Agric. Food Chem.*, **24**, p. 1075.
34. Morris, J. A. and Cagan, R. H. (1975). *Proc. Soc. Exp. Biol.*, **150**, p. 265.
35. Jirgensons, B. (1976). *Biochim. Biophys. Acta*, **446**, p. 255.
36. Wlodawer, A. and Hodgson, K. O. (1975). *Proc. Nat. Acad. Sci. USA*, **72**, p. 398.
37. Brouwer, J. N., van der Wel, H., Francke, A. and Henning, G. J. (1968). *Nature*, **220**, p. 373.
38. Kurihara, K. and Beidler, L. M. (1968). *Science*, **161**, p. 1241.
39. Kurihara, K. and Beidler, L. M. (1969). *Nature*, **222**, p. 1176.
40. van der Wel, H. and Loeve, K. (1972). *Eur. J. Biochem.*, **31**, p. 221.
41. Von Hippel, P. H. and Schleich, T. (1969). *Acc. Chem. Res.*, **2**(9), p. 257.
42. Anderson, H. T., Funakoshi, M. and Zotterman, Y. (1963). In: *Olfaction and Taste*, ed. Y. Zotterman, Vol. 1, Pergamon Press, London p. 177.
43. Miyake, M., Kamo, N., Kurihara, K. and Kobatake, Y. (1976). *Biochim. Biophys. Acta*, **436**, p. 856.
44. Ozeki, M. and Sato, M. (1972). *Comp. Biochem. Physiol.*, **41A**, p. 391.
45. Higginbotham, J. D. *Belg. Pat.* 84 985 *and* 841 924, *French Pat.* 2 309 636, *US Pat.* 4 011 206.
46. van der Wel, H. and Bel, J. (1976). *Chem. Senses Flav.*, **2**, p. 211.
47. Korver, O., van Gorkom, M. and van der Wel, H. (1973). *Eur. J. Biochem.*, **35**, p. 554.
48. van der Wel, H., van Soest, T. C. and Royers, E. C. (1975). *Febs Lett.*, **56**, p. 316.
49. Higginbotham, J. D. (1976). *Chem. and Ind.*, p. 262.

DISCUSSION

Birch: Could Mr Hough comment on the phenomenon of persistence. Although Professor Shallenberger has mentioned *impact time* it seems to me that neither chemists nor psychologists have given any degree of attention to this important variable.

Hough: The persistent sweetness of thaumatin is not satisfactorily explained by our current conceptions of sweetness and sweetness determinants. Our studies on the effect of salts on the taste of thaumatin would seem to suggest that the molecule is not released from the taste receptor, after initial stimulation of sweetness, which remains as a satisfactory explanation for the action of sucrose. This would imply that thaumatin may have a secondary, strong binding capability that restrains the molecule from being completely released.

Birch: So thaumatin is bound to the receptor at a different location from the ion-channel?

Hough: Yes.

Moskowitz: What is meant by sweetness estimation? It is wrong to say that a particular molecule is so many times sweeter than sucrose when what we mean is that at a lower concentration the molecule is a more efficient stimulant.

Hough: If one regards the intensity of sweetness as a constant, the differences in the sweetness experienced per unit stimulus molecule must be regarded in terms of efficiency. Thus our scales of estimated sweetness and sweetness factors, determined as a multiple of that of sucrose, are misnomers. In fact the scales should be reversed and one should take the 'sweetest' molecule as being the most efficient. The other molecules could be represented as being less efficient at stimulating and are hence less sweet. The problem is simply one of communicating a concept.

Moskowitz: As far as persistence is concerned this lasts for several minutes if the molecules remain in the mouth.

Hough: Yes, that is possible, but some reason must be applied to the ability of thaumatin to remain on the tongue for such a long period of time.

Bartoshuk: The 'persistent' sweet taste of the protein sweeteners, dihydrochalcones, etc. may need better terminology. In fact the DHC sweet taste adapts quickly under controlled stimulation. Water following DHC then has a sweet taste. The re-emergence of a sweet taste intermittently over a period of time following the initial exposure may be re-stimulation of the DHC sweet due to movement of DHC molecules.

Peer: Considering the sweetness of some D-amino acids two questions have occurred to me:

    1. You showed lists of bitter, sour and tasteless dipeptides. What is known about (sweet?) taste of dipeptides containing D-amino acid partners?

    2. Are there indications for the presence of D-amino acids in the chains of thaumatin and could this (partly) explain the sweet taste?

Hough: No, we have only carried out amino acid analyses, without carrying out studies into the isomeric forms of the component amino acids. There is a recent review by Y. Grugoz and J. Solms, Bitter peptides, occurrence and structure, *Chem. Senses and Flavour*, **2** (1976), 71–84.

10

The Important Volatile Flavour Components of Foods

H. E. NURSTEN

Department of Food Science, University of Reading, Reading, England

ABSTRACT

Leaving aside the very difficult question of how importance is to be assessed in relation to aroma, foods can be classified into 4 groups in terms of current knowledge of flavour volatiles:

1. *Those foods whose aroma resides largely in one compound, a so-called character-impact compound.*
2. *Those foods whose aroma is essentially due not to a single compound, but to a mixture of a small number of compounds. A character-impact compound may be present.*
3. *Those foods whose aroma can only be reproduced reasonably faithfully by the use of quite a large number of compounds. A character-impact compound is unlikely to be present.*
4. *Those foods whose aroma cannot be reasonably reproduced even by a complex mixture of specific compounds. No character-impact compound has been discovered or is likely to be.*

The chemical structures of important food volatiles discovered to date will be reviewed and examples of foods belonging to each of the above groups will be cited and discussed.

INTRODUCTION

The intention is to discuss the *important* volatile flavour components of foods. Important in what way? At such a symposium as this, sensory importance is paramount and that is the implication which the term 'important' is intended to have here.

Since the human nose can detect certain substances by smell over solutions at concentrations of 1 in 10^{12} or even lower, important here certainly does not need to mean quantitatively important. The literature, however, is most nearly comprehensive in terms of the qualitative analysis of foodstuffs (identification of components);[1] it gives fairly complete quantitative data, but, as regards organoleptic effects, there are all too many gaps.

In spite of these, it is well worthwhile to survey rapidly the gamut of important food odorants. The organoleptic importance of individual components to particular foods will here be stated as far as possible using the two terms devised by Jennings and Sevenants:[2] character-impact compound and contributory flavour compound. Spices, herbs, and essential oils will be omitted deliberately.

The following subdivisions will be used: hydroxy compounds, aldehydes, ketones, acids, esters, nitrogen compounds, sulphur compounds, oxygen heterocycles, nitrogen heterocycles, sulphur heterocycles, and, finally, other compounds.

The survey cannot be complete, not only because of limitations of time and space, but because of limitations in my knowledge and experience. However, academics do have an advantage in that they can afford to stick out their necks, since, even when shown to be mistaken, they are still fulfilling their function of advancing their subject. Those, particularly in industry, who have much of the knowledge and by far the most experience, are generally in a much more constrained position as regards disseminating them.

In general, references will only be cited for recent work, since earlier researches can be traced through Weurman's compilation.[1]

IMPORTANT FOOD VOLATILES

These will now be surveyed, subdivided as stated in the Introduction.

Hydroxy Compounds (Fig. 1)

There are only three alcohols to be considered: *cis*-3-hexenol, 1-octen-3-ol, and geosmin. The first has a green, leafy odour, which contributes to tomatoes and raspberries. The second is a contributor to mushroom aroma,[3] but also to that of green beans. The last has a powerful earthy odour, thought to be responsible for the odour of freshly ploughed soil and earthy-musty taints in water supplies. It is a contributor to beetroot flavour,[4,5] and can also cause a musty off-flavour in dry beans.[6]

Five phenols are also listed. Phenol itself contributes to Pont l'Evêque cheese.[7] Vinylguaiacol is present in many foods, but

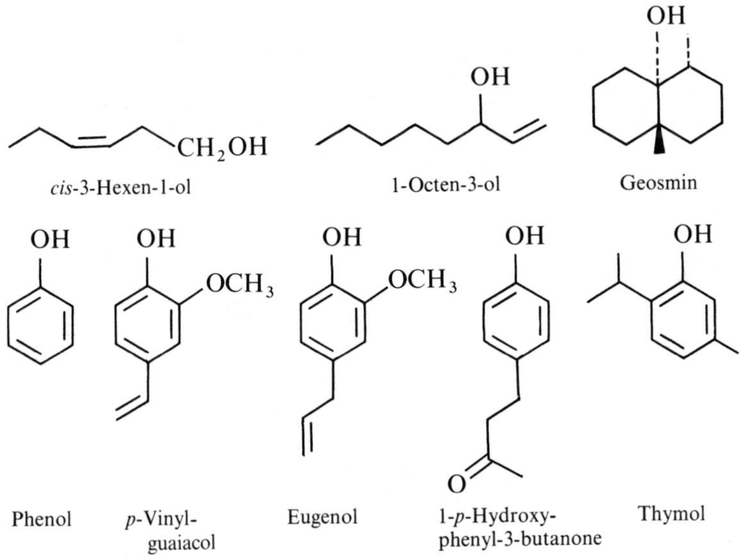

| *cis*-3-Hexen-1-ol | 1-Octen-3-ol | Geosmin |

| Phenol | *p*-Vinyl-guaiacol | Eugenol | 1-*p*-Hydroxy-phenyl-3-butanone | Thymol |

FIG. 1. Important food volatiles: hydroxy compounds.

important in smoked ones. Eugenol too is widely distributed and, although it is the character-impact compound of oil of cloves, it is included here as a contributor to banana flavour. 1-(*p*-Hydroxyphenyl)-3-butanone is the character-impact compound of raspberries and thymol is an important contributor to tangerines.

Aldehydes (Fig. 2)

The list is much longer and more interesting. Ethanal contributes to butter, and is present in many other foods, as is hexanal, which is known to contribute to apples. Similarly, *trans*-2-hexenal contributes to apples, bilberries and cucumbers. Benzaldehyde is a common constituent of foods, making a distinct contribution to prunoids, such as almonds, cherries and peaches. *cis*-4-Heptenal has been reported as the character-impact compound of cream, yet it is also responsible

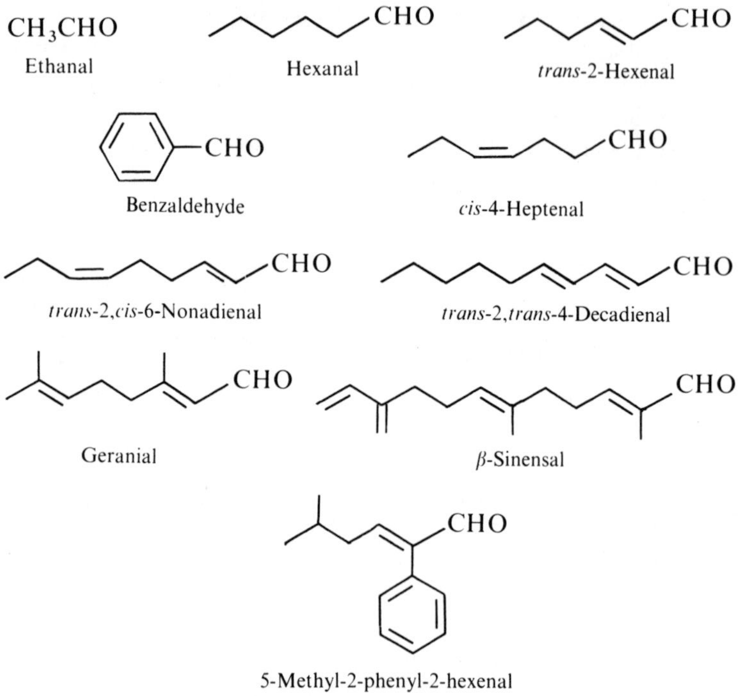

CH_3CHO

Ethanal

Hexanal

trans-2-Hexenal

Benzaldehyde

cis-4-Heptenal

trans-2,*cis*-6-Nonadienal

trans-2,*trans*-4-Decadienal

Geranial

β-Sinensal

5-Methyl-2-phenyl-2-hexenal

FIG. 2.   Important food volatiles: aldehydes.

for the cold-storage flavour which develops in cod.[8] *trans*-2,*cis*-6-Nonadienal is the character-impact compound of cucumbers, 2-nonenal contributing, as well as 2-hexenal. Two 2,4,6-nonatrienals have recently been isolated from blended dry beans.[9] 2,4-Decadienals have an oily aroma and are present in many foods, particularly those that have undergone processing. The *trans,trans*-isomer plays an important contributory role in the off-flavour of lamb fed on a lipid-protected diet.[10] Neral and geranial are the character-impact compounds of lemon and β-sinensal (note the 5 double bonds and molecular weight 218) is the character-impact compound of orange.

5-Methyl-2-phenyl-2-hexenal is worth recalling for two reasons; it is a contributor to chocolate aroma and it is the product of the interaction of two Strecker aldehydes, followed by loss of water.

Ketones (Fig. 3)

The character-impact compound of butter has long been known to

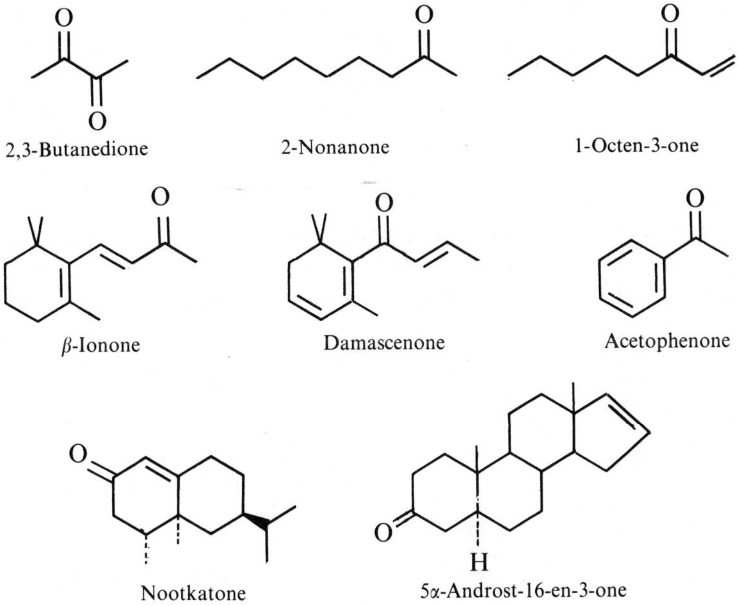

2,3-Butanedione   2-Nonanone   1-Octen-3-one

β-Ionone   Damascenone   Acetophenone

Nootkatone   5α-Androst-16-en-3-one

FIG. 3.   Important food volatiles: ketones.

be 2,3-butanedione; it contributes to celery and is present in many other foods. 2-Heptanone and 2-nonanone are the character-impact compounds of blue cheese. Acetophenone contributes to the flavour of Pont l'Evêque[7] and is present in many other foods. 1-Octen-3-one is the character-impact compound of boiled mushrooms, *Agaricus bisporus*,[3] and it has been found to be responsible for metallic off-odours in dairy products.

α- and β-Ionone contribute to raspberries and are wide-spread. Damascenone, clearly related chemically to the ionones and carotenes, is a much more recent discovery and contributes to raspberries, to cooked apples, and to tea. With nootkatone, molecular weight 218 is reached again. It is the character-impact compound of grapefruit. Even larger is 5α-androst-16-en-3-one with molecular weight 272, yet it has an intense urine-like odour, responsible for boar-taint. Women are more sensitive to it and find it more objectionable.[11]

Acids
Although some acids have powerful odours and must contribute to

many foods, specific examples are relatively rare. Acetic acid is clearly the character-impact compound of vinegar. 2-Methylbutyric acid contributes to mountain cranberries. Important to mutton odour (soo odour) are branched-chain acids, particularly 4-methyl-octanoic and -nonanoic, and unsaturated acids, such as 2-octenoic.[12]

Esters (Fig. 4)

Esters are generally characterised by fruitiness. Isopentyl acetate is the character-impact compound of bananas and ethyl 2-methylbuty-rate of Delicious apples. The latter and its 3-isomer are important

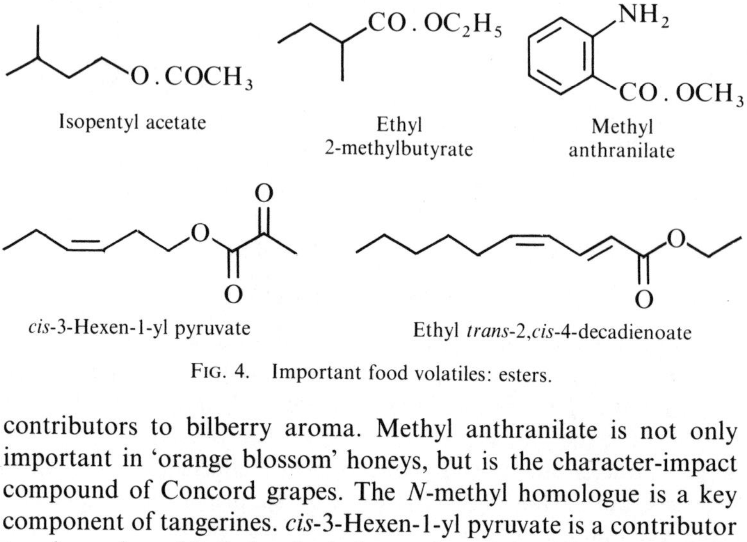

| Isopentyl acetate | Ethyl 2-methylbutyrate | Methyl anthranilate |

cis-3-Hexen-1-yl pyruvate   Ethyl *trans*-2,*cis*-4-decadienoate

FIG. 4.   Important food volatiles: esters.

contributors to bilberry aroma. Methyl anthranilate is not only important in 'orange blossom' honeys, but is the character-impact compound of Concord grapes. The *N*-methyl homologue is a key component of tangerines. *cis*-3-Hexen-1-yl pyruvate is a contributor to celery odour. Methyl and ethyl *trans*-2,*cis*-4-decadienoates are the character-impact compounds of Bartlett pears.

Nitrogen Compounds

Ammonia and amines are powerful odorants and contribute to a number of foods, especially fish and meat, but precise data are lacking. 28 amines which contribute to Chanakh cheese have been identified.[13]

Sulphur Compounds (Fig. 5)

Much information is available on sulphur compounds and this presentation will necessarily have to be selective. Sulphur compounds

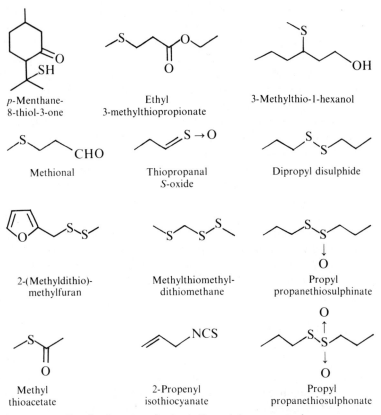

p-Menthane-
8-thiol-3-one

Ethyl
3-methylthiopropionate

3-Methylthio-1-hexanol

Methional

Thiopropanal
S-oxide

Dipropyl disulphide

2-(Methyldithio)-
methylfuran

Methylthiomethyl-
dithiomethane

Propyl
propanethiosulphinate

Methyl
thioacetate

2-Propenyl
isothiocyanate

Propyl
propanethiosulphonate

FIG. 5.   Important food volatiles: sulphur compounds.

tend to be powerful odorants and even hydrogen sulphide is no exception. It clearly contributes to foods, such as eggs and meat. Thiols, sulphides and disulphides contribute to many, particularly cooked, foods. Methanethiol content has a high correlation with Cheddar flavour.[14] *p*-Menthane-8-thiol-3-one, present in oil of buchu, possesses a blackcurrant odour.[15] Dimethyl sulphide is important in asparagus, cooked tomato and corn, and contributes to butter flavour. Pineapple has long been known to contain ethyl 3-methylthiopropionate, but 3-methylthio-1-hexanol has only just been isolated from yellow passionfruit, where it contributes a green, fatty, and sulphury note, typical of certain exotic fruits.[16] It is capable of imparting the character of the fresh fruit to juice. Methional, the

Strecker degradation product of methionine, contributes to many foods, but is associated particularly with potato.

Disulphides have distinctive odours. Whereas the dimethyl compound contributes to cabbage, the propyl and 1-propenyl compounds are characteristic of boiled onions, and the 2-propenyl compound of garlic. Very recently 2-(methyldithio)methylfuran has been shown to be of major importance to the aroma of white bread.[17] Methylthiomethyldithiomethane has been found in brassicas.[18] Thiosulphinates and thiosulphonates are important contributors to fresh onion, where thiopropanal S-oxide is the lachrymator.

Yet another class of sulphur compounds, thioesters, has been recently shown to be an important contributor to the characteristic odour of Pont l'Evêque.[7]

Isothiocyanates have long been known to be of significance. Not only is the 2-propenyl compound the character-impact compound of black mustard, but it also contributes to cabbage and horseradish. The latter contains in addition 2-phenylethyl isothiocyanate, which is the character-impact compound of watercress[19] and contributes also to garden cress.[20]

Oxygen Heterocycles (Fig. 6)

Furans are widespread, usually connected with the breakdown of carbohydrates. In a most useful review of heterocyclics in flavour chemistry, furans are cited as preponderating numerically.[21] Furaneol has been found to be an important contributor to pineapple, strawberry, and beef broth, and is present also in popcorn and roasted filberts. The ethyl homologue has just been shown to be intensely sweet and a major contributor to soy sauce.[22] Mesifurane, furaneol methyl ether, is the principal volatile component and character-impact compound of the arctic bramble, where furaneol also contributes.[23] Mesifurane had previously been found in canned mango.[24] 2-Thiomethylfuran has a strong roasted coffee aroma and contributes to meat. The importance of 2-(methyldithio)methylfuran to bread aroma has already been mentioned.[17]

Straight-chain lactones have long been known to contribute particularly to apricot, coconut, and peach. The character-impact compounds of celery are lactones of rather different structure, such as 3-isobutylidene-3a,4-dihydrophthalide. Many compounds contribute to the aroma of meat, amongst them lactones, e.g. that from 2,4-dihydroxy-3-methyl-2-hexenoic acid, and 2,4,5-trimethyloxazoline.

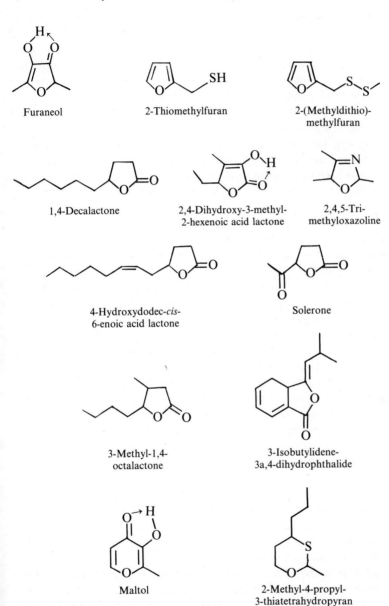

Furaneol

2-Thiomethylfuran

2-(Methyldithio)-
methylfuran

1,4-Decalactone

2,4-Dihydroxy-3-methyl-
2-hexenoic acid lactone

2,4,5-Tri-
methyloxazoline

4-Hydroxydodec-*cis*-
6-enoic acid lactone

Solerone

3-Methyl-1,4-
octalactone

3-Isobutylidene-
3a,4-dihydrophthalide

Maltol

2-Methyl-4-propyl-
3-thiatetrahydropyran

FIG. 6.   Important food volatiles: oxygen heterocycles.

An unsaturated lactone, that of 4-hydroxydodec-*cis*-6-enoic acid, provides the sweetness in odour of lamb fed a lipid-protected diet.[10] Solerone, 4-hydroxy-5-oxohexanoic acid lactone, is an important odorant in wine. A different lactone, 3-methyl-1,4-octalactone, finds its way into brandy from oak casks.[25] An extensive review of lactones in food has just appeared.[26]

Maltol, a γ-pyrone, has long been recognised as an important volatile, particularly in foods which have undergone heating. Two isomeric heterocycles, containing both oxygen and sulphur, namely *cis*- and *trans*-2-methyl-4-propyl-3-thiatetrahydropyran, have recently been isolated from yellow passionfruit. They have a strong and natural fruity odour, with a green and slightly burnt note.[16]

Nitrogen Heterocycles (Fig. 7)

Pyrroles and pyridines have been isolated from foods,[21] but here only indole is mentioned, since it has been shown to contribute to Pont l'Evêque.[7]

Pyrazines are one of the outstanding flavour discoveries of the last decade. Two types need to be distinguished: those substituted only with alkyl groups and those bearing additionally a methoxy group. The latter are the more powerful odorants. The 2-isobutyl-3-methoxy compound, its 2-s-butyl isomer, and its isopropyl homologue are widely distributed in raw vegetables, often occurring together.[27] The first dominates in green and red peppers, the second in carrot, parsnip, beetroot, and silverbeet, and the last in peas, pea shells, broad beans, potato, cucumber, and asparagus. The 2-s-butyl compound has also been found in boiled carrot;[28] the isobutyl isomer in an aroma fraction characteristic of Cabernet Sauvignon grapes.[29] In boiled potatoes, the current evidence points to 2-ethyl-3-methoxypyrazine as the character-impact compound.

Alkylpyrazines without a methoxy substituent are formed on heating in many foods. For example, 2-ethyl-3,6-dimethylpyrazine is among the most important volatiles of baked potato. Musty potato odour, which can develop in dairy products, has been traced to 2,5-dimethyl- and 2-isopropyl-3-methoxy-pyrazine,[30] yet the former and 2,3,5-trimethylpyrazine are thought to be main contributors of the weak nutty notes in American processed cheese.[31]

Thiazoles are quite widespread.[32] 2-Isobutylthiazole is an important contributor to tomato and interesting thiazoles have been found in dry bean and in potato products.

Sulphur Heterocycles (Fig. 7)

Thiophenes are quite widespread,[33] examples being the occurrence of dimethyl derivatives in onion oil and fried onion and the contribution by the 2-formyl compound to meat. 3,5-Dimethyl-1,2,4-trithiolane also contributes to meat, but lenthionine, a seven-membered heterocycle containing five sulphur atoms, is the character-impact compound of shiitake, a Japanese mushroom.

Other Compounds (Fig. 7)

Although the intention is not to be exhaustive, it is necessary to round off this survey by drawing attention to yet other facets of the chemistry of important food volatiles. Hydrogen cyanide is present in many prunoids: apricot kernels may contain as much as 0.18%![134] More and more halogenated compounds are being encountered; the extreme example is the favourite edible seaweed in Hawaii,[35] the essential oil of which is composed mainly of bromine and iodine containing haloforms. 2,3,4,6-Tetrachloroanisole and related compounds have been shown to be the cause of musty taint in chicken.[36]

There is no doubt but that the future still holds many surprises in

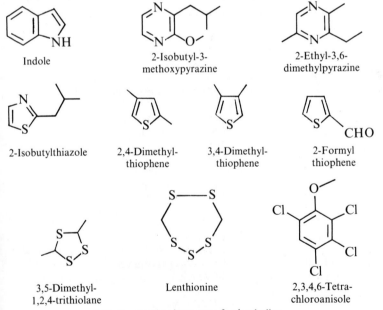

Indole

2-Isobutyl-3-methoxypyrazine

2-Ethyl-3,6-dimethylpyrazine

2-Isobutylthiazole

2,4-Dimethyl-thiophene

3,4-Dimethyl-thiophene

2-Formyl thiophene

3,5-Dimethyl-1,2,4-trithiolane

Lenthionine

2,3,4,6-Tetra-chloroanisole

FIG. 7. Further important food volatiles.

this fascinating area of research, but it is necessary to turn now to a consideration of individual foods, in order to see to what extent the volatiles surveyed above explain the perceived aromas.

CLASSIFICATION OF FOODS IN TERMS OF THEIR IMPORTANT VOLATILE CONSTITUENTS

In the Abstract, such a classification of foods was suggested, based essentially on the concepts of character-impact compounds and contributory flavour compounds. This clearly is a very rudimentary system, recognising only 3 levels of organoleptic importance, none, contributory, and character-impact. Refinement is highly desirable, but at least it is worth making a start.

Class 1

Table 1 shows a number of foods and the corresponding character-impact compounds which place them in this class. In some cases, such as watercress, the character-impact compound accounts virtually for all the odour, but this is not true to the same extent for the banana, for example. This class could be subdivided, since the aromas of some of the foods have more than one character-impact compound

TABLE 1

Some foods whose aroma resides largely in one compound

Food	Character-impact compound
Banana	Isopentyl acetate
Grape, Concord	Methyl anthranilate
Grapefruit	Nootkatone
Lemon	Citral
Pear	*trans*-2,*cis*-4-Decadienoates
Cucumber	*trans*-2,*cis*-6-Nonadienal
Green pepper	2-Isobutyl-3-methoxypyrazine
Potato, raw	2-Isopropyl-3-methoxypyrazine
Mushroom, boiled	1-Octen-3-one
Shiitake	Lenthionine
Beetroot	Geosmin
Garlic	Di-2-propenyl disulphide
Watercress	2-Phenylethyl isothiocyanate
Almonds	Benzaldehyde
Cheese, Blue	2-Heptanone and 2-Nonanone

(see pear and Blue cheese), but these are closely related to one another chemically and organoleptically (homologues in these instances).

Class 2

Table 2 shows a number of foods together with their character-impact and contributory flavour compounds. It should be noted that a character-impact compound does not necessarily have to be present, yet a reasonably faithful aroma can be produced from a mixture of a small number of compounds.

TABLE 2
Some foods whose aroma is due to a mixture of a small number of compounds

Food	Character-impact compound	Contributory flavour compounds
Apple, Delicious	Ethyl 2-methylbutyrate	Hexanal
		trans-2-Hexenal
Bilberries		Ethyl 2-methylbutyrate
		Ethyl 3-methylbutyrate
		trans-2-Hexenal
Raspberries	1-*p*-Hydroxyphenyl-3-butanone	*cis*-3-Hexen-1-ol
		Damascenone
		α- and β-Ionone
Tangerines		Methyl *N*-methylanthranilate
		Thymol
Tomatoes		Hexanal
		trans-2-Hexenal
		cis-3-Hexenal
		cis-3-Hexen-1-ol
		2-Isobutylthiazole
		Some high-boilers
Celery	3-Isobutylidene-3a,4-dihydrophthalide	*cis*-3-Hexen-1-yl pyruvate
	3-Isovalidene-3a,4-dihydrophthalide	2,3-Butadione
Onion, raw	Thiopropanal *S*-oxide (lachrymator)	Thiosulphinates
		Thiosulphonates
Onion, boiled	Propyl and 1-propenyl disulphides	
Cabbage, boiled	Dimethyl disulphide	2-Propenyl isothiocyanate
		Dimethyl trisulphide
Potato, boiled	2-Ethyl-3-methoxypyrazine	Methional
Butter	2,3-Butanedione	Ethanal
		Dimethyl sulphide

The most recent study of tomatoes[37] shows the presence of some relatively high-boiling volatiles with strong tomato-like odours, which may well turn out to be character-impact compounds.

Fried onions are not included in Table 2. Dimethylthiophenes had been thought to be important contributors, but this is no longer tenable.[38]

Roasted groundnut belongs to this class, but its aroma is due relatively non-specifically to a complex mixture of pyrazines. A character-impact chemical class is present rather than a character-impact compound.

Class 3

This class comprises those foods whose aroma can only be reproduced reasonably faithfully by the use of quite a large number of compounds. Usually no character-impact compound has been found.

Examples are apricot and peach, blackcurrant, lime, passionfruit, leek,[39] pineapple, brazil nut,[40] walnut,[41] roast beef and other cooked meats, bread, coffee and tea.

Class 4

This, the last class, comprises those foods whose aroma cannot be reasonably reproduced even by a complex mixture of specific compounds from amongst the volatiles identified.

The prime example is strawberry, but chocolate is another. Cloudberry is a recently investigated case: a mixture of 50 of the over 80 components identified compared very unfavourably with the aroma of the fresh berries.[42] In these instances no natural character-impact compound has been identified to date and the likelihood of one being discovered is very low.

The above classification is bound to be controversial and is only intended as a means of clarifying the state of the art that has been reached. Detailed discussion should now follow, leading to a refinement of concepts, which in turn will form the basis of future progress.

REFERENCES

1. van Straten, S. and de Vrijer, F. (1973). *Lists of Volatile Compounds in Food*, 3rd edn. Report No. R.4030. Central Institute for Nutrition and Food Research TNO, Zeist. Supplements 1–6 (1975).
2. Jennings, W. G. and Sevenants, M. R. (1964). *J. Fd. Sci.*, **29**, p. 158.

3. Cronin, D. A. and Ward, M. K. (1971). *J. Sci. Fd. Agric.*, **22**, p. 477.
4. Murray, K. E., Bannister, B. A. and Buttery, R. G. (1975). *Chemy Ind.*, p. 973.
5. Acree, T. E., Lee, C. Y., Butts, R. M. and Barnard, J. (1976). *J. agric. Fd. Chem.*, **24**, p. 430.
6. Buttery, R. G., Guadagni, D. G. and Ling, L. C. (1976). *J. agric. Fd. Chem.*, **24**, p. 419; *cf.* Buttery, R. G. and Garibaldi, J. A., *ibid.*, p. 1246.
7. Dumont, J. P., Degas, C. and Adda, J. (1976). *Lait*, **553/4**, p. 177.
8. McGill, A. S., Hardy, R., Burt, J. R. and Gunstone, F. (1974). *J. Sci. Fd. Agric.*, **25**, p. 1477.
9. Buttery, R. G. (1975). *J. agric. Fd. Chem.*, **23**, p. 1003.
10. Park, R. J., Murray, K. E. and Stanley, G. (1974). *Chemy Ind.*, p. 380.
11. Patterson, R. L. S. (1968). *J. Sci. Fd. Agric.*, **19**, p. 31; Griffiths, N. M. and Patterson, R. L. S. (1970). *Ibid.*, **21**, p. 4.
12. Wong, E., Johnson, C. B. and Nixon, N. L. (1975). *Chemy Ind.*, p. 40; Wong, E., Nixon, N. L. and Johnson, C. B. (1975). *J. agric. Fd. Chem.*, **23**, p. 495.
13. Magak'yan, D. T. (1976). *Prikl. Biokhim. Mikrobiol.*, **12**, p. 253; *Chem. Abstr.*, **85**, 19232.
14. Manning, D. J., Chapman, H. R. and Hosking, Z. D. (1976). *J. Dairy Res.*, **43**, p. 313.
15. Sundt, E., Willhalm, B., Chappaz, R. and Ohloff, G. (1971). *Helv. chim. Acta*, **54**, p. 1801.
16. Winter, M., Furrer, A. and Willhalm, B. (1976). *Helv. chim. Acta*, **59**, p. 1613.
17. Mulders, E. J., Kleipool, R. J. C. and ten Noever de Brauw, M. C. (1976). *Chemy Ind.*, p. 613.
18. Buttery, R. G., Guadagni, D. G., Ling, L. C., Seifert, R. M. and Lipton, W. (1976). *J. agric. Fd. Chem.*, **24**, p. 829.
19. MacLeod, A. J. and Islam, R. (1975). *J. Sci. Fd. Agric.*, **26**, p. 1545.
20. MacLeod, A. J. and Islam, R. (1976). *J. Sci. Fd. Agric.*, **27**, p. 909.
21. Flament, I. (1975). In: *Aroma Research*, eds. H. Maarse and P. J. Groenen, Centre for Agricultural Publishing and Documentation, Wageningen, p. 221.
22. Nunomura, N., Sasaki, M., Asao, Y. and Yokutsuka, T. (1976). *Agric. biol. Chem.*, **40**, pp. 485, 491.
23. Kallio, H. (1976). *J. Fd. Sci.*, **41**, pp. 555, 563.
24. Hunter, G. L. K., Bucek, W. A. and Radford, T. (1974). *J. Fd. Sci.*, **39**, p. 900.
25. Pisarnitskii, A. F., Egorov, I. A. and Gavrilov, A. I. (1976). *Prikl. Biokhim. Mikrobiol.*, **12**, p. 192: *Chem. Abstr.*, **85**, 31582.
26. Maga, J. A. (1976). *Critical Rev. Fd. Sci. Nutr.*, **8**, p. 1.
27. Murray, K. E. and Whitfield, F. B. (1975). *J. Sci. Fd. Agric.*, **26**, p. 973.
28. Cronin, D. A. and Stanton, P. (1976). *J. Sci. Fd. Agric.*, **27**, p. 145.
29. Bayenove, C., Cordonnier, R. and Dubois, P. (1975). *Compt. rend.*, **281D**, p. 75.
30. Morgan, M. E. (1976). *Biotech. Bioeng.*, **18**, p. 953.
31. Lin, S. S. (1976). *J. agric. Fd. Chem.*, **24**, p. 1252.

32. Maga, J. A. (1975). *Critical Rev. Fd. Sci. Nutr.*, **6**, p. 153.
33. Maga, J. A. (1975). *Critical Rev. Fd. Sci. Nutr.*, **6**, p. 241.
34. Stoewsand, G. S., Anderson, J. L. and Lamb, R. C. (1975). *J. Fd. Sci.*, **40**, p. 1107.
35. Burreson, B. J., Moore, R. E. and Roller, P. P. (1976). *J. agric. Fd. Chem.*, **24**, p. 856.
36. Curtis, R. F., Dennis, C., Gee, J. M., Gee, M. G., Griffiths, N. M., Land, D. G., Peel, J. L. and Robinson, D. (1974). *J. Sci. Fd. Agric.* **25**, p. 811.
37. Dirinck, P., Schreyen, L., van Wassenhove, F. and Schamp, N. (1976). *J. Sci. Fd. Agric.*, **27**, p. 499.
38. Galetto, W. G. and Hoffman, P. G. (1976). *J. agric. Fd. Chem.*, **24**, p. 852; *cf.* p. 854.
39. Schreyen, L., Dirinck, P., van Wassenhove, F. and Schamp, N. (1976). *J. agric. Fd. Chem.*, **24**, pp. 336, 1147.
40. Clark, R. G. and Nursten, H. E. (1976). *J. Sci. Fd. Agric.*, **27**, p. 713.
41. Clark, R. G. and Nursten, H. E. (1976). *J. Sci. Fd. Agric.*, **27**, p. 902.
42. Honkanen, E. and Pyysalo, T. (1976). *Z. Lebensm. Unters.-Forsch.*, **160**, p. 393.

DISCUSSION

Questioner: What exactly is the taste described as metallic?

Nursten: It is the taste obtained when a small piece of metal, e.g. iron, finds its way into the mouth. Foil, e.g. sweet wrappings, can be the cause, but the term has become associated particularly with oxidative rancidity.

McCracken: In the food industry a proportion of, e.g. processed foods are prepared in open cooking vessels. Volatile flavours may therefore be lost to the atmosphere. Do you have any general comments regarding the loss of volatile flavours, e.g. time/temperature conditions?

Nursten: Preparation in open vessels clearly allows loss of volatiles and this will increase with time and with temperature. However, it must be borne in mind that loss of some volatiles can be beneficial. It is important, therefore, to study each case individually and to determine which are the significant volatiles, the manner in which they are significant, and what happens to them in processing.

Harper: How often do the authors of the papers on which you have drawn report the details of their sensory techniques?

Nursten: The best ones do very fully, but for the majority the sensory information is better described as asides rather than data. The situation is improving and the emphasis which symposia such as this place on high standards of sensory assessment encourages improvement.

11

A Short History of Sensory Analysis in the United Kingdom

Roland Harper

*Department of Food Science, University of Reading,
Reading, England*

ABSTRACT

So far, no one has written a history of the development of sensory analysis in the United Kingdom. An earlier review by the author contained only 35 references (19 from the UK). The origins of sensory analysis must be lost in antiquity. The present survey goes back only to 1753 when the sensory attributes of quality in food were well documented in a series of 'Instructions for Marketting'. Progress and expansion, as opposed to academic interest in the subject, has been greatly affected by economic pressures, some of which are noted. With a few conspicuous exceptions the major expansion in the applications of sensory analysis in the United Kingdom was delayed until well after the end of food rationing in 1955. Choice is only possible when there is more than enough food to meet mere necessities. However, the pressures for systematic methods of sensory analysis have often come from the demands of importers rather than from internal pressures from the producing countries. Apart from the appearance of occasional studies and reports the co-ordination of interest and application of sensory analysis in the United Kingdom has been stimulated by the activities of Committee FA/-/2 (Sensory Analysis) of the British Standards Institution. This development took place in 1968. It was influenced by the prior activities of a corresponding Working Group (now a Sub-Committee) of the International Standards Organisation, the aim being to provide specialist advice to commodity committees. Although any review must be selective, some of the events which have taken place in the United Kingdom since the late 1930s are noted and summarised. This review ends with a reference to the recent Symposium

(*January* 1977) *on Sensory Quality Control arranged jointly by the Sensory Panel of the Food Group of the Society of Chemical Industry and the Institute of Food Science and Technology* (*UK*).

INTRODUCTION: SOME EARLY DEVELOPMENTS

The material presented here has been drawn from a number of different sources, including several published bibliographies[1-5] which have been scanned visually. The earliest document noted is a section taken from the 1753 edition of 'The Lady's Companion'[6] and is entitled 'Directions for Marketting'. This clearly indicates how sophisticated an 18th century housewife might be expected to become and how she might be trained as her own 'sensory analyst'. Two quotations from this section are given below, taken respectively from pages 404 and 407.

'*To choose beef* (Old English usage transliterated)
True ox-beef has an open grain, and the fat, if young, is of a crumbly or oily smoothness, except it be the brisket and neck pieces, with such others as are very fibrous. The lean ought to be of a pleasant carnation red, the fat inclining to white rather than yellow, and the suet very white.

Cow beef has a closer grain, the fat is whiter, the bones less, and the lean of a paler colour. If it be young and tender, the dent made by pressing it with the finger will rise again in a little time.

Bull-beef is of a deeper red, a closer grain, and firmer than either of the former, harder to be indented with your finger and rising again sooner. The fat is gross and fibrous and of a strong rank scent. If it be old, it will be so very tough, that your pinching of it will scarcely make any impression. If it be fresh, it will be of a lively colour, but if stale, of a dark dusty colour, and very clammy. If it be bruised, the part affected will look of a blackish or more dusty colour than the rest.'

'*To choose eggs*
When you buy eggs hold them up against the sun, or a candle, and if the whites appear clear and fair, and the yolk round, they are good; but if muddy or cloudy, and the yolk broken, they are naught. Or put the great end to your tongue; if it feels warm, it is new; but if cold, it is stale. Or take the egg, and put it into a pan of cold water; the fresher it is the sooner it will sink to the bottom; but if wrotten, or addled, it will

swim on the surface of the water. The best way to keep them is in bran or meal.'

The evolution of any subject results from the interplay of many different forces. In addition to the influence of particular individuals, economic forces often trigger off developments which may have been seen as academically interesting and important, but which have remained stagnant in terms of growth and application. This has been true of developments relating to sensory analysis in the United Kingdom, at least until a decade or so ago. Going back to the middle of the last century, the development of the railways and other forms of transport produced a number of changes which necessitated the development of new forms of appraisal and control as a substitute for that of the well trained housewife, or the individual craftsmen or small trader. The large wholesaler, sometimes referred to as 'a factor' and the specialist grocer were the first to emerge and both of them would be knowledgeable about the foods they sold and they were often aware of differences in local tastes. The sending of choice varieties of cheeses to certain of the London clubs might be regarded as a specific example of this. As the scale of the developing food industry has increased there have been further changes. The tasks of discrimination and control passed from the responsibility of the owner to the manager (and perhaps his wife). Then in the 1920s or early 1930s, the food chemist took over responsibility for many of these functions. His training and disciplines emphasised what could be measured by physical or chemical methods, with a partial neglect of the sensory bases of quality in food. However, even as early as the 1930s there were signs of the beginning of a movement 'back to the senses'. For example, the importance of quality as a selling point in the eyes of the consumer became recognised in British Agriculture which was in a depressed state at that time. This is illustrated by the establishment in 1934 by the Ministry of Agriculture and Fisheries of a National Mark Scheme.[7]

However, some products have a longer history of systematic specification and control involving sensory aspects. One of the best examples is the development of methods of grading dairy products, which also developed in response to the needs of commerce. In the first instance this was in the interests of international trade. Thus, Sutherland Thomson has outlined the development of systematic methods of grading by New Zealand to meet the needs of the export trade with the United Kingdom, as early as 1894.[8] The dairy industry and associated research provide one of the prior examples of developments in sensory analysis. The current state of the art was reviewed in 1957[9] and again recently.[10] However, reverting to the previous time-sequence, the period covering World War II and extending until about 1955 when food rationing ended was essentially one of retrogression rather than advancement. For example, during this period grading cheese was simplified so as to allow for only three categories: Grade I, fit for keeping; Grade II, fit for immediate consumption; and Grade III, fit for processing. Under conditions of shortages and rationing the consumer has no choice, except to do without, and in this context questions of high quality and all but the most extreme forms of loss of palatability become trivial. (1955 was the first date in personal records after the beginning of the war that a sample of butter was returned to the grocer for replacement because it was defective. The butter had been stored close to the firelighters in a small grocer's shop!) The same year the schemes for grading dairy products were revised and improved. However, general developments since the end of the war will be discussed separately.

THE GROWTH OF THE LITERATURE

At the time of writing well over 230 relevant references have been assembled. This particular sample has been classified into five-year groups, the results being given in Table 1. The main conclusions from this analysis are that apart from a sizeable group of contributions immediately before World War II, the bulk of the literature is post-war and only during the last decade has the growth-rate shown signs of a progressive increase. In fact, there is an apparent drop in the number of papers during the period 1951–55 which could be attributed to the ending of financial support from the grant-giving agencies of the programme of psychophysical research at the National Institute for Research in Dairying about 1952. The contribution of individual institutions has not been examined in detail, but the impression is that a few well-known Research Institutes have been responsible for the bulk of the publications, with University Departments a long way second and, with the exception of the dairy industry and studies of changes in the freshness of fish, only a few contributions from the food industry itself. There would be little variation in the actual significance of individual papers coming from each of these three sources.

Since the end of World War II there have been nearly twenty Symposia or collected papers relating to sensory analysis and its development. The first of these took place in 1947 and was entitled

TABLE 1

The growth of the literature relating to sensory analysis in the UK. The cumulative total refers to the end of each five-year period

	n	Total (Cumulative)		n	Total (Cumulative)
1971–75	52	(238)	1931–35	1	(10)
1966–70	38	(186)	1926–30	1	(9)
1961–65	32	(148)	1921–25	2	(8)
1956–60	33	(116)	1916–20	0	(6)
1951–55	24	(83)	1911–15	1	(6)
1946–50	32	(59)	1906–10	2	(5)
1941–45	4	(27)	1901–05	0	(5)
1936–40	13	(23)	before 1900	3	(3)

'Organoleptic tests in the food industry'. The term 'Organoleptic' has recently been defined as follows:[11]

'Relating to an attribute of a product perceptible by the sense organs'.

Although a number of experts regard the term as archaic and argue against its continued use, it is one of the terms included in the glossary of terms recently published by the British Standards Institution and accepted by the International Standards Organisation. The 1947 Symposium included a review of the experience of a number of people who had contributed to new technological developments during the war in the processing and preservation of foods. Thus, for example, Bate-Smith outlined the development of a scoring system for dried egg, and the establishment of a minimal score above which 75 % of the customers would accept the product. In spite of criticisms, dried egg played an important part in the diet of people at war, in the UK. At one stage, Bate-Smith had looked upon taste-tests as something temporary, to be replaced in due course by physical or chemical tests yet to be developed. However, in the light of experience he changed his views and thus became one of the pioneers of sensory analysis. Thus in 1947 he wrote:

'Both sorts of tests† and also hybrids between them have their value in control and research in the food industry, and are capable of being built up into standardised disciplines. I feel that we are at the litmus stage of organoleptic testing. We can, I am sure, look forward to an advance in technique not less than that represented by the advance from litmus paper to electrometric titration in a more familiar field of analysis.[12]

Space does not permit a detailed review of each Symposium which has taken place in the United Kingdom since 1947; most of these are listed in Appendix I. Although by no means all of these Symposia were limited to those who have a professional interest in the sensory analysis of food, this has become one of the main sources of information. The most recent is the Symposium on 'Sensory Quality Control' arranged jointly by the Sensory Panel of the Food Group of the Society of Chemical Industry and the Institute of Food Science and Technology (UK), in January 1977. When the proceedings are published this will very considerably redress the balance of papers on the use of sensory analysis in the food industry.

PSYCHO-RHEOLOGY AND ITS SUCCESSORS

No history of the development of sensory analysis in the UK would be complete without reference to G.W. Scott Blair, for many years head of the Physics Department at the National Institute for Research in Dairying. Not only was he the pioneer of Rheology—the science of measurement of the properties of complex materials which deform or flow under pressure—but he also pioneered what he referred to as 'Psycho-rheology'.[13] This deals with the relation between human responses to various materials and the measurement of the underlying properties. The term, which is still used, anticipates what is now described as 'Sensory-Instrumental Correlation'. Psycho-rheology was chosen by analogy with the already well-established subject of Psychophysics (relating physical measurements to the various

† Bate-Smith was referring here to quantitative descriptive tests and to preference tests, respectively.

sensations which we experience, especially those of sight and hearing), a discipline first formalised as long ago as 1860.

The literature of psychophysics has contributed much to the concepts and methods of sensory analysis. In the late 1930s Scott Blair met Katz, a distinguished psychologist with a special interest in the human senses and perception. After the war Katz became Professor of Psychology in the University of Stockholm, but at the time referred to he was a refugee from Germany. Among the tasks he undertook in this capacity was a study of the skills of expert bakers.[14,15] For example, he demonstrated experimentally that the expert baker could detect differences in water content between two doughs as little as 1–2% from differences in stickiness. On his appointment to the NIRD Scott Blair saw the possibilities of similar investigations relating to dairy products, including questions of body and texture. He initiated a programme of psycho-rheological research which, apart from an interruption during the war, continued from about 1938 to 1952. This programme had a number of different facets including the following:

(1) The development of special instruments for measuring the rheological properties of complex materials especially dairy products.

(2) Fundamental studies concerned with measuring the powers of discrimination of the human hand when manipulating model systems with properties similar to many dairy products. Such actions simulate certain of the skills involved in traditional methods of cheese making and cheese grading.

(3) A variety of field studies involving the use of some of these instrumental tests and sensory assessments of the essential qualities of dairy products.

Scott Blair's collaborators included Coppen, Harper, Baron, Sheppard and Prentice, each of whom made important contributions to the whole programme. The first phase included a number of different studies of man's ability to distinguish between the firmness of pairs of samples of rubber and other materials with 'cheese-like' properties.[16–23] The first field studies of relevance were undertaken by Harper and Baron[24,25] and included two investigations in which approximately 200 cheeses from continuous factory production were tested by up to 12 instrumental tests and up to 6 sensory tests. The analysis of the data included the use of what are now referred to as multi-dimensional statistical methods. This was the first time these particular methods had ever been used with data relating to food. The analyses were carried out without the aid of computers. Many interesting points emerged from these studies including the multi-dimensional nature of cheese quality. That is at least three and possibly more types of variation are involved. Certain tests were demonstrated to measure the same 'properties' as others, and were eliminated. In other instances gaps in the selection of tests were demonstrated statistically, and certain tests were found to be largely independent of the sensory qualities which they had been designed to measure. The best example of this was the 'crumbliness' of Cheshire cheeses, an essential quality distinctive of the variety which can best be assessed by breaking down a small portion of cheese between finger and thumb. It is of interest historically to add that one of the war-time problems on which Scott Blair's advice was sought was how to make Cheshire cheeses more Cheddar-like so that the cheese ration could be taken in a single piece and not as a collection of small particles. The multi-dimensional studies of cheese have been summarised.[26] Similar techniques were employed by Prentice to choose between a number of alternative tests for measuring the properties of fats (especially margarine and butter) and this was the origin of the FIRA/NIRD Extruder.[27, 28] Sheppard's contributions began with a continuation of the discrimination tasks, but later included several studies on terminology, scales and scoring systems.[29-32] However, by the time the programme was disbanded in the early 1950s Sheppard had already turned his attention to a number of consumer studies.

Apart from a few review papers, studies of rheological properties of foods and their sensory correlates were interrupted for a number of years. The technique of Magnitude Estimation was applied to a set of materials very similar to the early discrimination studies. This particular study was made in the Psychophysics Laboratories at Harvard University and reported by Harper and Stevens in 1963.[33] The main conclusion was that the firmness of the compliant materials handled was a power-law function of the measured stimuli with an exponent of 0·8 when the firmness was expressed according to the rules of Magnitude Estimation, a psychophysical procedure developed earlier by Stevens. Designating the physical stimulus by Φ and the sensory response by Ψ this relationship is expressed by the equation:

$$\Psi = k\Phi^n$$

After an interval of a number of years, further investigations in this area were first reported by Wood, in a contribution to the second Symposium on 'Rheology and Texture of Foodstuffs'. During the intervening years international activities expanded considerably as indicated by the appearance of the Journal of Texture Studies. By 1968 instrumental measurements had greatly improved since the pioneer studies in Reading and the time was now ripe for further investigations. Logically, the situation is simple in those instances in which similar materials are compared with one another and where there is a high, linear correlation between a particular stimulus measure and the numbers assigned to represent the intensity or degree to which the corresponding quality is present. In many practical instances this is not so. Two important complications arise. One is to be found in those instances in which the sensory property evaluated is related to more than one separately measurable rheological property. The second arises when the rheological properties change in the course of testing, or differ from one product or material to another. Scott Blair anticipated these problems in a number of different ways. Not only did he postulate the existence of 'quasi-properties' (i.e. properties which might change in the course of testing), but he also carried out matching and discrimination experiments using test-samples which differed qualitatively. At that stage (in the late 1940s) these studies were highly academic and entirely fundamental. Wood[34-36] developed this subject experimentally and Shama and Sherman[37] have been able to identify the area or region on a graphical representation of the rate of stress against the rate strain for a number of fluid foodstuffs which corresponds with the manner in which that product behaves when probed by hand or mouth in sensory tests. Thus different bands have been identified in principle for the relevant measurements corresponding respectively with visual assessment, the assessment by stirring, or the mouthfeel of the samples appraised. This development, together with the use of multi-dimensional statistical methods of analysis, must represent two of the most important developments in the complex area of sensory-instrumental correlation one aim of which is the calibration of the instrument by the assessors. Note should also be taken of the extension of Shama and Sherman's approach by Barry and Grace[38,39] to cosmetic creams and the way they feel in 'topical application'.

A brief reference must be made to the subject of descriptive terminology. This has been far less intensively investigated with textural qualities than with odour qualities (see below). Here it is necessary to declare a personal interest which may differ from one investigator to another. Most scientific investigators place prior emphasis upon what instruments can measure, and orientate (or even train) their assessors to make judgements within this framework. Personally, I take the view that the starting point should be spontaneous usage and the task is then to determine which instrumental measurements correspond to the changes in the sensations or qualities which the user has already identified and named. In fact, the truth is somewhere between the two approaches, particularly when in practice the various qualities may have to be defined by actual samples and variations between them. Sherman[40] has set out details of his physically orientated system and Jowitt[41] has proposed a series of useful working definitions. Throughout sensory analyses the relative effectiveness of sensory and instrumental methods should be demonstrated experimentally rather than assumed.

ODOUR CHARACTERISATION AND ODOUR CLASSIFICATION

Studies of odour characterisation and odour classification, and their practical application in various profiling systems represent another important development which merits separate consideration. Personal interest in this dates back to the NIRD phase (1946–50) when in spite of the major commitment with rheology and texture the excellent library facilities provided access to the international literature concerned with taste testing and food grading. Several reviews of this literature were published[42–45] about this time. Contact with the pioneer work by Cheesman and his colleagues,[46–48] also being carried out in Reading, drew attention to the potentialities of olfactory research. Cheesman's studies, which were later to be transferred to Tasmania, were concerned with the interaction between different odours, as indicated by the influence on the threshold for one odour stimulus by the presence of another. This information provided one measure of odour similarity. Two odours which interfered with one another would be defined as in some degree similar, whereas two odours which did not interfere with one another would not be similar.

On transferring personally to the recently established Department of Psychology in the University of Leeds, one of the first steps was to acquire from America the Crocker-Henderson Odour Classification Set, with its 32 separate test-tubes containing individual chemicals representing the Crocker-Henderson system of four major qualities: *fragrant, acid, burnt* and *capryllic* in varying degrees. These odour stimuli formed the basis of a number of early studies of odour characterisation and established a growing interest in the subject.[49] A documentary exercise (undertaken by my wife) consisted of extracting from the Concise Oxford Dictionary, which included over 200 000 words and their definitions, those words which were used to describe taste, odours and textures. The analysis and classification of these words formed the basis of a paper to the first post-war Symposium in the UK on problems of perception. Repeated attempts at that time to publish this failed, but it was eventually published in 1972 in a revised form.[50] This event well-illustrates the importance of fashions in science and the fact that there is a particular point in time which is favourable for particular developments.

By the early 1960s interest in odour characterisation was beginning to crystallise more definitely, but it became evident that for useful work the most up-to-date controls of the odour stimuli (as well as on the methods of sensory evaluation) were necessary. Since 1947, the possibility of collaboration with Bate-Smith had repeatedly been explored but it was not until 1964 that this became possible financially. The Low Temperature Research Station in Cambridge, one of the pioneer institutions in what has subsequently become known as food science, was about to close down, most of the staff eventually being transferred either to the Agriculture Research Council's Meat Research Institute in Langford (near Bristol) or to the sister organisation, the Food Research Institute in Norwich. A multi-disciplinary research team was thus established in Norwich involving members of the Flavour Group from Cambridge in addition to myself. For the next three years this group was concerned with the intensive study of odour characterisation and classification.

Many aspects of the work have already been fully reported. They include a glossary containing the systematic descriptions of 45 odour stimuli, single chemical substances of high purity,[51] and a reciprocal type of analysis consisting of those substances which best represent the 44 selected odour qualities.[52] Two different groups of assessors were used, one consisting of experienced persons (experienced in smelling odours, but not experts in the perfumery sense), the other group were novices. Important preliminary information had been obtained previously by presenting many of these stimuli to a number of persons totalling over 400 attending a Meeting of the British Association for the Advancement of Science in Cambridge. Several positive outcomes of these studies were achieved. The technique of odour characterisation using a set of simple rating scales (0–5) including each of the 44 selected qualities was pushed to the limit and still found to be effective and discriminating. The literature on odour characterisation and odour classification was surveyed and published in book form.[53]

In addition, several different types of analysis using multi-dimensional statistical methods were carried out. However, the contractual period was strictly limited and these multi-disciplinary studies were discontinued in 1967. In fact, none of the multi-dimensional studies has been published in full. Statistical analyses were carried out in collaboration with Gower (Rothamsted Experimental Station) who had already developed his own form of Principal Co-ordinates Analysis. The more the results are examined ten years later the more points of interest are discovered. The available data can also be analysed in many different ways which have not yet been undertaken, including an estimation of the nature of differences between individuals.

Since 1968 a number of other developments have eventually taken place, and others are still in progress. Between 1973 and 1975 further studies were carried out in Reading, some consisting of additional analyses of the Norwich data and others involving a new collection of odours and terms presented by means of a special olfactometer designed and constructed by Piggott.[54, 55] This work was supported by British Gas. An undergraduate study comparing the memories triggered off by odours with those resulting from tactile stimuli is also in progress.

OTHER INVESTIGATIONS

The preceding sections have been largely concerned with developments with which I have been directly associated. Attention is now turned to a number of other investigations, which equally well illustrate important steps in the history of sensory analysis in the UK.

Even these are selective and some additional topics which also need consideration are listed in the final section.

Fish Freshness Studies

Only a brief reference is made to the studies of fish freshness, which have been continued practically without interruption for over 30 years. These have been carried out at Torry Research Station in Aberdeen and constitute one of the best documented examples of sensory analysis and its development. In this case, the deterioration in fish quality is followed with the aid of a set of score sheets covering each of the main aspects of quality, appearance, aroma, taste and texture both before and after cooking in a standard manner. The terms developed for describing changes in the odour were used in building up the comprehensive list of 44 terms referred to in the previous section. One illustration of the effectiveness of this scoring system is illustrated by a personal experience in Chile in 1968 when a series of fish differing in the number of days they had been kept on ice were placed on display at the Fisheries Research Institute in Santiago for the benefit of a group of M.Sc. students (postgraduate) from the Institute of Food Science and Technology. The scores assigned to the fish by these untrained students simply following the instructions corresponded perfectly with the number of days the same fish had been kept on ice. The scheme has been extended and adapted in the United Kingdom for use by the trade, including the catering industry. A fish freshness meter has recently been developed and marketed. This is based upon the changes in electrical properties of the fish during staling and has been calibrated against panel data obtained from different samples of fish which have been kept on ice for varying lengths of time.

Profiling Beers and Ciders

Another important development is the profiling of beers and ciders. The relevant literature goes back at least to 1925,[58] although most of the research leading to practicable systems has taken place during the last few years. Practice relating to sensory quality control in the brewery has been summarised by Wren[59] and Clapperton has developed the subject both in terms of fundamental research and international standardisation of the necessary terminology.[60,61] Considerable attention has been given in these studies to the choice of a number of reference standards which define the various terms.

Somewhat similar investigations relating to ciders and perries have been reported by Williams.[62]

Terminology in General

In principle, the problems of terminology are the same whether these concern taste, odour or texture. Those relating to colour and sound have been developed much more systematically than those relating to the other senses. Glossaries of terms are available in a number of different languages. The latest addition is the Glossary of Terms used in Sensory Analysis published by the British Standards Institution as a result of lengthy deliberations by the BSI Committee on Sensory Analysis.[11] Terms relating the methods of sensory analysis are included as well as a selection of descriptive terms. The definitions given are based upon a consensus principle. This glossary has also formed the basis of discussion and some degree of agreement by the corresponding Committee of the International Standards Organisation. In each instance, attention has been concentrated upon verbal definitions. Definitions in terms of agreed reference standards have not yet been considered.

Methodology and Statistics

Methodology and statistics cover a wide range of topics, including certain aspects of consumer studies. The British Standards Institution Committee on Sensory Analysis deliberately excluded consumer preferences from its deliberations; these are directed primarily at informing other commodity committees. However, in the last analysis the consumer cannot be excluded from the implications of the sensory analysis of food. One of the first studies in the United Kingdom of consumer preferences which employed the method of paired comparisons was published as long ago as 1937. This is one of the pre-war references.[63] Finney's text book 'Probit Analysis'[64] dealt with the use of the normal (probability) response curve which is applicable to measurements of sensitivity. The applications of Signal Detection Theory, first developed in relation to visual and auditory sensitivity in the military context of detecting and recognising faint signals, is only just beginning to penetrate into the literature of sensory analysis in the UK. These techniques tend to be time-consuming since they involve large amounts of response data, and short cut techniques are not yet fully worked out. Harries[65-67] has been concerned with a number of statistical contributions, dating back to about 1953. His early contributions were made as a member of the Ministry of Agriculture Fisheries and Food. During the past few years these activities have continued at the Meat Research Institute. Whereas some investigators—including the present author—have stressed the link with psychophysics, Harries has repeatedly stressed that sensory testing may be regarded as a form of biological assay. The more traditional aspects of statistics have been outlined and discussed by a number of individuals including Wadsworth[68] and Pridmore.[69] In treating statistical aspects both Gregson[70,71] and Steiner[72] have given particular attention to Difference Tests (The Triangular test and/or Paired Comparisons) which tend to be under represented in many of the traditional textbooks of statistics.

Reference has already been made to the first occasions on which Multi-dimensional Statistical Methods were applied to data consisting of tests and assessments of food. With the development of computers the task of applying these methods has become almost routine. Calculations which in the late 1940s took several weeks or even months to complete can now be carried out in microseconds, once the data have been punched onto the tape and fed into the computer. The use of these methods in odour characterisation and odour classification has already been outlined. More recent developments, involving the use of somewhat similar methods or derivatives of them to deal with the differences between judges or assessors as individuals or groups have been reported by Banfield and Harries[73] in connection with quality in meat, and Palmer[74] has examined individual differences in the use of terminology employed in evaluating quality in tea.

The method of Magnitude Estimation has also been touched upon. This is a system for quantifying human judgements (sensations and/or preferences) using a form of Ratio Scale. A ratio scale is open ended, as opposed to the closed or bounded function of the extremes of the ordinary Rating Scale. However, Magnitude Estimation has certain other defects which are reflected most readily in individual differences in the use of numbers and in the effect on the functional relationship between sensation and stimulus magnitude resulting from the particular range of stimuli employed. One of the most ardent critics of the method is Poulton.[75,76] The problems associated with the development of sensory scales have also been discussed critically by Treisman and his colleagues.[77-79]

SUMMING UP

It will be obvious that the history of any subject cannot be dealt with comprehensively in a short article. The present review inevitably reflects personal interests. Before concluding, some of the additional contributions which should be included in a balanced history are noted:

(1) Individual papers by Moncrieff, who was probably the first to write a book 'The Chemical Senses'[80] and whose studies of odour preferences should also be noted.[81]

(2) Recent investigations from the National Institute for Research in Dairying on the effects of various processes on the flavour and acceptability of dairy products.

(3) Investigations by Birch and his colleagues from the National College of Food Technology on the relation between chemical structure and taste qualities.[82,83] This seems to be the only group in the UK actively investigating this particular problem.

(4) Note should also be taken of the psychophysical studies of the sense of taste by O'Mahony[84–86] (Bristol University). Much of his emphasis has been placed on methodology, including the variability of sense experience and its quantification, when carried out under highly controlled conditions. It is difficult to appraise the full significance of these studies, since under practical conditions many important aspects of perception are more stable than the (peripheral) pattern of stimuli which give rise to them. This has been clearly demonstrated in vision, but the corresponding experiments have not been formulated with taste and smell.

(6) Only a passing reference has been made to the work of the Meat Research Institute (Langford near Bristol), which is relevant and important.

(7) Note also the genetically orientated studies of taste and smell illustrated by the summary by Kalmus and Hubbard.[87]

(8) An increasing number of investigations will appear on particular commodities. Most of those of a routine nature and those primarily concerned with instrumental aspects rather than sensory aspects have been omitted.

A complete list of supplementary material could be continued much further. There are certain extensive bibliographies such as those of the International Food Information Service which can now be scanned satisfactorily only by computer. This has not yet been done. The process of sensory analysis is being influenced more and more by special interest groups instead of the individual pioneers who were largely responsible for the early developments. Among these groups is the Sensory Panel of the Food Group of the Society of Chemical Industry established in 1974. A previous attempt to establish a group such as this was first made in 1966–67, but came to nothing. Developments in the United Kingdom have also been very much influenced by the establishments of the British Standards Institution Committee on Sensory Analysis (Committee FA/-/2.). The BSI Glossary published in 1975 has already been noted. The final draft of a similar document dealing with the various methods of sensory analysis has recently appeared and forms a part of the UK Contribution to the activities of the International Standards Organisation.[88] Apart from the 'case studies' included in the developing literature, these two documents provide the most comprehensive outline of the principles and practices of sensory analysis now available in the United Kingdom and are recommended as a guide to all. An appraisal of future needs and trends requires more reflection and further consideration in the future. Undoubtedly, sensory analysis is here to stay. One of the next developments will be in terms of some form of professional standards relating to the applications within the food industry. In a sense this suggestion follows a recent demand for a critical analysis of the mode of presentation and the general standard of what is currently being reported in the literature of sensory analysis[89] and which will contribute to its future history.

SELECTED REFERENCES

The following list includes nearly 90 references, just under half those assembled to date representing UK sources. As a rough estimate, further searching might be expected to increase the total number available to about 300, to the end of 1976. The first five references represent bibliographic or abstract sources. The scale of the literature and the problems of selection are illustrated by the total number of entries in certain of these bibliographies. That prepared by Drake and Johansson contains over 2000 *annotated* references, whereas the Harvey's Bibliography includes over 8000 titles.

Chemoreception Abstracts now includes between 300 and 400 items per quarter, but only a small proportion of these are concerned with the sensory analysis of food. Stringent selection is necessary from most of these bibliographies.

1. Paschal, D. (1952). *Odours and the Sense of Smell:* A Bibliography 320 BC–1947. Airkem, New York.
2. Michels, K. M., Philips, D. S., Wright, R. H. and Pustek, J. Jr. *Percept. Motor Skills.*, **15,** p. 475.
3. Drake, B. and Johansson, B. (1969). *Sensory Evaluation of Food: Annotated Bibliography.* Report No. 255, Swedish Food Institute, Göteborg (2 volumes).
3a. *Ibid.* Supplement 1968–73.
4. Krudy, E. and Rollo, S. (eds., 1973). *Chemoreception Abstracts.* Published quarterly. Information Retrieval Ltd., London, European Chemoreception Research Organisation.
5. O'Mahony, M. and Thompson, J. (eds., 1975) *The Harvey's Bibliography of Taste.* Harvey's, Bristol.
6. Anon (1753). *The Lady's Companion: Or an Infallible Guide to the Fair Sex.* 6th Edition. Printed for J. Hodges and R. Baldwin, London. Vol. 2, p. 408.
7. Heath, Ambrose and Cottingham Taylor, D. D. (1936). *The National Mark Calendar of Cooking.* Ministry of Agriculture and Fisheries, London.
8. Thomson, G. Sutherland (1925). *Grading Dairy Products.* Crosby Lockwood, London.
9. Anon. (1957). *J. Soc. Dairy Technol.*, **10,** p. 50.
10. Presswood, J. B. (in press). *Proc. Symp. on Sensory Quality Control.*
11. Anon. (1975). *Glossary of Terms Relating to the Sensory Analysis of Food.* B.S. 5098:1975. British Standards Institution, London.
12. Bate-Smith, E. C. (1949). *J. Soc. Chem. Ind.*, **68,** p. 78.
13. Scott Blair, G. W. (1938). *Dairy Ind.*, Dec. Reprint.
14. Katz, D. (1937). *Cereal Chem.*, **14,** p. 382.
15. Katz, D. (1938). *Occup. Psychol.*, **12,** p. 139.
16. Coppen, F. M. V. *Brit. J. Psychol.*, **32,** p. 231.
17. Harper, R. (1947). *Amer. J. Psychol.*, **60,** p. 554.
18. Harper, R. (1949). *Amer. J. Psychol.*, **62,** p. 553.
19. Harper, R. (1952). *Brit. J. Psychol.*, *Monog. Supp. No.* 28, Cambridge University Press.
20. Scott Blair, G. W. and Coppen, F. M. V. (1939). *Proc. Roy. Soc. (B)*, **128,** p. 109.
21. Scott Blair, G. W. and Coppen, F. M. V. (1940). *Brit. J. Psychol.*, **31,** p. 61.
22. Scott Blair, G. W. and Coppen, F. M. V. (1942). *Amer. J. Psychol.*, **55,** p. 215.
23. Scott Blair, G. W. and Coppen, F. M. V. (1943). *Amer. J. Psychol.*, **56,** p. 241.
24. Harper, R. and Baron, M. (1948). *Nature*, **162,** p. 821.

25. Harper, R. and Baron, M. (1949). *J. Dairy Res.*, **16**, p. 363.
26. Harper, R. (1956). *Appl. Stat.*, **5**, p. 32.
27. Prentice, J. H. (1956). *BFMIRA Research Report No.* 69.
28. Prentice, J. H. (1959). *BFMIRA Research Report No.* 94.
29. Sheppard, D. (1953). *Quart. J. Exp. Psychol.*, **5**, p. 1.
30. Sheppard, D. (1953). *Lab. Pract.*, **2**, p. 488.
31. Sheppard, D. (1954). *Lab. Pract.*, **3**, pp. 53 & 101.
32. Sheppard, D. (1954). *Fd. Res.*, **20**, p. 114.
33. Harper, R. and Stevens, S. S. (1963). *Quart. J. Exp. Psychol.*, **16**, p. 215.
34. Wood, F. W. (1968). *Rheology and Texture of Foodstuffs*, S.C.I. Monograph No. 27, Society of Chemical Industry, London p. 40.
35. Wood, F. W. (1974). *Die Starke*, **4**, p. 127.
36. Wood, F. W. (1974). *Proc. IV. Int. Cong. Food Sci. and Technol.*, **2** p. 273.
37. Shama, F. and Sherman, P. (1973). *J. Text. Stud.*, **4**, p. 111.
38. Barry, B. W. and Grace, A. J. (1971). *J. Pharm. Sci.*, **60**, p. 814.
39. Barry, B. W. and Grace, A. J. (1972). *J. Pharm. Sci.*, **61**, p. 335.
40. Sherman, P. (1969). *J. Fd. Sci.*, **34**, p. 458.
41. Jowitt, R. (1974). *J. Text. Stud.*, **5**, p. 351.
42. Harper, R. (1949). *Food*, **18**, p. 207.
43. Harper, R. (1950). *Food*, **19**, p. 371.
44. Harper, R. (1954). *Dairy Ind.*, **19**, p. 307.
45. Harper, R. (1955). *Appl. Stat.*, **4**, p. 145.
46. Cheesman, G. H. and Mayne, S. (1953). *Quart. J. Exp. Psychol.*, **5**, p. 22.
47. Cheesman, G. H. and Townsend, M. J. (1956). *Quart. J. Exp. Psychol.*, **8**, p. 8.
48. Cheesman, G. H. and Kirby, H. M. (1959). *Quart. J. Exp. Psychol.*, **11**, p. 115.
49. Patterson, D. (1956). B.A. Thesis, University of Leeds.
50. Harper, R. (1972). *Proc. Inst. Food Sci. and Technol.* (UK), **5**, p. 211.
51. Harper, R., Bate-Smith, E. C., Land, D. G. and Griffiths, N. M. (1968). *Perfum. Essent. Oil Rec.*, **59**, p. 22.
52. Harper, R., Land, D. G. and Griffiths, N. M. (1968). *Brit. J. Psychol.*, **59**, p. 231.
53. Harper, R., Bate-Smith, E. C. and Land, D. G. (1968). *Odour Description and Odour Classification*. J. & A. Churchill, London.
54. Piggott, J. R. and Harper, R. (1975). *J. Chem. Senses and Flav.*, **1**, p. 307.
55. Piggott, J. (1975). Ph.D. Thesis, University of Reading.
56. Reay, G. A. and Shewan, J. M. (1949). *Advanc. in Food Res.*, **2**, p. 343.
57. Spencer, R. and Baines, C. R. (1965). *Proc. 1st. Cong. Food Sci. and Technol.*, **3**, p. 253.
58. Hyde, G. W. (1925). *J. Inst. Brew.*, **31**, p. 246.
59. Wren, J. (1972). *J. Inst. Brew.*, **78**, p. 69.
60. Clapperton, J. F. (1973). *J. Inst. Brew.*, **79**, p. 495.
61. Clapperton, J. F., Dalgliesh, C. E. and Meilgard, M. C. (1976). *J. Inst. Brew.*, **82**, p. 7.
62. Williams, A. A. (1975). *J. Sci. Fd. Agric.*, **26**, p. 567.
63. Ferguson, H. H. (1937). *Occup. Psychol.*, **11**, p. 399.

64. Finney, D. J. (1947, and subsequent editions) *Probit Analysis*. Cambridge University Press.
65. Harries, J. M. (1953). *J. Sci. Fd. Agric.*, **4**, p. 477.
66. Harries, J. M. (1955). *J. Inst. Biol.*, **2**, p. 25.
67. Harries, J. M. (1956). *Fd. Technol.*, **10**, p. 80.
68. Wadsworth, R. N. (1952). *Appl. Stat.*, **1**, p. 169.
69. Pridmore, W. A. (1971). *J. Soc. Cosmet. Chem.*, **22**, p. 211.
70. Gregson, R. A. M. (1960). *Occup. Psychol.*, **34**, p. 247.
71. Gregson, R. A. M. (1962). *J. Fd. Sci.*, **27**, p. 376.
72. Steiner, E. H. (1966). *J. Fd. Technol.*, **4**, p. 93.
73. Banfield, C. F. and Harries, J. M. (1975). *J. Fd. Technol.*, **10**, p. 1.
74. Palmer, D. H. (1974). *J. Sci. Fd. Agric.*, **25**, p. 153.
75. Poulton, E. C. (1968). *Psychol. Bull.*, **69**, p. 1.
76. Poulton, E. C. (1976). *Bull. Brit. Psych. Soc.*, **29**, p. 385.
77. Treisman, M. (1960). *Nature*, **198**, p. 914.
78. Treisman, M. (1964). *Quart. J. Exp. Psychol.*, **16**, pp. 11 & 387.
79. Treisman, M. and Watts, T. R. (1966). *Psychol. Bull.*, **66**, p. 438.
80. Moncrieff, R. W. (1951, 2nd edn.) *The Chemical Senses*. Leonard Hill Ltd, London.
81. Moncrieff, R. W. (1966). *Odour Preferences*. Leonard Hill Ltd, London.
82. Birch, G. G., Cowell, N. D. and Eyton, D. (1970). *Fd. Technol.*, **5**, p. 277.
83. Birch, G. G., Lee, G. K. and Rolfe, E. J. (1970). *J. Sci. Fd. Agric.*, **20**, p. 650.
84. O'Mahony, M. (1972). *Perception*, **1**, p. 209.
85. O'Mahony, M. (1974). *J. Fd. Technol.*, **9**, p. 1.
86. O'Mahony, M., Ivory, H. and King, R. (1974). *Perception*, **3**, p. 185.
87. Kalmus, H. and Hubbard, S. J. (1960). *The Chemical Senses in Health and Disease*. C. C. Thomson, Springfield, Ill.
88. Anon. (1976). Third draft standard *Sensory Analysis of Food: General Methodology* B.S.I. Committee F.A./-/2.
89. Invited lecture by Prof. R. M. Pangborn, introducing a Sensory Day in the Second Congress of the European Chemoreception Research Organisation.

DISCUSSION

Bartoshuk: Are there any links with Lord Adrian and the Cambridge School of Physiology that produced Carl Pfaffmann, Lloyd Beidler and Y. Zotterman, leaders in the physiology of taste?

Harper: Adrian was the first speaker in the symposium on flavour assessment in 1953. I have said there are many omissions and Adrian of course is one of them. A point I would like to make is that somewhere around 1962 I made my first visit to the United States, which was in fact arranged by Carl Pfaffmann, at a meeting in Denver, Colorado, when the subject was sensory factors in palatability of food. Over that same period I spent some time with S. S. Stevens of Harvard. At that time we applied for the first time the technique of magnitude estimation to squeezing materials with food-like consistency. Actually they were india-rubber but that's all right. My Ph.D. thesis was centred round the pieces of india-rubber!

Moskowitz: Were there any connections between the pharmaceutical and food industries?

Harper: Whereas my own personal contact with the pharmaceutical industry is minimal, Dr Bate-Smith was in close touch with developments in this area. The reference to *materia medica* is very relevant historically, including the contribution of Linnaeus to odour classification as well as the paper by Greaves (1828) to which Howard Moskowitz has already drawn my attention.

Nursten: Yesterday afternoon I drew attention to the relative lack of proper sensory data in the work on the chemical aspects of food aroma. For the chemical work, one could draw up a family tree paralleling that of Dr Harper's for the sensory work. The two coalesce in places, for example, at FRI, and I wish to stress the importance of the assembly of such interdisciplinary teams. The excellent work which resulted in that and other instances sets the standard. As long as those less fortunately endowed appreciate the importance of contact with the disciplines missing from their individual teams, advice can usually be obtained. It is in establishing such contacts that this and other symposia play a vital role.

Howgate: A comment on the history of sensory analysis at Torry. The scale for measuring freshness of fish was published in 1953, though the scale was in use before that. We are still using the scale today at Torry without modification, though of course the panel is not the same. However, I am sure, though this is difficult to prove, that the present panel is behaving in the same way as the original. There is an element of apostolic succession here and the hands have been laid on my head.

Harper: Thank you for this comment. My own contact with the Torry Fish Freshness scale goes back to about 1947 and this, along with cheese-grading, have been the two most often quoted examples of the use of sensory techniques. I appreciate that the history of the method goes back earlier than about 1947, although my own records began about then.

12

New Uses of Magnitude Estimation

Howard R. Moskowitz and John W. Chandler

MPI Sensory Testing, Inc., New York, USA

ABSTRACT

Magnitude estimation has been applied to four new areas concerned with consumer responses to food items. These areas are: (1) The rescaling of descriptor words traditionally used for product evaluation, to determine more quantitatively numerical values for traditional category and descriptor scale points; (2) Application of magnitude estimation to product development via the Eclipse method, which uses both factorial designs of product variation and regression analyses to suggest ingredient formulations which correspond to consumer-estimated 'ideal' or 'favourite' products; (3) Use of magnitude estimation to develop tolerance curves, indicating estimated change of liking for changes in sensory levels of specific product attributes (i.e. how will liking change with changes in sweetness, in tartness, in colour, etc.); and (4) Use of magnitude estimation to develop a psychological 'demand' curve for products. Specific examples of each application illustrate the current use of the method, and future direction for other, continuing research.

INTRODUCTION

The emergence of the 'new psychophysics'[1] into the mainstream of psychology in particular, and science in general, has brought with it a very powerful subjective measuring technique. The technique is known generically as 'magnitude estimation'. It allows experimenters to gather ratings from panellists, with the important property that ratios of these magnitude estimates reflect ratios of perceptions. For the first time, for instance, a panellist can quantify his or her perceived sweetness in such a way that the ratios of numbers the panellist assigns can be compared to ratios of actual concentration. This ratio scale property is a significant advance over the traditional methods of category scaling, wherein the panellist is forced to select numbers from a limited scale (e.g., 1–5 or 1–9) to match gradations in perceived stimulus intensity. In addition, ratio scaling is a significant advance over the classic method of threshold evaluations. Threshold determinations require that the panellist report when he detects stimuli. The lowest concentration at which detection occurs is the threshold. Although detection procedures have become increasingly refined during the past decades[2] nonetheless they do not allow the experimenter to quantify relative subjective magnitudes. The panellist, in fact, is allowed simply to act as a balancing instrument, who detects and signals the presence of (or fails to signal) a stimulus.

PSYCHOPHYSICAL LAWS

Perhaps the most important contribution scientifically that ratio scaling and magnitude estimation have made is that they focus attention upon the existence of equations which relate perceived sensory intensity to objectively measured physical intensity. These equations often turn out to be power functions, of the form $S = k I^n$ (S = sensory intensity, assessed by magnitude estimation, I = physical intensity objectively measured by instruments, n = rate-of-growth parameter, k = multiplicative constant). If the exponent n exceeds $1 \cdot 0$, then sensory intensity grows faster than physical intensity (i.e., it accelerates). In contrast, if n is less than $1 \cdot 0$, then sensory intensity grows more slowly than physical intensity (i.e., it decelerates). Finally, if n equals $1 \cdot 0$, then sensory intensity grows as rapidly as physical intensity.

These psychophysical power functions have been reported for a number of sensory continua pertaining to sensations and to food related perceptions in particular. Table 1 presents a list of these exponents for different sensory modalities.[3]

As they are currently constituted, these psychophysical equations provide only a modest bank of basic scientific information to the product developer. Most of the equations have been obtained by

TABLE 1

Representative exponents of the power functions relating psychological magnitude to stimulus magnitude

Continuum	Exponent	Stimulus condition
Loudness	0·60	binaural
Loudness	0·54	monaural
Brightness	0·33	5° target—dark-adapted eye
Brightness	0·50	point source—dark-adapted eye
Lightness	1·20	reflectance of grey papers
Smell	0·55	coffee odour
Smell	0·60	heptane
Taste	0·80	saccharin
Taste	1·30	sucrose
Taste	1·30	salt
Temperature	1·00	cold—on arm
Temperature	1·50	warmth—on arm
Vibration	0·95	60 cps—on finger
Vibration	0·60	250 cps—on finger
Duration	1·10	white-noise stimulus
Repetition rate	1·00	light, sound, touch and shocks
Finger span	1·30	thickness of wood blocks
Pressure on palm	1·10	static force on skin
Heaviness	1·45	lifted weights
Force of handgrip	1·70	precision hand dynamometer
Vocal effort	1·10	sound pressure of vocalisation
Electric shock	3·50	60 cps—through fingers
Tactile roughness	1·50	felt diameter of emery grits
Tactile hardness	0·80	rubber squeezed between fingers
Visual velocity	1·20	moving spot of light
Visual length	1·00	projected line of light
Visual area	0·70	projected square of light

experimenters using pure taste, smell or texture stimuli, since the experimenter's aim in the first place was to learn how we process simple physical information and transform that information into simple, well defined, perceptual magnitudes. Knowledge that perceived sweetness of sucrose (as well as of other carbohydrate sugars) grows as an accelerating function of concentration,[4] and that the perceived sweetness of saccharin and cyclamate grows as decelerating functions of concentration[5] provides some clues for the product developer about what is likely to happen when he increases or decreases the amount of sweetener in a product. What the product developer lacks, however, is an understanding of what will happen to *his particular* product, as well as what descriptor terms apply to the sensory shifts (i.e., does the product that loses half its sweetness then diminish from moderately sweet to slightly sweet, or from very sweet to moderately sweet, etc.).

FOOD EVALUATION APPLICATIONS

The body of this paper concerns new applications of the method of magnitude estimation, based upon extensive testing with consumers, in situations where the experimenter's aims have been dictated by the exigencies of real product needs, rather than by the desire to obtain additional information about sensory processes. The applications are, by their very nature, structured to conform with product development and marketing requirements. However, in all cases and approaches reported, the same precision of experimental design and execution has been set up as ordinarily would be done for studies on sensory functioning assessed by magnitude estimation.

Application 1: Re-scaling of Other Scales

Quite often product developers use limited scales, such as a 1–5 category scale to indicate degrees of sensory magnitude (1 = least, 5 = most).[6] The product developers often have no idea about the validity of the scales as sensory measuring instruments, nor do they know whether the psychological differences between adjacent scale points are really equal. That is, is the difference in sweetness intensity between a 1 and 2 equal to that between a 2 and 3? Stevens and Galanter[7] in their extensive comparison of ratio (or magnitude estimation) scales and category scales for a dozen continua pointed out the non-linearities that are characteristic of category scales. Their studies assessed the relation between category and magnitude estimation scales for simple sensory continua.

The aim of this first series of experiments was to compare category and magnitude estimation scales for continua and attributes that impact on consumer acceptance of real foods. The comparison indicates the relation between the two scales.

In the typical experiments whose results are reported here, consumers were recruited for the specific evaluation of a set of similar products (e.g., flavoured still or carbonated drinks, flavoured sauces, etc.). The consumers were initially unfamiliar with the method of magnitude estimation, and an introductory 20-min session was spent briefing the consumers how to assign magnitude estimates to reflect sensory intensities (e.g., sweetness and tartness in beverages, hardness of crackers, flavour of tomato in a sauce, etc.). In addition, the same consumers were also briefed on how to assign magnitude estimates to reflect hedonic values, with positive numbers (or numbers prefaced by an L) to reflect increasing degrees of liking, and negative numbers (or numbers prefaced by a D) to reflect increasing degrees of disliking. 0 meant neutrality (neither liking nor disliking).

At the end of product evaluation session, the same consumers were shown a series of verbal scales (e.g., extremely sweet, very sweet, moderately sweet, slightly sweet, and not sweet at all), and were instructed to assign magnitude estimates to these concepts, as if the concepts themselves referred to actual products. That is, the consumers were told to assume that they were now tasting a product that is 'extremely sweet', etc. What magnitude estimate, then, would they call such a product, given the magnitude estimates they had been using for other sweet products during the actual evaluation.[8]

This approach of allowing consumers to assign magnitude estimates to concepts of sensory intensity (as well as hedonic tone) provides some important information about the following aspects of sensory scaling:

(1) What magnitude scale value corresponds to each category label?

(2) Are the categories equally spaced, or do they exhibit equal ratios, or neither?

(3) Do different category sequences, for different sensory attributes (e.g., sweetness, bitterness) exhibit similar magnitude estimation scale values, or does each sensory continuum exhibit its own unique set of scale values, even for identical gradations in adjectives (i.e., are extremely sweet and extremely bitter equal in sensory magnitude, as judged this way, or are they different?)

(4) Are bipolar scales (e.g., hedonics) equal and opposite. Is 'like extremely' equal to, but opposite in sign, from 'dislike extremely?' Are the scales symmetric?

Table 2 shows the average magnitude estimates given to varying scale values. The results are taken from a number of studies in which

TABLE 2

A sample of calibration scales for magnitude estimates

1. *Sweetness of sauce with* 3 *replicate sessions* (*pivot = average magnitude estimate*)

	Replicate 1	Replicate 2	Replicate 3
Extremely sweet	183·4	184·5	176·4
Very sweet	134·4	137·8	139·6
Moderately sweet	93·9	94·2	97·1
Slightly sweet	59·0	54·9	57·0
Barely sweet	14·3	22·5	15·9

2. *Flavour intensity* (*pivot = extremely strong*) (*product: sauce*)

Extremely strong	100·00
Very strong	76·00
Moderately strong	53·4
Slightly strong	34·1
Not at all perceivable	0

3. *Degree of consistency* (*pivot = average magnitude estimate to all categories*) (*product: sauce*)

Extremely	159·3
Very	128·5
Moderately	100·0
Slightly	70·9

4. *Degree of colour deepness* (*pivot = extremely strong*) (*product: pudding*)

Extremely	100·0
Very	81·8
Moderately	61·7
Slightly	20·2
None at all	0

5. *Liking/disliking* (*pivot = average of magnitude estimates*)

Unipolar		Bipolar	
Like extremely	143·3	Like extremely	185·1
Like very much	99·7	Like very much	137·5
Like moderately	85·3	Like moderately	103·4
Like slightly	73·9	Like slightly	59·3
Like barely	49·3	Neither like nor dislike	0
Do not like at all	0	Dislike slightly	−54·0
		Dislike moderately	−85·8
		Dislike very much	−101·5
		Dislike extremely	−137·2

the consumers did the scale point evaluations after they had evaluated a set of test products. In addition to showing average magnitude estimates corresponding to categories, Table 2 shows scales for the same attributes replicated on three different days.

[For computational purposes, and to reduce the inter-individual variation due to size of numbers, each observer's magnitude estimates, both for the products, and for the calibrating values, were divided by a pivot number. Each observer's pivot number was different and was defined as (a) the average magnitude estimate given to the non-zero calibration values, or (b) the value given to 'moderate' or to 'extreme'. In Table 2, the definition of the pivot value is shown as either a or b.]

The important things about the calibration scale shown in Table 2 are:

(a)   The category intervals are not equal to each other. That is, the perceived separation between 'extremely' and 'very' on an attribute is not equal to the separation between 'very' and 'moderately'. Hence, as a first approximation, the category scale is not an equal-interval scale, when magnitude estimation is used as the measuring instrument.

(b)   In a given study, if different sensory attributes (i.e., flavour, sweetness, etc.) are evaluated, using the same set of modifying adjectives (i.e., extremely sweet, extremely strong flavour, very sweet, very strong flavour, etc.) then the calibrating scale values are similar. The calibrating scale values will change, however, if more and intermediate adjectives are used, i.e., between 'slightly' and 'none at all', include 'very barely', then the category scale values tend to change.

(c)   Surprisingly, bipolar scales, especially for hedonics (liking versus disliking) are neither equal interval, nor are they symmetric with each other. 'Like extremely' is often assigned a greater positive number than 'dislike extremely' is assigned a negative number. Whether this asymmetry is a characteristic of different 'liking' versus 'disliking' scales that we ordinarily use, or an artefact of the scaling, remains for further exploration. However, empirically, it would be very exciting to demonstrate that positive and negative hedonics behave as two different sets of scales, which may be non-linearly related to each other.

Application 2: Discovering and Developing Perceptual Laws for Foods

Although magnitude estimation procedures were originally developed for psychophysical analysis of simple, 'pure' stimuli which could be well controlled in the laboratory, they find extensive application in the sensory evaluation of foods. One can use magnitude estimation in two different ways. First, the scaling procedures can serve as an adjunct to, or even eventually replace, many current scaling methods which rely upon rank order evaluations (for acceptance, flavour, etc.), or category evaluation (e.g., 'excellent-to-poor' category scales). Even if the experimenter does not know the physical constitution of his product, he can still use the magnitude estimation method to quantify how much sweeter is one product than another, or how well liked is one specific product, compared to the competitive frame of other products against which it is positioned and marketed. Second, if the experimenter has available to him the physical constitutions of foods, then he may be able to discover laws or at least empirical relations between consumer perceptions and physical aspects of products.

Traditional experiments in the perception of taste, smell and texture, usually using model food systems (e.g., sucrose solutions, rubber foam samples) often find that power functions relate physical magnitude to sensory magnitude, as Table 1 shows for a general range of continua.

Experimenters working with real food systems, and who use magnitude estimation methods, are rarely faced with such simple systems in which the experimenter has systematically varied only one or at most two constituents. In such cases, where artificial variations have been made for actual food materials (e.g., varying sucrose or flavouring level in fruit flavoured still beverages), the power function reproduces itself,[9,10] but the basic information is of limited value because it has been obtained on a range of variations that a product developer would not usually produce. Table 3 presents some of the findings for the direct scaling of some actual food systems, where the experimenter was able to artificially create a range of product variations. As expected, the results are in line with what usually has been previously found.

When real food products are encountered, which comprise a half a dozen or more constituents, then difficulties ensue if the experimenter attempts to learn about the invariant laws of food product perception. For one, there are many potential combinations of products which

TABLE 3
Psychophysical functions for real foods

Food/attribute	Exponent	Reference
Appearance		
1. Perceived size of grind in hamburger	0·55	Moskowitz[14]
Texture in mouth		
1. Hardness of space cubes (vs. modulus of elasticity)	0·41	Moskowitz *et al.*[15]
2. Hardness of space cubes (vs. ultimate strength)	0·61	
3. Crunchiness of space cubes (vs. modulus of elasticity)	0·55	
4. Crunchiness of space cubes (vs. ultimate strength)	0·72	
Aroma		
1. Coffee odour	0·55	Stevens[16]
2. Pork	0·46	Moskowitz[17]
3. Cheddar cheese	0·20	Moskowitz[17]
4. Grapefruit	0·44	Moskowitz[17]
5. California orange	0·52	
Flavour in mouth		
1. Amount of mayonnaise	1·2	Moskowitz[14]
2. Amount of cherry flavour	1·2	Moskowitz[14]
3. Coffee flavour	0·75	Stone and Harder[18]
Taste in mouth		
1. Amount of sweetness in cherry beverage	1·2	Moskowitz *et al.*[19]

the experimenter can investigate. (For 5 ingredients, each of which can be varied at 3 levels, high, medium and low, there are $3^5 = 243$ different combinations. For more ingredients, or for a finer mesh of levels, there are many more potential combinations which are likely candidates for assessment.) Hence, in a research programme, effort must be made to limit the range of samples. This pragmatic limitation also reduces the likelihood that an experimenter can truly determine the laws governing product perception, even for that specific product and its limited set of variations. Second, even were the experimenter able to produce all of the products, and have a brave group of observers evaluate them, the types of product interactions might be so overwhelming that a fundamental understanding of how we perceive the product versus its constituents might be elusive, if not impossible.

Recently, Moskowitz and Gatty,[11] Moskowitz and Rauch[12] and Moskowitz, Stanley and Chandler[13] have suggested a more pragmatic approach, which is entitled the 'Eclipse Method'. The premises of Eclipse are:

(a) For complicated products (whether natural or fabricated) it might well be impossible to ascertain the fundamental laws governing the relation between product constitution and consumer perception, at least in terms of invariant, 'true' quantitative relations.

(b) Nonetheless, if an experimenter has selected a series of product variations from the larger set of potential options (e.g., through a fractional factorial design, which covers the full range of ingredient variation with a minimal set of products), then the experimenter may eventually be able to construct *ad hoc* mathematical relations between a specific consumer perception (e.g., spiciness of a gravy mix), and physical ingredients. Note that these *ad hoc* relations account for the data, but may not necessarily reflect 'true' underlying relations between variables. Such underlying relations or 'laws' could only be obtained by much more arduous work. These *ad hoc* relations simply summarise the relations, in a statistical sense.

(c) Having obtained equations which relate each sensory percept to a well defined combination of physical variation, the experimenter can now 'read out' or predict, with greater or lesser accuracy, the profile of a product, in the same category whose ingredients are known and accounted for. Given a physical recipe, and the set of equations, the experimenter should be able to deduce what is the likely consumer profile, using the equations.

(d) During the data acquisition phase, the consumers who evaluate the test products also provide a profile of a product in the same category they would like to have. This profile of the 'Ideal' product is provided in the same language of attributes and with the same magnitude estimation scale, as consumers had used for evaluating actual physical products.

(e) The experimenter can now mathematically 'turn around' the regression equations. Knowledge of the equations had allowed him to predict responses, given formulations

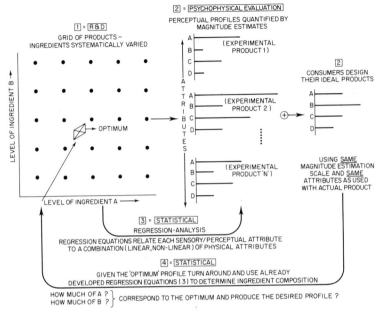

FIG. 1. Schematic lay-out of the Eclipse method for product development. The schematic lay-out shows the series of steps, beginning with (1) a set of possible product formulations, and continuing through (2) sensory profiling of existing product formulations and ideal formulations by magnitude estimation, and finishing with (3) developing equations to relate physical formulations to perceptions of products, and (4) relate perceptions of an ideal, desired product to physical formulations.

(physical variables). Turning around the equations allows the experimenter to predict formulations, given responses. That is—by turning around the equations, the dependent variables are the profiles of the product a person would like to have, and the coefficients are the formulation components which are solved for statistically.

Figure 1 illustrates a schematic lay-out of the Eclipse method. All steps are fairly straightforward, and are as follows:

(1) Recognition of the range of ingredient variation, and selection of which ingredients are to be varied.

(2) Selection of a representative group of product variations (usually by the factorial design).

(3) Development of an appropriate set of descriptor terms for

evaluation of the product by consumers, and selection of the proper group of consumers.

(4)   Obtaining magnitude estimates for each attribute, from the consumers, who evaluate all of the experimental products.

(5)   At the end of the same experimental test session, obtaining magnitude estimates for a hypothetical product whose sensory profile is of interest, using the same attributes and magnitude estimation scale as used for product evaluation.

(6)   Developing the *ad hoc* regression equations which predict sensory magnitude from physical magnitude.

(7)   Turning the regression equations around, in order to obtain a series of equations in which the ingredient levels are the unknowns.

(8)   'Plugging in' the desired sensory perceptions, corresponding to the ideal product, and then solving the 'turned around' equation for that set of ingredients which would have produced the perceptions.

To illustrate the method, consider Table 4. The food product (disguised) was a pudding, which could be varied in the amount of chocolate flavouring, and the amount of brown food colouring added to it. The aim was to determine the ideal recipe for this two dimensional case (in effect, the same approach would be followed, whether there are two, or ten or more different ingredients).

An initial experimental design was developed, which considered 6 levels of brown colour × 5 levels of flavour strength.

Respondents were recruited from chocolate pudding users, in the Northeast United States, paid for their participation, and instructed in the method. (A useful clarifying and instructional device is to show the respondents different sized shapes and ask for magnitude estimates of size or show different word concepts and ask them to estimate the magnitude of liking or disliking of these concepts.)

A series of analyses was done to assess the following:

(a)   Relation between colour and chocolate flavour (independent variables) and three sensory variables: colour richness, flavour strength and product sweetness.

Table 4 shows the set of three equations for the product tested.

(b)   In the same experiment, the consumers also profiled the chocolate pudding product that they would most like to have.

TABLE 4

Eclipse development of chocolate pudding

---

(1) *Experimental formulations*

Food colouring (relative units)

		2·5	5·0	7·5	10·0	15·0	22·5
		A	B	C	D	E	F
Chocolate flavouring	5a	⊗	⊗	⊗	⊗	⊗	⊗
(Relative units)	7·5b	⊗	⊗	⊗	⊗	⊗	⊗
	10·0c	⊗	⊗	⊗	⊗	⊗	⊗
	15·0d	⊗	⊗	⊗	⊗	⊗	⊗
	22·5e	⊗	⊗	⊗	⊗	⊗	⊗

(2) *Forward going equations*

$$\text{Sweetness} = 24\cdot4 \text{ (chocolate flavour)} + 6\cdot10 \text{ (colour)} - 35\cdot6$$
$$R = 0\cdot47 \quad F(2,3657) = 537\cdot5$$
$$\text{Flavour strength} = 53\cdot45 \text{ (chocolate flavour)} + 2\cdot44 \text{ (colour)} - 69\cdot03$$
$$R = 0\cdot76 \quad F(2,3657) = 2\,533\cdot38$$
$$\text{Colour (brownness)} = 4\cdot42 \text{ (chocolate flavour)} + 40\cdot30 \text{ (colour)} - 47\cdot46$$
$$R = 0\cdot67 \quad F(2,3657) = 1\,563\cdot80$$

(3) *Ideal profile*

$$\text{Flavour intensity} = 96\cdot2$$
$$\text{Sweetness} = 124\cdot3$$
$$\text{Brownness} = 128\cdot9$$

(4) *'Backwards' regression equation*

$$\text{Sweetness} = 24\cdot4(F) + 6\cdot10(C) - 35\cdot6 = 124\cdot3$$
$$\text{Flavour intensity} = 53\cdot45(F) + 2\cdot44(C) - 69\cdot03 = 96\cdot2$$
$$\text{Colour (brownness)} = 4\cdot42(F) + 40\cdot30(C) - 47\cdot46 = 128\cdot9$$

To make 'ideal' use:

$$F = 16\cdot75 = \text{chocolate flavour}$$
$$C = 22\cdot7 = \text{amount of colouring}$$

Its profile in the magnitude estimation scale is also shown in Table 4.

(c) The equations were turned around. Now, physical colour level and chocolate flavouring level were the unknown quantities. The predictor equations were turned around, as shown in Table 4, and the set of equations was solved to provide a product recipe that produced the desired chocolate pudding product.

The Eclipse method is still in its infancy. There are many food ingredient systems that show severe interactions. A simple linear system, like the one that was used for chocolate pudding may not work in many instances. To predict, for instance, overall sweetness might require non-linear terms, such as the complicated equation:

$$\text{Sweetness} = k_1 (\text{chocolate}) + k_2 (\text{colour}) + k_3 (\text{chocolate/colour}) + k_4$$

The non-linear, interaction term, (chocolate flavour)/(colour) is easy to estimate when we relate perceived sweetness to a combination of physical constituents (in Phase I, or the 'forward going phase' of Eclipse). However, that same interaction term becomes a troublesome one when we try to predict the chocolate flavour level and the colour levels which satisfy the consumer's desired sweetness, flavour and colour perceptions. More complex mathematics, with non-linear equations and approximate solutions, will be required to solve these equations, once the sensory levels are fixed, and the physical variables become the ones whose solution is desired.

Applications 3 and 4: Tolerance Curves and Demand Functions for Products

A third area of applied research using magnitude estimation can be conveniently called 'tolerance' analysis. Tolerance analysis comprises two components:

(1)   Given sensory (or physical) variations in a product, what is the relation between sensory variation and acceptance (liking/disliking) of a product.

(2)   Given price variations in a product, what is the propensity to buy the product, as cost for the product increases. This second tolerance curve is also known in economics as the demand curve.

Sensory Tolerance Curves

From an increasing bank of data with commercial product variations, it appears that consumers can accurately and reliably estimate how much their liking for a product will change if the product's *sensory* attributes are changed systematically. They must, however, have judged a number of product variations beforehand.

A typical experiment will illustrate what happens when a consumer is faced with the question of how much he or she will like a product with varying changes in the product's sensory character. Prior to asking that question, the consumer is exposed to a number of product variations, which he/she assesses for the sensory attributes in question. This initial part of the study is the typical product evaluation. At the end of the evaluations, the consumers provide two additional sets of ratings:

(a) Magnitude estimates which correspond to sensory gradations (i.e., on their own scale, for a beverage, what magnitude estimate corresponds to extremely sweet, very sweet, moderately sweet, etc., and like extremely, like very much...neutral...dislike very much, etc.). These correspond to the 'calibration scaling'.

(b) Estimated liking or disliking (on their own liking scale) for products that are assumed to have 'an extremely sweet taste', 'a very sweet taste', 'a moderately sweet taste', etc. That is, the consumer provides (a) calibrating magnitude estimates to indicate the scale value that corresponds to a descriptor word (extremely sweet, for example), and (b) liking/disliking estimates (on their own scales) to correspond to a product that would have such a sensory intensity.

In the actual experiment, these two evaluations are done separately. Furthermore, the consumer is instructed in the second part (liking ratings for sensory variations) to assign numbers assuming that the only sensory information that he/she has about a product is that the product possesses the particular sensory attribute at the stated level. Nothing else about the product is known.

Figure 2 shows tolerance curves for three products.
(A) A catsup with variations in tomato flavour.
(B) A carbonated, fruit flavoured beverage, with variations in sweetness.
(C) A candy product, with variations in hardness.

From these data, as well as from others, some interesting patterns emerge:

(a) Individuals have a moderately good idea of their tolerance for product variations in quality. They seem to be able to gauge hedonics when 'too little' or 'too much' is sensorially presented. These tolerance curves agree, for the most part, with empirical data (if other sensory and physical factors are held constant).

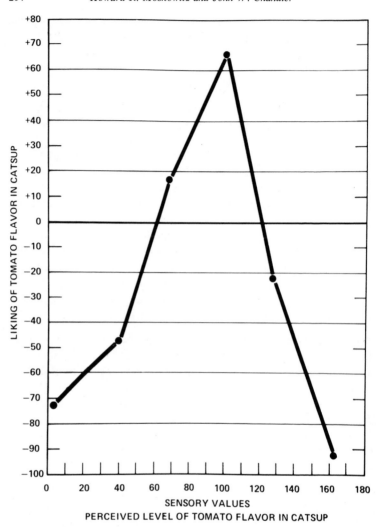

2A.

FIG. 2A–2C. Tolerance curves for product variations (Fig. 2A = variations in the tomato flavour of tomato catsup; Fig. 2B = variations in the sweetness of fruit flavoured beverages; Fig. 2C = variations in the hardness of candy). The abscissa is sensory magnitude (on a ratio scale). The ordinate is the respondent's magnitude estimate of liking (+) or disliking (−) of the product, given that the product possesses the specified sensory characteristic. Nothing else, except for this sensory magnitude, is specified in *verbally describing* the product.

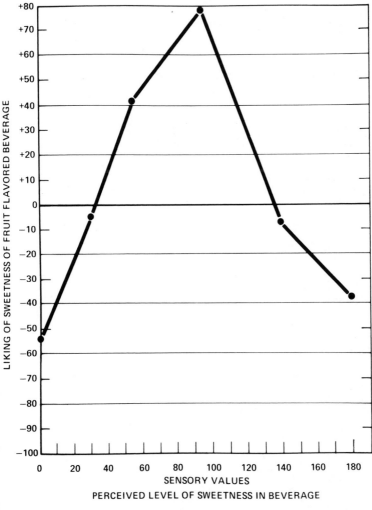

LIKING OF SWEETNESS OF FRUIT FLAVORED BEVERAGE

SENSORY VALUES

PERCEIVED LEVEL OF SWEETNESS IN BEVERAGE

FIG. 2B.

(b) Individuals from different regions of the US show similar tolerance curves for some attributes (most often those attributes which are visual, such as liking for saturation of a beverage colour), and quite different tolerance curves for other attributes (most often flavour and sweetness). These differences are statistically significant (by analysis of

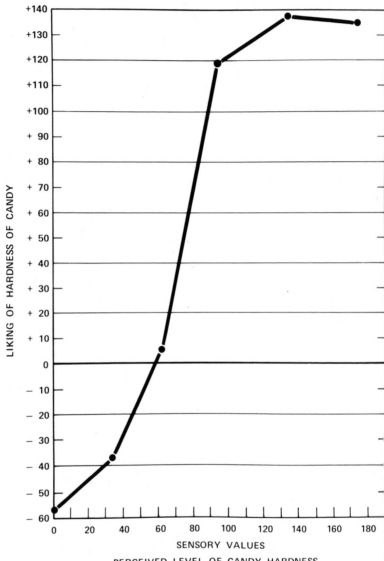

FIG. 2C.

variance), and show up as interactions between respondent group and specific sensory level.

(c) The shape of the tolerance curves differ from one attribute to another, even within the same product. Apparently, estimated hedonic functions for different attributes are quite different in shape.

Demand Curves

Individuals also appear to be able to estimate 'intent' to purchase a product for given product prices. Estimated intent to purchase (by magnitude estimation) provides ratio-scale values, or cardinal utility values in the economist's terms, against which price can be plotted.

In a series of experiments with actual food products, we have explored the nature of these demand curves, for two types of product: (a) the best product that the consumer tasted in a specific test session, and (b) the 'ideal' product that the consumer would like to have, were he/she able to design the sensory characteristics of such a product. The probe questions again occur after respondents have had experience with actual product variations, and after they have grown accustomed to using magnitude estimation. The consumers are instructed to estimate the following (in dollars and cents):

(1) The highest amount of money a manufacturer could charge for the product, and yet the consumers would still definitely purchase the product.

(2) The highest amount of money a manufacturer could charge for the product, and yet the consumer would probably purchase it, etc. (The categories are definitely purchase, probably purchase, might purchase, probably not purchase, definitely not purchase.)

In addition, the consumers are instructed to estimate the magnitude estimation equivalent of each of the 5 categories: 'definitely purchase', 'probably purchase', 'might purchase', 'probably not purchase', 'definitely not purchase'.

The results from these evaluations are: (for a given product)
(a) A set of categories of purchase intent, and the magnitude estimation value corresponding to each category.
(b) An average dollar value corresponding to the categories, for the product, above which the product no longer falls into the purchase interest category (i.e., above a certain dollar value, a

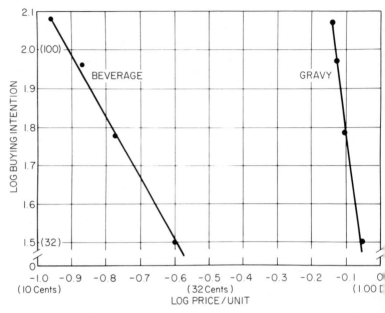

FIG. 3. Demand curve for two products. The abscissa represents the relative intent to purchase for each of 4 of the 5 categories (definitely purchase, might purchase, might or might not purchase, might not purchase). The spacing corresponds to spacing from magnitude estimation scaling of the category terms. The ordinate represents the highest dollar and cents value at which the item falls into the purchase intent category. Both co-ordinates are logarithmically spaced.

product would no longer fall into the 'definitely purchase' category, but would fall down to the 'probably purchase' category).

Figure 3 shows the results of two of these studies, one for an unsweetened dry mix beverage which sells at approximately 6¢/quart and another which is a gravy sauce that sells for approximately 65¢/can. Both curves pertain to a single actual product.

The shape of the psychological demand curve is different from one product category to another (i.e., from beverage to sauce), which indicates different elasticities for different product categories. Ideally, a large number of such products must be evaluated by this procedure in order to develop a necessary data base on the psychological aspects of product pricing. These two products represent a start in that direction.

AN OVERVIEW

The studies presented here reflect a potential new direction in consumer research to which magnitude estimation may make a contribution. Virtually all of the ideas discussed have appeared, at one time or another, in other disciplines. The optimisation method reflects a modification of optimisation procedures for quality control and process development. The tolerance curves reflect the sensory analogues of tolerance curves in quality control. (Magnitude estimation scaling has a distinct advantage, however. By psychophysical scaling, these sensory tolerance curves can be translated back into physical constituent tolerance curves. That way, the sensory perception can be used to guide product quality control. The curves could be expressed in physical measurables, but the curves are derived from sensory measures.) Finally, the demand curves are derived in a rather straightforward way from economics textbooks. Each of the uses of the scaling procedures may provide profitable research avenues which hopefully will act as a catalyst for further research and development of products in particular, and knowledge of consumer behaviour, in general.

REFERENCES

1. Stevens, S. S. (1953). *Science*, **118**, p. 576.
2. Swets, J. A. (ed.) (1964). *Signal Detection and Recognition by Human Observers*. Wiley, New York.
3. Stevens, S. S. (1962). *Second Public Klopsteg Lecture*, Northwestern University, Evanston, Illinois, USA.
4. Moskowitz, H. R. (1971). *Am. J. Psychol.*, **84**, p. 385.
5. Moskowitz, H. R. (1970). *Percept. & Psychophys.*, **8**, p. 40.
6. Amerine, M. A., Pangborn, R. M. and Roessler, E. B. (1965). *Principles of Sensory Evaluation of Food*. Academic Press, New York.
7. Stevens, S. S. and Galanter, E. (1957). *J. Exp. Psychol.*, **54**, p. 377.
8. Moskowitz, H. R. and Toscano, V. (1976). *Candy & Snack Industry*, April, p. 28.
9. Moskowitz, H. R., Kluter, R. A., Westerling, J. and Jacobs, H. L. (1974). *Science*, **184**, p. 583.
10. Moskowitz, H. R. (1976). *Paper presented at the Master Brewers Association, Technical Meeting, Lake Buena Vista, Florida*.
11. Moskowitz, H. R. and Gatty, R. (1976). *Paper presented to the Workshop on New Ingredients. American Chemical Society, Division of Agricultural and Food Chemistry, San Francisco, Ca.*

12. Moskowitz, H. R. and Rauch, D. (1976). *Paper presented to the Product Testing Group, Chesebrough Pond's, Greenwich, Conn.*
13. Moskowitz, H. R., Stanley, D. W. and Chandler, J. W. (1977). *Can. J. Food Sci. & Technol.*, in press.
14. Moskowitz, H. R. (1972). *J. Applied Psychol.*, **56**, p. 60.
15. Moskowitz, H. R., Segars, R. A., Kapsalis, J. G. and Kluter, R. A. (1974). *J. Food Sci.*, **39**, p. 200.
16. Stevens, S. S. (1962). *Second Public Klopsteg Lecture, Northwestern University, Evanston, Illinois, USA.*
17. Moskowitz, H. R. (1977). *Chemical Senses and Nutrition* (ed. M. R. Kare and O. Maller), in press.
18. Stone, L. A. and Harder, R. E. (1969). *Psychonom. Sci.*, **15**, p. 105.
19. Moskowitz, H. R., Kluter, R. A., Westerling, J. and Jacobs, H. L. (1974). *Science*, **184**, p. 573.

DISCUSSION

Francis: Why do you invent new terms, e.g. 'deepness of colour' rather than use accepted terms?

Moskowitz: When we evaluate products the consumer's language is different from our language. We who are sitting in the laboratory milling around with products and instruments have a limited time to present a series of products to consumers who can rank them on the basis of deepness of colour. The behaviour is consistent from time to time. Ask the consumer what is going on and the consumer hasn't the faintest idea. He cannot give you an answer. It just seems to be that that's deeper than that. If you do it twenty-five times the same answer comes out. So something is going on. The premise, therefore, is that we cannot look at the consumer's language *per se*. We have got to use the structure of that behaviour and translate back into the world of ingredients.

Sherman: With reference to the study of the influence of price on the acceptability of a range of beverages and sauces, have parallel tests been made on these commodities in which, in one series, consumers are not acquainted with the commodity prices and, in the other series, the prices are made known? If such tests have been made, how much does the knowledge of price influence product acceptability?

Moskowitz: When you do that you do what is called a regression analysis. You have intent to purchase, which is a psychological variable. The second variable is stated price, and the third variable is the degree of liking. You can literally trade off degree of liking and price to get an estimated intent to purchase. You can also trade off acceptability units for price units.

Harper: How are mixtures of odours described?

Moskowitz: Initially for any kind of research you have a focus group and some words seem to come out consistently. We are looking at the possibility of using Eclipse as a method for producing odour quality. Given a series of ingredients of various qualities and mixing them in various combinations could you produce a given quality? Given the qualities of the components and various mixtures could you produce the recipe of constituents? I don't know if it will work.

Harries: How does 'goal programming' differ, if at all, from the standard techniques of linear programming?

Moskowitz: Goal programming says 'I have a given goal I want to produce'. It is called multi-objective. I want to achieve this within a range of allowable formulations. The goal is the perception of the product, the profile of the ideal product. The constraints are that the ingredients cannot be higher or lower than a given level. Given various ingredients you can predict a perception. If I have a number of these things set I can define a region, and the goal programming method lets you get as close to that region as you possibly can. It is a new method of programming. You are trying to come to a goal, trying to come as close as possible to a given profile of perception.

Williams: You said that the consumer can use what terms he likes provided he can describe the ideal product in the same terms. How do you define the ideal product?

Moskowitz: You can show the person an advertisment, you can show the person the word 'ideal', you can show the person a concept board or you can have an evaluation of a competitor product.

13

Optimisation of Sensory Attributes Through Quality Assurance

R. LANGLAIS, M. LAUSTER, G. LOHRE and E. KUGLER

Coca-Cola GmbH, Essen, West Germany

ABSTRACT

The quality of a finished product (or its ingredients) is a compromise between many factors, one of which is a high level of sensory appeal. Modern instrumental techniques provide support to the flavour chemist in ensuring optimal organoleptic characteristics for his product.

An example which deals with the organoleptic evaluation and instrumental analysis of several cold-pressed Sicilian lemon oils will serve as an illustration. A clear discrimination between these oils is possible by quantitative gas liquid chromatography (GLC). Although sensory analysis may yield equivocal results, instrumental analysis does not make sensory analysis superfluous: they are complementary.

INTRODUCTION

Among the factors that determine the marketing success of a product, a soft drink for instance, consumer acceptability is of major importance. The optimisation of the sensory properties of the beverage may be achieved by using only sensory methods. Given the compositional variation of natural ingredients it is the flavour chemist's task to indicate the best means of maintaining the desired organoleptic characteristics of the product or ingredients. Nowadays instrumental analytical methods are available to support the sensory methods; aromatising substances are, for instance, characterised by both sensory and instrumental analysis. Table 1 shows the methods most commonly used.

Physico–chemical methods alone, however sophisticated, cannot adequately determine and describe physiological effects like smell and taste. A trend to substitute sensory analysis by more and more refined instrumental techniques cannot be ignored. In recent years promising results have been obtained in the various fields of essential oils,[1] coffee[2] and tea.[3] Yet sensory evaluation of finished products or their ingredients is still indispensable as testified to in numerous publications by renowned authors (*see*, for example, refs. 4 and 5).

TABLE 1

Analytical methods used in the evaluation of soft drinks and their ingredients

Sensory analysis	Instrumental analysis
Monadic test	Colour measurement
Rank order test	Acid titration
Paired comparison test	Brix determination
Replicate pair test	Turbidity measurement
Triangle test	Viscosity measurement
Dilution test	Gas chromatography
	High-pressure liquid chromatography
	Thin layer chromatography
	Carbonation measurement

Whereas the methods and results of instrumental analysis can be standardised, the results of sensory analysis are necessarily imperfect, dependent as they are on human beings, themselves subject to all kinds of variables which may influence their sensory performance. Consequently, results related directly to these impressions can be highly biased.

A greater objectivity of test participants' statements and better reproducibility of their judgements can be achieved by systematic and intensive training, backed by appropriate statistical evaluation of the results. Performance profiles for every panel member should be derived since these profiles allow the composition of the test-panel to be selected in a rational manner.[6]

The relationship of sensory and instrumental analysis as applied in maintaining the quality of certain flavour ingredients will now be described.

COMPARATIVE SENSORY AND INSTRUMENTAL EVALUATION OF SOME COMMERCIAL COLD-PRESSED SICILIAN LEMON OILS

In the past the criteria for evaluating essential oils were lacking in objectivity. Decisions on the type, quality and origin of essential oils were reached mainly on the basis of the buyer's expertise and possibly also on his long-term relationship with and trust in the supplier.

The physical or chemical tests carried out on the oils in those days were few and the decisions to purchase such oils were based primarily on sensory evaluation. Accurate instrumental analysis is now available to assist in the choice of essential oils for a particular product.

It is well known that cheap citral produced either from lemon grass or by synthesis was sometimes added to lemon oils as a flavour booster. Other synthetic compounds also found their way into 'natural' oils for improving or strengthening the aroma or even to correct or cover up off-flavour.

The enormous progress made in the last 25 years in analytical techniques together with the improvement in sensory methods, have made possible a more objective evaluation of essential oils.

Combining the instrumental techniques with the sensory methods enables the flavour chemist to better achieve two objectives, viz. (1) to distinguish between a number of similar oils and to make an appropriate selection for optimising the product's organoleptic properties; (2) to help in maintaining the high level of organoleptic appeal in the face of compositional variation of the natural ingredients over the course of time.

Table 2 shows the evaluation methods used in our comparative study.

TABLE 2
Evaluation methods for essential oils

Sensory evaluation	Instrumental analysis
Triangle test Double triangle test Blotter test	Optical rotation Refractive Index Specific Gravity UV spectra Gas chromatography

INSTRUMENTATION AND MATERIALS

(1)   The essential oils were evaluated at a level of 100 ppm, in a solution of 10% sucrose and 0·2% citric acid (w/v) and dispersed by means of a hand-homogeniser. The six oils were coded A–F throughout.

(2)   A trained panel of seven to ten persons carried out the sensory evaluation; the triangle test was used throughout.

(3)   The essential oils were evaluated by triangle tests.

(4)   Optical rotations were determined with a Perkin Elmer Polarimeter (model 241).

(5)   Refractive indices were determined with a Zeiss refractometer (Type No. 26751).

(6)   Densities were determined with a Heraeus digital DMA 10 instrument.

(7)   UV spectra were obtained using a Perkin Elmer Model 124 D double beam spectrophotometer.

(8)   A Carlo Erba Model GI (Milano, Italy) gas chromatograph, equipped with a flame ionisation detector (FID) was employed. The injection port and the detector were operated at 200 °C. Hydrogen pressure and air pressure were 0·5 atm and 1·5 atm, respectively. Commercially available purified nitrogen was used as a carrier gas at a pressure of 1·3 atm, with a split ratio of 1 : 50. The quantity of sample injected was 0·2 μl. The temperature was programmed from 50–200 °C at a rate of 2 °C min^{-1}. The glass-capillary column was 50 m long with an internal diameter of 0·3 mm and coated with polypropylene glycol (PPG).[7]

(9)   A Perkin Elmer Model 56 recorder (range 1 mV; 5 mm min^{-1} chart speed) was operated in conjunction with an Infotronics Model CRS-101 (automatic digital integrator) and a Teleprint Model 390 (Teleprint GmbH, Eschborn, Frankfurt am Main). Punched tapes were processed by a Teletype Corporation reader.

RESULTS AND DISCUSSION

Instrumental Analysis

General methods

The results of the classical analyses are presented below together

TABLE 3
Comparison of physical data

Lemon oil	Optical rotation 25 °C $[\alpha]_D$	Refractive index 20 °C n_D	Density 25 °C	CD value	Sediment[a]
A	+ 58·84°	1·4739	0·8497	0·12	+
B	+ 59·06°	1·4743	0·8502	0·27	+
C	+ 59·18°	1·4744	0·8499	0·33	+ +
D	+ 59·24°	1·4748	0·8502	0·46	+ + +
E	+ 59·48°	1·4750	0·8513	0·68	+ + +
F	+ 61·02°	1·4749	0·8513	0·64	—
Literature values[b]	57–65·63°	1·4742–1·4755	0·8490–0·8550	0·200–0·670	—

[a] Amount of sediment observed in the bottles after a certain refrigeration period (12–14 hours over night at + 2 °C).
[b] *See* reference 8.

with brief comments. In the presentation of results the order of the samples is in correlation with the results of quantitative GLC.

Table 3 shows the optical rotation, the density, the refractive index and the CD values[8] of the lemon oils. The values quoted in Table 3 indicate that the majority of the routine physical analyses of lemon oils provide insufficient information for their discrimination.

Most of the results fall within the generally accepted range of values for a good quality lemon oil,[8] free of any adulterants.

Most valuable is the determination of the CD values[8] which are derived from the UV spectra and represent one of the physical characteristics of citrus essential oils. In our case, the CD values happen to correlate with the quantitative GLC data.

It would be misleading to use only those criteria shown in Table 3 as distinctive marks of quality. The UV spectra give an indication of the character of the oil and allow the detection of possible adulterations only within the limits governing the spectroscopic method. For example, the addition of minor amounts of coumarin to oil A increases its CD value and renders it spectroscopically similar to oil C or D.

Generally speaking, the spectrophotometric measurements may be used to discriminate between a number of cold-pressed lemon oils; they do not allow the direct detection of adulterants nor the contribution of individual components to the calculated CD values.

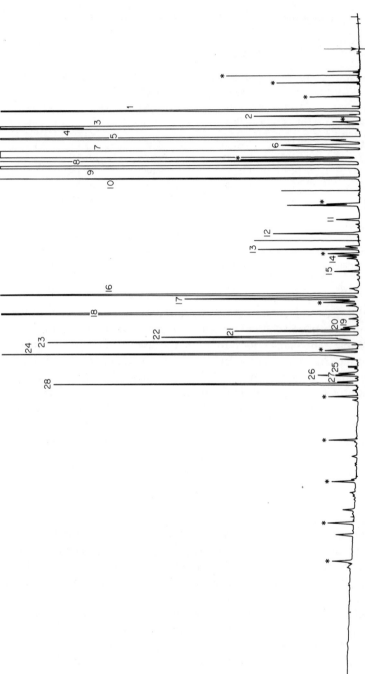

Fig. 1. Cold pressed Sicilian lemon oil + c. 7% of n-paraffins. (*C-7 to C-20 in equal proportions); 0·2 mm³, standard conditions (see Instrumentation and Materials)

Gas–liquid chromatography (GLC)

Chromatograms were quantitatively evaluated by our GLC/ computer system. Each sample was chromatographed five times, and the mean peak areas were calculated, together with the standard deviation, the 95% tolerance limits and the retention indices. These are needed for the identification of the peaks common to all 30 chromatograms and for their identification with compounds of known retention indices (disc file). Only those peaks occurring in all of the chromatograms were used for later evaluation. Figure 1 shows a representative gas chromatogram of one of the lemon oils; Table 4 lists the mean peak areas of each oil series, with the corresponding standard deviation for each peak.[7]

A close look at some of the major peak areas, for example of limonene, α-pinene, β-pinene, reveals certain trends. In the oil series A–E the peak areas for α-pinene (peak 1) clearly decrease, while those for β-pinene (peak 2) increase. Similar trends may be followed systematically all over the chromatograms and a simplified picture of these findings is given in Table 5.

Of a total of 28 peaks, five (peaks 2, 8, 11, 20, 24) do not behave in a linear fashion but show only an overall increase. The two oils E and F are seen to be very similar. By comparing the 95% tolerance limits of the peak areas with each other a comparison of the quantitative peak data can be made more accurate and bias minimised.

Table 6 shows the 95% tolerance limits for each of the six lemon

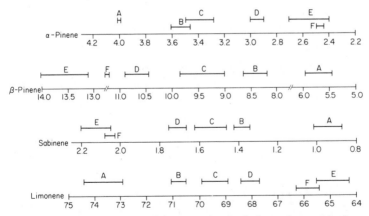

FIG. 2. Graphical presentation of the 95% tolerance limits (peak area %) of some major terpenes.

TABLE 4

Comparison of mean peak areas (%) of commercial lemon oils (n = 5)

Sample		A		B		C		D		E		S		Compounds (tentative identification by means of retention indices)
Peak no.	Retention index	Area	Standard deviation	Area	Standard deviation	Area	Standard deviation	Area	Standard deviation	Area	Standard deviation	Area	Standard deviation	
1	956·3	4·03706	0·01964	3·54364	0·02319	3·38988	0·03918	3·03215	0·02048	2·57404	0·06095	2·47363	0·00853	α-Pinene/α-Thujene
2	975·8	0·01779	0·00322	0·12177	0·00378	0·10748	0·00121	0·08769	0·00002	0·05859	0·00112	0·05554	0·00010	?
3	1015·2	5·62937	0·05778	8·42581	0·08347	9·43741	0·14732	10·69769	0·07953	13·59535	0·15634	12·42184	0·01292	β-Pinene
4	1018·7	0·99987	0·03966	1·38088	0·01715	1·54344	0·02940	1·72349	0·01333	2·14084	0·02896	2·05888	0·00765	Sabinene
5	1048·6	2·05233	0·09646	1·82255	0·02231	1·79266	0·07321	1·64316	0·02062	1·48980	0·02079	1·52891	0·00190	β-Myrcene
6	1065·6	0·48442	0·00977	0·34037	0·00244	0·33059	0·00712	0·26711	0·00334	0·14681	0·00291	0·16261	0·00079	?
7	1093·3	73·72083	0·27277	70·78530	0·08651	69·43802	0·17557	68·11207	0·11442	64·95838	0·22603	65·85930	0·16358	Limonene
8	1103·1	0·43826	0·01622	0·48209	0·00807	0·32503	0·00377	0·36158	0·01748	0·47469	0·12262	0·35104	0·00471	p-Cymene/α-Terpinene
9	1118·5	7·14513	0·01633	7·93126	0·02142	8·41899	0·03576	8·87301	0·01300	9·54958	0·07942	9·55087	0·03656	γ-Terpinene
10	1144·0	0·47324	0·00309	0·41236	0·00197	0·41476	0·00284	0·39710	0·00037	0·32747	0·00854	0·35780	0·00238	Terpinolene
11	1232·6	0·02252	0·00133	0·02642	0·00081	0·02446	0·00022	0·02776	0·00120	0·03245	0·00125	0·03822	0·00051	Terpinene-1-ol
12	1259·2	0·11482	0·00275	0·10431	0·00220	0·11150	0·00114	0·11066	0·00394	0·09280	0·01028	0·09286	0·00547	Citronellal
13	1290·6	0·15234	0·00236	0·12836	0·00319	0·12253	0·00117	0·11500	0·00025	0·09516	0·00346	0·11173	0·00009	Linalool
14	1305·0	0·01323	0·00284	0·02075	0·00430	0·02598	0·00254	0·02929	0·00071	0·03418	0·00002	0·02601	0·00177	Decanal
15	1335·9	0·02210	0·00001	0·02520	0·00014	0·02737	0·00028	0·02851	0·00159	0·03196	0·00096	0·03205	0·00066	Terpinene-4-ol
16	1384·3	0·97122	0·00957	0·83800	0·01258	0·85494	0·01007	0·82987	0·03234	0·70929	0·02015	0·85689	0·00609	Neral
17	1391·8	0·32880	0·00112	0·24303	0·00487	0·22494	0·00155	0·19883	0·00700	0·12765	0·00860	0·16529	0·00167	α-Terpineol
18	1423·0	1·58058	0·02230	1·40342	0·02467	1·38635	0·02132	1·37005	0·05965	1·20113	0·02318	1·46865	0·01402	Geranial
19	1453·3	0·01087	0·00061	0·01439	0·00178	0·01464	0·00101	0·01603	0·00121	0·01939	0·00245	0·02468	0·00247	?
20	1456·7	0·00640	0·00028	0·01008	0·00063	0·00943	0·00106	0·01185	0·00154	0·01627	0·00437	0·02078	0·00104	Citronellyl acetate
21	1459·3	0·11183	0·00384	0·12862	0·00431	0·14195	0·00446	0·15695	0·00191	0·17902	0·01198	0·21579	0·00260	Terpinyl acetate
22	1471·6	0·11206	0·00384	0·17720	0·00867	0·20876	0·00878	0·24968	0·02104	0·33609	0·02847	0·36209	0·00209	Nerol
23	1482·1	0·45539	0·02482	0·40992	0·00993	0·40743	0·00981	0·39957	0·02980	0·35275	0·01174	0·40572	0·00174	Neryl acetate
24	1507·0	0·40091	0·01299	0·46056	0·04428	0·44734	0·01518	0·53938	0·02690	0·52526	0·04285	0·44546	0·00438	Geranyl + Decyl acetate
25	1549·3	0·01133	0·00051	0·01713	0·00221	0·01924	0·00083	0·02042	0·00110	0·02426	0·00290	0·01004	0·00130	?
26	1553·2	0·02495	0·00260	0·03130	0·00318	0·04077	0·00123	0·04442	0·00178	0·05080	0·00752	0·06549	0·00705	Valencene
27	1567·4	0·01064	0·00040	0·01559	0·00114	0·01812	0·00048	0·02039	0·00258	0·02693	0·00391	0·03727	0·00068	?
28	1570·7	0·21384	0·00890	0·31375	0·01600	0·36112	0·01742	0·40241	0·01632	0·48236	0·04870	0·51194	0·00716	β-Bisabolene

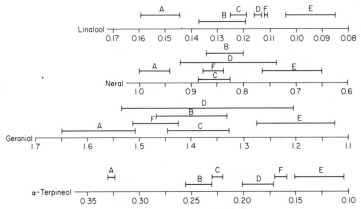

FIG. 3. Graphical presentation of the 95% tolerance limits (peak area %) of some major oxygenated compounds.

oils, in the form of the upper (U) and the lower (L) peak area percentages. These limits indicate the reproducibility of the analyses. From this table some terpenes and oxygenated compounds which are known to contribute to the overall flavour were singled out. Their 95% tolerance limits are illustrated graphically in Figs. 2 and 3.

The only important exception in this respect is citral: it is present at almost the same level in all six samples.

Sensory Analysis

Blotter test of pure lemon oils

The lemon oils were tested on two different days using the triangle test; the codings alternated for the odd sample (AAB and BBA). The number of possible test-permutations (30) was limited to no more than six, based on the preliminary data gained from the instrumental analysis.

(a)   E v. F
(b)   C v. D
(c)   A v. B
(d)   A v. E
(e)   B v. D
(f)   F v. C

The results were unequivocal only for those tests in which E was compared with F and A with E. The seven panel members were able to select the odd sample in both cases.

TABLE 5
Trends in peak area observed from oils A to E

Peak	Name	< Increasing > Decreasing
1	α-Pinene	>
2	?	<
3	β-Pinene	<
4	Sabinene	<
5	β-Myrcene	>
6	?	>
7	Limonene	>
8	p-Cymene α-Terpinene	Equivocal
9	γ-Terpinene	<
10	Terpinolene	>
11	Terpinene-1-ol	<
12	Citronellal	Stable
13	Linalool	>
14	Decanal	<
15	Terpinene-4-ol	<
16	Neral	>
17	α-Terpineol	>
18	Geranial	>
19	?	<
20	Citronellyl acetate	Equivocal
21	Terpinyl acetate	<
22	Nerol	<
23	Neryl acetate	>
24	Geranyl + Decyl acetate	Equivocal
25	?	<
26	Valencene	<
27	?	<
28	β-Bisabolene	<

No significant results were obtained for the other triangle tests.

The same tests were repeated three days later with identical results. Thus, it can be concluded that there are obvious sensory differences between some of the oils. Furthermore, E was preferred over F, as the latter was found to be less characteristic of lemon, due to a distinct orange note.

Triangle tests of oils at beverage dilution level

The same experimental design as for the blotter tests was chosen for

TABLE 6

95% tolerance limits (n = 5) of mean peak areas of commercial lemon oils (L = lower limit; U = upper limit)

Peak no.	Retention index	A Peak areas (%)		B Peak areas (%)		C Peak areas (%)		D Peak areas (%)		E Peak areas (%)		F Peak areas (%)		Compounds (tentative identification by means of retention indices only)
		L	U	L	U	L	U	L	U	L	U	L	U	
1	953·1	3·974 60	4·099 51	3·469 89	3·617 39	3·280 96	3·498 80	2·967 01	3·097 29	2·404 61	2·743 47	2·444 93	2·497 33	α-Pinene/α-Thujene
2	976·6	0·008 84	0·026 75	0·111 25	0·132 28	0·104 13	0·110 84	0·087 48	0·087 90	0·055 47	0·061 72	0·055 12	0·055 97	?
3	1014·0	5·445 64	5·813 10	8·193 77	8·657 85	9·027 85	9·846 97	10·476 59	10·918 78	13·160 72	14·029 98	12·380 76	12·462 93	β-Pinene
4	1017·2	0·889 61	1·110 12	1·333 20	1·428 57	1·461 70	1·625 17	1·686 44	1·760 53	2·060 33	2·221 35	2·037 60	2·080 15	Sabinene
5	1046·2	1·784 17	2·320 49	1·760 52	1·884 57	1·589 13	1·996 20	1·577 58	1·708 74	1·432 01	1·547 59	1·522 89	1·534 94	β-Myrcene
6	1065·6	0·457 26	0·511 59	0·332 62	0·348 11	0·310 80	0·350 39	0·257 84	0·276 39	0·137 55	0·156 07	0·160 10	0·165 13	?
7	1090·7	72·962 54	74·479 12	70·544 79	71·025 80	68·949 92	69·926 11	67·748 20	68·475 93	64·330 00	65·586 75	65·404 56	66·314 04	Limonene
8	1102·3	0·393 18	0·483 35	0·456 42	0·507 75	0·314 55	0·335 51	0·312 98	0·410 18	0·133 81	0·815 56	0·336 07	0·366 00	p-Cymene/α-Terpinene
9	1118·8	7·093 20	7·197 05	7·871 70	7·990 82	8·319 57	8·518 41	8·831 67	8·914 34	9·328 79	9·770 36	9·449 24	9·652 51	γ-Terpinene
10	1143·4	0·463 41	0·483 08	0·406 89	0·417 84	0·406 88	0·422 65	0·395 50	0·398 71	0·303 73	0·351 21	0·351 17	0·364 43	Terpinolene
11	1231·7	0·018 27	0·026 76	0·024 18	0·028 67	0·023 85	0·025 07	0·024 42	0·031 11	0·028 97	0·035 93	0·036 58	0·039 85	Terpinene-1-ol
12	1258·7	0·106 07	0·123 57	0·098 18	0·110 43	0·108 34	0·114 66	0·099 70	0·121 63	0·064 22	0·121 39	0·077 66	0·108 06	Citronellal
13	1290·5	0·144 82	0·159 86	0·119 49	0·137 24	0·119 27	0·125 79	0·113 91	0·116 08	0·085 55	0·104 77	0·111 35	0·112 11	Linalool
14	1304·4	0·005 33	0·021 13	0·008 79	0·032 70	0·018 92	0·033 03	0·027 03	0·031 54	0·033 90	0·034 47	0·021 09	0·030 92	Decanal
15	1335·4	0·022 03	0·022 17	0·024 74	0·025 66	0·026 60	0·028 13	0·024 09	0·032 93	0·029 29	0·034 63	0·030 21	0·033 90	Terpinene-4-ol
16	1383·5	0·940 78	1·001 65	0·803 02	0·872 98	0·826 95	0·882 93	0·739 98	0·919 77	0·653 28	0·765 30	0·837 54	0·876 24	Neral
17	1391·4	0·324 01	0·333 60	0·229 49	0·256 57	0·220 64	0·292 24	0·179 36	0·218 30	0·103 73	0·151 57	0·159 99	0·170 60	α-Terpineol
18	1422·0	1·509 68	1·651 49	1·334 83	1·472 01	1·327 07	1·445 63	1·204 21	1·535 89	1·127 41	1·274 84	1·424 07	1·513 23	Geranial
19	1453·0	0·008 92	0·012 82	0·009 45	0·019 33	0·011 82	0·017 46	0·012 19	0·019 88	0·012 57	0·026 21	0·017 82	0·031 54	?
20	1455·7	0·005 50	0·007 30	0·008 08	0·012 08	0·006 49	0·012 38	0·007 57	0·016 12	0·004 13	0·028 40	0·017 46	0·024 10	Citronellyl acetate
21	1459·9	0·099 61	0·124 05	0·116 65	0·140 59	0·129 55	0·154 35	0·148 73	0·165 17	0·145 71	0·212 33	0·207 54	0·224 05	Terpinyl acetate
22	1472·0	0·099 86	0·124 25	0·153 10	0·201 29	0·184 36	0·233 16	0·191 19	0·308 17	0·256 95	0·415 23	0·355 44	0·368 74	Nerol
23	1481·4	0·376 45	0·534 34	0·382 31	0·437 52	0·380 15	0·434 71	0·316 71	0·482 42	0·315 42	0·390 07	0·398 22	0·413 22	Neryl acetate
24	1506·4	0·359 61	0·442 20	0·337 45	0·583 67	0·399 07	0·495 60	0·464 59	0·614 17	0·406 13	0·644 39	0·431 52	0·459 40	Geranyl + Decyl acetate
25	1549·5	0·009 70	0·012 95	0·010 97	0·023 28	0·016 94	0·021 54	0·016 94	0·023 90	0·016 20	0·032 32	0·005 91	0·014 16	?
26	1553·2	0·016 67	0·033 24	0·022 46	0·040 15	0·037 35	0·044 20	0·038 75	0·050 09	0·029 89	0·071 70	0·045 90	0·085 08	Valencene
27	1567·0	0·009 37	0·011 92	0·012 43	0·018 75	0·016 79	0·019 44	0·013 22	0·027 56	0·016 06	0·037 80	0·035 10	0·039 43	?
28	1571·3	0·185 54	0·242 14	0·269 26	0·358 25	0·312 69	0·409 55	0·350 51	0·454 30	0·346 98	0·617 75	0·489 16	0·534 73	β-Bisabolene

the triangle tests. Thus, for the reasons outlined before, the following tests were carried out:

(a)   E v. F
(b)   C v. D
(c)   A v. B
(d)   A v. E
(e)   B v. D
(f)   F v. C

Definite differences could be established between the two beverages made from oils E and F and between those made from oils E and A. In both cases, all six members of the expert panel were able to distinguish the odd sample. In the first comparison sample E was preferred over F, again due to the latter's untypical orange note.

The rest of the triangle test did not give any statistically significant results. The panel was unable to discriminate between the beverages.

SUMMARY

1. After the product optimisation has been achieved, both instrumental and sensory methods are used for maintaining quality.

2. It may be demonstrated that an instrumental match of essential oils does not guarantee an organoleptic match; the instrumental equality of oils E and F on the one hand and their sensory inequality on the other testify to these findings.

3. Small panels can be less sensitive than glass-capillary GLC in detecting compositional changes.

4. The conventional routine-type analytical procedures provide data which are in good agreement with values found in the literature. Discrimination of minor changes was not possible.

5. In order to prevent the use of adulterated oils, limiting values for results of instrumental analysis have to be established. At the same time, a very strong emphasis is put on organoleptic equality: if samples match a previously set standard instrumentally, a rejection is still possible on an organoleptic basis. Conversely, if sensory analysis yields acceptable results but the compositional variation exceeds the standard values, rejection is automatic.

REFERENCES

1. Zlatkis, A. and Gostecnik, G. (1975). *J. Chromatogr.* **106,** p. 73.
2. Gianturco, M., Biggers, R. and Ridling, B. (1974). *J. Agric. Food Chem.,* **22,** p. 758.
3. Biggers, R., Hilton, J. and Gianturco, M. (1969). *J. Chromatogr. Sci.,* **7,** p. 453.
4. Amerine, A., Pangborn, R. and Roessler, B. (1965). *Principles of Sensory Evaluation of Food,* Academic Press, New York.
5. Jellinek, G. (1968). *Gordian,* **68,** p. 9.
6. Lohre, G. Food Technology Thesis (unpublished) (1974). Vocational College Lippe, Lemgo, West Germany.
7. Kugler, E., Langlais, R., Halang, W. and Hufschmidt, M. (1975). *Chromatographia,* **8,** p. 468.
8. Kesterson, J., Hendrikson, R. and Braddok, J. (1971). In: *Florida Citrus Oils,* ed. J. W. Siles. Bulletin 749 of the Agricultural Exp. Stat. Inst. of Food and Agric. Sciences, pp. 96 and 116.

DISCUSSION

Baxter: In view of the lack of correlation between the GC analysis figures and panel discrimination for these samples, did you consider using coupled gas chromatographic–odour port techniques to relate the sensory aspects with the presence or absence of specific components?

Langlais: That could be done but are you sure that what you inject is going to come out of the effluent? It takes you two days to go through these samples and I am not such an expert as to be unbiased in sitting two days on a hot effluent! We have used the effluent method in other cases but I would not go into it for these examples.

Nursten: I must reinforce the point Dr Baxter is making. High priority needs to be given to determining which of the chromatographic peaks detected by Dr Langlais are the organoleptically important ones. The chances of then obtaining a good correlation of some function of the concentration of these substances with the overall sensory assessments should be considerably increased.

Knights: Isn't it likely that the 'different' constituent in oil 'E' was obscured by one of the larger detected peaks? If so odour assessment would have detected this.

Langlais: In this series of oils we did not detect any possibility of this.

14

Some Factors Affecting the Objective Study of Food Texture

J. G. Brennan and R. Jowitt

National College of Food Technology, University of Reading, Weybridge, Surrey, England

ABSTRACT

In spite of their importance and widespread use, difficulties still arise in defining texture and related textural attributes as applied to the quality of food. Sensory and instrumental methods of texture measurement are the subjects of continuing research. In the former case methods of texture profiling have been developed and improvements in panel organisation and training reported.

Instrumental methods of texture measurement can be grouped into three classes: empirical, imitative and fundamental. Empirical methods usually involve measurement of the resistance to deformation offered by the sample. The properties measured are not well defined and the results cannot easily be expressed in fundamental terms. Such results are dependent on probe geometry, rate of deformation and sample size. This dependence is exemplified by results obtained using a simple cylindrical probe and a Kramer Shear Cell mounted on an Instron Universal Test Machine. The need to calibrate empirical instruments is another limitation on their use.

Imitative instruments attempt to simulate to some extent the action of the jaws and/or teeth when masticating food in the mouth. The General Foods Texturometer is a well-known instrument in this category. A detailed analysis of the action of this instrument revealed a high initial stress as its characteristic feature. However there is no clear evidence available to suggest that the results from this instrument are any more meaningful than those obtained from other empirical instruments.

Fundamental methods are intended to measure one or more well-defined physical properties of the sample and to relate these to the textural characteristics of the food. The complex and variable structure of foods and the wide spectrum of rheological behaviour which they exhibit give rise to difficulties in applying such fundamental methods. The application of such methods and the difficulties encountered are exemplified by results obtained when attempting to measure crispness and brittleness of biscuits.

While a great deal of further work needs to be done it is felt that a more fundamental approach to texture measurement in foods is likely to be more fruitful in increasing our understanding of the subject and lead to the development of more useful methods of measurement.

INTRODUCTION

Having received comparatively little serious attention for many decades the subject of food texture has come to be regarded as a suitable topic for research in many parts of the world in the last twenty years. A great deal of activity has taken place involving studies of the factors affecting the textural characteristics of specific foodstuffs, the design of instruments and procedures for assessing such characteristics and correlating the results obtained by sensory methods with those obtained by the use of instruments. The approach to this work varies from fundamental on the one hand to extremely empirical on the other. In recent years more and more workers in this field are adopting the more fundamental approach.

Texture Terminology

In spite of the widespread use of the word texture and other terms to describe specific textural attributes of foods, by the consuming public as well as those involved in the systematic study of food quality, there are still no internationally accepted definitions of such terms. This lack of standardisation in texture terminology can lead to difficulty in interpreting the results from consumer surveys and trained sensory panels and may impair progress in cooperative research in this field. The authors have been concerned with this problem in recent years. Jowitt[1] published a discussion paper on this topic in 1974. Both authors contributed to the deliberations of the sub-committee which prepared the British Standards Institution's 'Glossary of terms relating to sensory analysis of food'[2] which includes definitions for the terms texture, structure and consistency. It is hoped that further useful discussion on texture terminology will take place during this symposium.

Texture Measurement

Both sensory and instrumental methods of texture measurement are the subjects of continuing research. In the former case the texture profile method developed by Szczesniak and co-workers[3-5] has been widely applied and modifications have been suggested.[6] Information on the training of sensory panels for texture work has become more widely available.[7]

Instrumental methods of texture measurement usually involve deformation of the test sample by means of a probe and the measurement of the resistance to deformation offered by the sample. A limited amount of work has been done recently on the use of sonic techniques for texture measurement. Studies of the structure and chemical analysis, particularly of the structural components, of foods also contribute information on the textural features of foods.

FACTORS AFFECTING TEXTURE MEASUREMENT BY INSTRUMENTAL MEANS

Methods of food texture measurement which involve deformation of the sample may be conveniently classified into three categories, namely empirical, imitative and fundamental.[8]

Empirical Methods

These methods measure physical characteristics which are usually ill-defined and the results are often expressed in arbitrary units. The type of action featured in empirical instruments includes: penetration, shear, compression, cutting and mixing. The pattern of forces exerted on the test sample is usually quite complex and often difficult to establish. The results are dependent on probe geometry, sample size and rate of deformation. These points may be illustrated by the results of some work carried out at the National College of Food Technology.[9]

An Instron Universal Test Machine, floor model TT-BM, was used in this work. A right-cylindrical probe was made to descend vertically

at a constant speed of 2×10^{-2} m min^{-1} on to a cylindrical sample of
the material, 25·5 mm in diameter and 15·0 mm high. The test sample
was supported on a load cell and a load-deformation trace was
obtained during each test. Each test was replicated ten times. A
number of measurements was derived from the trace and used as

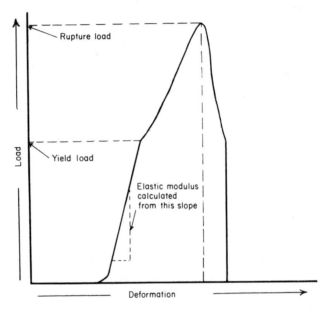

FIG. 1.   Typical load–deformation trace obtained during a puncture test using a right,
cylindrical probe.

indices of physical properties of the sample. Those reported here are:
(1) elastic modulus calculated from the straight line portion of the
curve as small deformations (2) yield load, which is the load registered
at the yield point of the sample, and (3) rupture load, which is the
maximum load registered before gross structural breakdown occurs.
These measurements are shown in Fig. 1. The effect of varying the
probe diameter was studied initially and some of these results are
shown in Table 1. The figures in that table represent the mean values
of ten replicates. Increasing the probe diameter from 13·0 mm to
25·5 mm resulted in all three properties decreasing in value. Further
increase in probe diameter, beyond 25·5 mm which was the diameter
of the test sample, had little effect on the results. This pattern is more
definite in the case of the elastic modulus and yield load than it is with

TABLE 1

Influence of probe diameter on the physical properties of various materials as determined by a puncture/compression test. Cylindrical test pieces used, 25·5 mm diameter, 15·0 mm high. Crosshead speed constant at $2 \times 10^{-2} m \, min^{-1}$.

Test material	Probe diameter (mm)					
Physical property[a]	13·0	18·0	25·5	32·0	40·0	50·0
Rubber						
$E \times 10^5 \, N \, m^{-2}$	3·6	3·3	1·9	1·9	1·9	1·8
Raw potato						
$E \times 10^5 \, N \, m^{-2}$	101·6	76·3	55·3	59·1	49·6	50·3
$Y \times 10^4 \, kg \, m^{-2}$	6·5	4·9	3·3	3·2	3·2	3·1
$R \times 10^4 \, kg \, m^{-2}$	15·9	15·2	12·7	14·3	13·9	13·2
Raw apple						
$E \times 10^5 \, N \, m^{-2}$	36·6	29·5	17·6	17·7	17·5	17·6
$Y \times 10^4 \, kg \, m^{-2}$	2·5	2·0	1·3	1·3	1·3	1·3
$R \times 10^4 \, kg \, m^{-2}$	3·5	3·1	2·2	2·2	2·1	2·1
Cheese (Edam)						
$E \times 10^5 \, N \, m^{-2}$	4·3	3·5	2·4	2·4	2·4	2·4
$Y \times 10^3 \, kg \, m^{-2}$	3·8	2·8	0·8	0·9	0·8	0·8
$R \times 10^3 \, kg \, m^{-2}$	11·1	10·6	9·8	12·0	11·6	11·8
Cake (madeira)						
$E \times 10^4 \, N \, m^{-2}$	11·9	9·7	6·4	5·5	6·8	6·5
$Y \times 10^2 \, kg \, m^{-2}$	9·8	6·3	4·9	5·3	5·1	4·9
$R \times 10^2 \, kg \, m^{-2}$	15·8	13·8	6·7	7·8	7·8	7·1

[a] E = Modulus of elasticity; Y = yield load; R = rupture load.

rupture load. The results for this last property were less reproducible than the other two. This influence of probe diameter may be attributable to the relative contributions made by shear and compressive resistances during the puncture test. To study this a further series of tests was carried out. Each test consisted of three steps as follows:

(1) A hollow, sharp-edged, cylindrical probe was made to shear through the sample at a constant rate and a load-deformation trace obtained.

(2) The cylindrical plug formed in the first step was replaced into the annular ring of the test material and compressed at a constant rate using a solid cylindrical probe of the same

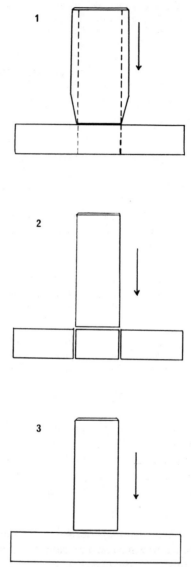

FIG. 2.   Principle of the three-step puncture test: (1) shear; (2) compression; (3) puncture.

diameter as the plug (and the internal diameter of the hollow probe). A load-deformation trace was again obtained.

(3)   In the third step another sample of the material under test was subjected to a puncture test using the same, solid, cylindrical probe as in (2) above and a load-deformation trace recorded.

Step (1) was designed to apply mainly shear force; step (2) 'restrained' compression and step (3) is a puncture test. The principle of the three-step test is shown in Fig. 2. Load–deformation (depth of penetration) curves were plotted for the three steps as shown in Fig. 3. In addition a fourth curve, representing the sum of the loads recorded in steps (1) and (2) at different penetration depths, was drawn for each test.

Edam cheese, raw potato and madeira cake were among the foods tested in this manner. The general pattern of the load–deformation curves appeared to be the same. At low penetration depths both shear and compression forces contributed to the total load registered in the puncture test. As the penetration depth increased the influence of the shear component became proportionately less. In most cases the curve representing the sum of the shear and compression loads obtained from steps (1) and (2) followed that obtained in the puncture test quite closely, as shown in Fig. 3 where the curves for Edam cheese are presented.

A further experiment was carried out in which matching sets of hollow and solid cylindrical probes of different diameters were used to study the influence of probe diameter on the load patterns in a puncture test. The results indicated that as the probe diameter was increased the compression component of the total load increased relative to the shear component at all stages in the test. Again the results for Edam cheese in Fig. 3 show this trend. This is to be expected from a consideration of the geometry of a cylindrical probe. The compressive resistance should be related to the square of the probe diameter while the shear resistance would be related to its circumference and so to its diameter. The influence of probe diameter on the pattern of forces could account for the variation in results with changing probe diameter shown in Table 1.

The influence of the rate of deformation on the results obtained in a puncture test was also briefly investigated. Because of restrictions imposed by the response of the recorder fitted to the Instron machine at the time, the maximum crosshead speed used was $0.1 \, \text{m min}^{-1}$.

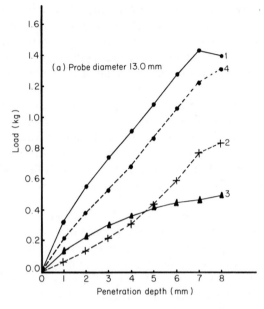

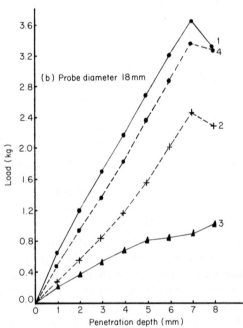

Fig. 3a

Fig. 3b

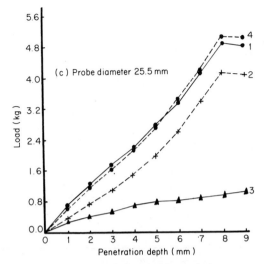

FIG. 3c

FIG. 3. Contribution of shear and compression forces during a puncture test using probes of different diameters: (1) puncture; (2) compression; (3) shear; (4) shear + compression. Test material, Edam cheese; cylindrical samples 35 mm in diameter, 14 mm thick, crosshead speed 2×10^{-2} m min^{-1}.

Variations in crosshead speed in the range 0·01 to 0·1 m min^{-1} had little effect on the results obtained with a variety of foods. However at higher speeds one might expect speed variation to have more influence on such results. Other aspects associated with the rate of deformation may need consideration. It may be that to obtain results from empirical tests which accurately reflect sensory properties of foods rates of deformation similar to those that occur during mastication should be employed. Most empirical tests involve subjecting the sample to a constant rate of deformation. It may be that this is not the best way to test for some properties such as brittleness or crispness. Further work is necessary to study these factors.

The influence of sample size on the results obtained from empirical tests can be demonstrated by reference to some work done on the Kramer Shear Cell mounted on the Instron Universal Test Machine. In this cell, which has been described in the literature,[10] a set of parallel blades is made to shear through the test sample contained in a box-like cell fitted with upper and lower horizontal grids through which the blades pass. A load cell measures the resistance offered by the sample and the result is presented in the form of a load–time trace

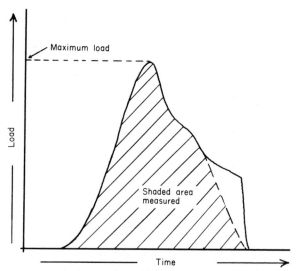

FIG. 4.   Typical load–time trace obtained from the Kramer Shear Cell mounted on the Instron Universal Test Machine.

such as that shown in Fig. 4. In the work reported here the maximum load registered and the area under the load–time curve were measured.

The foods tested included potato (cooked in boiling water for 10 min), raw banana and madeira cake. Each material was diced into cubes of uniform size and these were filled into the cell in a random fashion. The weight of sample used was varied from 10 to 120 g. The results varied from product to product. In the case of banana and cake a linear relationship between maximum load and sample weight was found to exist but not in the case of the cooked potato. In the case of all three materials the area under the curve varied linearly with sample weight. These results are at variance with others reported in the literature by Szczesniak[11] and DeMan.[12]

The results discussed above demonstrate some of the limitations of the empirical approach to instrumental measurement of texture. Results from such tests are very much dependent on instrument design, sample size and test conditions. They can be seldom expressed in fundamental units and it is difficult to predict the effects of altering probe size, rate of deformation or sample size without extended experimentation. It is essential to specify the geometrical characteristics of the instrument, the sample and the test conditions when reporting results. It is usually difficult to relate two sets of results, even if the action is the same, when the geometry is not.

Another limitation is the need to standardise empirical instruments. One approach is to use a sample of food which has been assessed by sensory methods to calibrate a 'master' instrument. This instrument is then used to calibrate a few other 'reference' instruments and these in turn are used to calibrate the instruments in the field. Thus a hierarchy of instruments is built up. Such a system is used in this country for pea tenderometers. Non-food materials such as asbestos, spun protein fibres, beeswax, filter paper, rubber and plastic have also been used as standards. Standardisation of empirical instruments can be time-consuming and a serious source of error.

Imitative Methods

These methods are essentially empirical with the added feature that they attempt to simulate to some extent the mechanical process the food undergoes during mastication. In practice to date this has been limited to tooth-shaped probes and/or an action similar to that of the human jaw. Little attention has been paid to the levels of forces, the type of forces and the rates of deformation featured in imitative instruments. The General Foods Texturometer is a well-known instrument in this category. It was first described by Friedman *et al.*[13] The principle of this instrument is shown in Fig. 5. The sample is

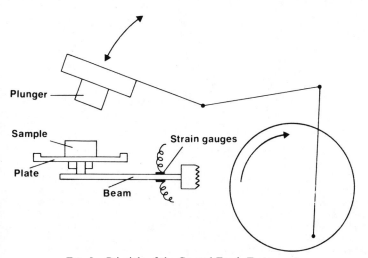

FIG. 5. Principle of the General Foods Texturometer.

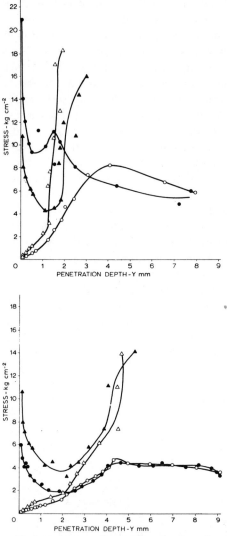

Fig. 6. Relationship between stress (kg cm^{-2}) and penetration depth (Y mm) for several food samples (12·8 mm thick × 26·0 mm in diameter) of: (a) ▲—▲ English carrots (arctuate motion); △—△ English carrots (vertical motion); ●—● Golden Delicious apples complete with skin (arctuate motion); ○—○ Golden Delicious apples complete with skin (vertical motion). (b) ▲—▲ McVitie's Rich Tea biscuits (arctuate motion); △—△ McVitie's Rich Tea biscuits (vertical motion); ●—● New Zealand Cheddar cheese (arctuate motion); ○—○ New Zealand Cheddar cheese (vertical motion). (From Brennan *et al.*[16])

located on a plate which is supported on a beam fixed at one end. The probe descends on to the sample, describing an arc as it does so. The resistance offered by the sample causes the beam to deflect, the extent of which being measured by strain gauges cemented to the beam. The output from the strain gauges is processed to produce a load–time trace. Details of test procedure, of the interpretation of the traces and of some experience with this instrument have been reported.[13, 14] The action of this instrument is intended to simulate the movement of the jaw when biting down on a food sample in the mouth. A detailed study of this action was undertaken[9, 15, 16] which showed that during the early stages of each cycle stresses developed by the Texturometer probe are high compared with those developed by a probe of similar geometry descending vertically on to the sample (Fig. 6). The difference decreases as the penetration depth increases and becomes negligible when the whole cross-sectional area of the plunger is in contact with the sample.

When an incisor tooth was used as the probe tip the stress–penetration depth curves were similar to those resulting from the action of the cylindrical Texturometer probe. It was thought that this feature of the instrument might account to some extent for the good correlations between the maximum load registered by this instrument and sensory panel assessments of 'hardness' and 'firmness' of a range of foods reported in the literature.[14] A correlation study undertaken with cheese as the test food revealed no significant difference between the results obtained with the Texturometer probe and a probe moving vertically. However when the stress at a low penetration depth was used as an index of 'firmness' the probe describing the arc gave results which correlated better with sensory 'firmness' than did the probe with the vertical movement. Further work is needed to establish the value of this feature of the Texturometer. However to date there is little evidence to suggest that the results from the Texturometer traces, interpreted in the manner proposed by the inventors,[13] are more useful as indices of textural features of foods than results obtained from simpler instruments featuring vertically moving probes.

Imitative methods in general suffer from the same limitations as empirical methods in that all test conditions need to be specified, interpretation of the results can be difficult and calibration of instruments is necessary. It is felt that a truly imitative instrument which will yield results more representative of the assessment of food in the mouth must await the outcome of further research involving the masticatory process.

Fundamental Methods

These methods measure one or more well-defined physical property of the food under test. This property must then be shown to relate to some textural property as assessed sensorily. The structure of foods varies from product to product and this variation gives rise to a wide spectrum of rheological behaviour in foods. Few foods exhibit ideal behaviour and obey the simple physical laws that characterise the behaviour of inanimate materials. For these reasons many difficulties are encountered when attempting to apply a fundamental approach to texture measurement. Nevertheless many attempts have been made to do so with varying degrees of success. Some of these are discussed in the literature.[8, 17, 18]

A study of crispness and brittleness in biscuits, undertaken at the National College of Food Technology, involved the use of sensory methods and both empirical and fundamental instrumental techniques.[15, 19] Experimental work with sensory panels and interviews confirmed the view generally expressed in the literature that crispness and brittleness are important characteristics of friable foods. Tests involving a number of biscuit types demonstrated that the panelists were able to distinguish clearly between brittleness and crispness in most cases. In a certain few biscuit types one characteristic could mask the other. Agreed definitions were developed for the textural characteristics brittleness, crispness and hardness. Another definition for 'bend deformation' using the hands proved to be of little value. The characteristics of crispness and brittleness were distinguished from each other by means of the method of mastication. Crispness involved the use of the molars to assess the rate of breakdown of the samples. The rate at which large particles moved away from the front teeth on biting was the index of brittleness. In the main study five biscuit types were tested. To investigate variations within each biscuit type, samples of each were equilibrated at seven different relative humidities to introduce small changes in moisture content. Sensory tests revealed that the textural characteristic of crispness was the most sensitive in distinguishing between samples of biscuit of the same type but with different moisture contents. Significant differences between the sensory characteristics were revealed only at relatively high moisture contents. Although less sensitive than crispness, hardness also proved to be an index of moisture content and the results were more reproducible than those for crispness.

In addition to these sensory studies, samples of the five biscuit types, conditioned at seven different relative humidities, were subjected to the following series of instrumental tests: (a) a simple beam, centre load, end support, bend test, (b) a cantilever beam, end load, bend test, (c) a direct shear test, (d) a uniaxial compression test, (e) a 'bulk' compression test, (f) a uniaxial tension test, (g) a Charpy impact test and (h) an FMBRA biscuit texture meter test. The principles of tests (a)–(g) are illustrated in Fig. 7. These were adopted from procedures used for testing non-food materials of a brittle nature. In the case of each test a number of different quantities was determined directly or derived and used to characterise the samples. Test (h) involves measuring the time taken for a circular saw to cut into a stack of biscuits to a constant depth.[20]

All these results were analysed statistically for reproducibility and the ability of each method to quantify variations within each biscuit type and between biscuit types. These instrumental results were correlated with those obtained by sensory panel work. A detailed discussion of these results is beyond the scope of this paper but some general conclusions are as follows. Apart from the shear test all the instrumental tests were equally capable of quantifying within sample variations for all five types of biscuit. The instrumental results correlated best with the sensory properties hardness and crispness. The results obtained from the Charpy impact test and the FMBRA biscuit texture meter were in most cases the most reproducible and also correlated well with sensory hardness and crispness. These results suggest that these instruments could be useful as quality control tools. The results also confirmed the findings of other workers in this field that the slope of the load–deformation curve is a good index of sensory crispness in friable foods. In addition it was found that the fracture force and ultimate stress at the point of failure of the sample were good indicators of variations in sensory crispness within biscuit types that contained partly gelatinised starch/protein matrix. Attempts to relate brittleness in the biscuits to the concepts and criteria of brittleness in engineering materials using the results from the bend, tension and impact tests failed in all but one biscuit type. The crispbread sample did satisfy all the criteria for brittleness. The failure of the other biscuit types to exhibit true brittle characteristics was attributed to their structures, in particular the thinness of the cell

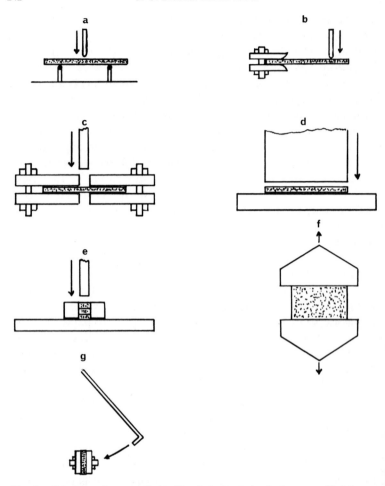

FIG. 7.   Principles of tests applied to biscuits in the study of crispness and brittleness.
(a) Centre load, end support bend test; (b) end load, end support bend test; (c) shear
test; (d) uniaxial compression test; (e) bulk compression test; (f) uniaxial tension test;
(g) Charpy impact test.

walls and the blunt, ovoidal shape of the cracks and air cells present.
Only the results from the cantilever bend test and the Charpy impact
test seemed to distinguish crispness from brittleness in the samples
and further work is necessary to develop instrumental tests to make
this distinction, established by sensory methods, as clear as possible.
    While the results of this work were not as conclusive as might have

been hoped they do serve to illustrate the difficulties as well as the advantages of the fundamental approach to texture measurement. Difficulties were encountered in designing the tests and the instruments themselves. Some of the results did not follow a clear pattern which made their interpretation difficult. On the other hand these results and those obtained from studies of the structure and chemical composition of the biscuit samples add to our knowledge of the behaviour of friable foods under stress and indicate the direction in which further work should point towards methods which will measure more accurately the textural characteristics of such foods.

GENERAL DISCUSSION

It is, after all, not surprising that, after millions of years of evolution, Man's senses have developed to such an extent that even with his unique intellect he cannot match them with his artefacts. He is nearest of all perhaps in his optical instrumentation, a little less close with his advanced analytical tools which cannot yet fully describe the flavour and aroma of foods in terms of their components. Right at the end of the line stands texture measurement, furthest of all from an adequate description of the textural sensations experienced by the consumer.

Despite useful progress in some areas such as liquid and semi-liquid foods, meat, peas and baked goods, texture measurement sometimes appears to owe as much to luck as to good judgement and this is less a reflection on the quality of research on the subject than on the complexity of the interaction between food and eater during mastication.

It was no doubt recognition of the complexity of this process which led to devices which attempted to simulate mechanically the biting or chewing action of mastication. However, it now seems clear that the operations performed on food, and the signals received by the brain as a result of them during mastication, are such that any correlation between imitative measurement of texture and sensory evaluation is probably quite coincidental and is no more capable of extrapolation or generalisation than other empirical measurements are. What is more, such instruments really teach us very little about the real nature of food texture.

Empirical instruments have proliferated mainly because of a one-to-one relationship which has emerged between the response of certain foods to the particular action of a particular instrument and a predominating physical characteristic which is largely responsible for the particular texture of such foods. Where this physical characteristic is a simple one, such as the shear resistance of meat or peas which correlates well with tenderness, then clearly the instruments deserve their place in objective texture measurement. However, when the characteristic is more complex, as it appears to be for instance in the case of crispness, one is more than a little uneasy in relying on even highly-correlating but nonetheless empirical tests such as the FMBRA biscuit texture meter for any measurements except under conditions corresponding closely to those used to calibrate the instrument.

Which leaves us with 'fundamental' measurements and the instruments and techniques for making them. It is probably no coincidence that in recent years many research and production establishments have installed materials testing machines such as the 'Instron' or the 'Ottawa' in the general trend 'back to fundamentals'.

Granted, such machines with suitable attachments can be used for many of the empirical tests established over the years for specific foods, but in the writers' view the main value of such instruments is that they do enable some basic property measurements to be made in the search for both correlation *and* explanation of sensory, texture characteristics.

Finally a word on terminology. Lord Kelvin said last century:[21] When you can measure what you are speaking about and express it in numbers, you know something about it; but when you cannot measure it, when you cannot express it in numbers, your knowledge is of a meagre and unsatisfactory kind.

This is, of course, what texture measurement is all about, but it is even worse when there is uncertainty regarding *what* one is speaking about, which can arise if a word means different things to different people or the same thing is referred to by different names by different people. This is still too often the case with food texture terminology. How the consumer describes the texture of food products is outside the control of the food technologist—even though it is of considerable interest and importance to him—but the terminology of the food texture investigator needs to be defined as explicitly as any other terminology used in science and that with careful recognition of definitions in other fields of study likely to interact with food texture work.

Perhaps there is some justification for envying colleagues concerned with the scientific study of the *appearance*—especially the colour—of foods where internationally-recognised numerical systems exist for specifying, more or less exactly, the colour, say, of a food in terms of the proportions of three primary colours and a brightness factor. Unfortunately no one has yet discovered a 'texture prism' which would enable us to separate the constituent texture components from each other but perhaps an investigation into the possible existence of 'texture primaries' might lead one to a position of being able to specify a finite number of such constituents some of which might be mutually exclusive and some of which might co-exist in the same food. They could then hopefully be measured, quantified and specified as constituting the 'texture profile' of any food. If they were also definable in objective physical terms the way to measuring the total texture characteristic of a food by instrumental means would then be open to us.

As already mentioned[3–6] some useful progress in this direction has been made but clearly there is still a long way to go.

REFERENCES

1. Jowitt, R. (1974). *J. Texture Studies*, **5,** p. 351.
2. British Standards Institution (1975). *Glossary of Terms Relating to Sensory Analysis of Food*, B.S. 5098, London.
3. Szczesniak, A. S. (1963). *J. Food Sci.*, **28,** p. 385.
4. Brandt, M. A., Skinner, E. Z. and Coleman, J. A. (1963). *J. Food Sci.*, **28,** p. 404.
5. Szczesniak, A. S., Brandt, M. A. and Friedman, H. H. (1963). *J. Food Sci.*, **28,** p. 397.
6. Sherman, P. (1969). *J. Food Sci.*, **34,** p. 458.
7. Civille, G. V. and Szczesniak, A. S. (1973). *J. Texture Studies*, **4,** p. 204.
8. Brennan, J. G. (1976). *Process Chem. Engng.*, **29,** p. 31.
9. Mughsi, O. A. (1971). Ph.D. Thesis, Nat. Coll. Food Technol., Univ. Reading.
10. Kramer, A., Aamlid, K., Guyer, R. B. and Rogers, H. (1951). *Food Engng.*, **23,** p. 112.
11. Szczesniak, A. S., Hambaugh, P. R. and Black, H. W. (1970). *J. Texture Studies*, **1,** p. 356.
12. DeMan, J. M. (1969). *Can. Inst. Food Technol. J.*, **2,** p. 76.
13. Friedman, H. H., Whitney, J. E. and Szczesniak, A. S. (1963). *J. Food Sci.*, **28,** p. 390.
14. Brennan, J. G., Mughsi, O. A. and Jowitt, R. (1970). *J. Texture Studies*, **1,** p. 167.

15. Williams, A. (1975). Ph.D. Thesis, Nat. Coll. Food Technol., Univ. Reading.
16. Brennan, J. G., Jowitt, R. and Williams, A. (1975). *J. Texture Studies*, **6**, p. 83.
17. Kramer, A. and Szczesniak, A. S. (eds.) (1973). *Texture Measurements of Foods*, D. Reidel Publishing Company, Dordrecht.
18. Mohsenin, N. N. (1970). *Physical Properties of Plant and Animal Materials*, Gordon and Breach Science Publishers, New York.
19. Brennan, J. G., Jowitt, R. and Williams, A. (1975). *Proceedings IV Int. Cong. Food Sci. Technol.*, Madrid, 1974, **2**, p. 62.
20. Francis, B. and Hastings, W. R. (1963). BBIRA Rep. No. 61, Chorleywood.
21. Thomson, *Sir* William. A Lecture: *Electrical units of measurement*, presented to Inst. C.E., 3rd May, 1883; in: *Popular Lectures and Addresses*, Vol. 1, p. 73; also in *Practical Applications of Electricity*—a series of lectures delivered at the Inst. C.E.

DISCUSSION

Ruhul Amin: Since texture is a complex term, ranging from mouthfulness to appearance, do you think several fundamental properties need to be considered to give the characteristic texture of the food? To represent the texture profile which a sensory panel may perceive, more accurately, as many as possible fundamental properties need to be considered.

Brennan: I think we all agree that texture is a complex property. We are not attempting to measure texture *per se* by one physical test. What we are saying is that it may be possible to relate one fundamental physical test to one particular attribute. A biscuit does exhibit the various criteria of brittleness and it seems reasonable that if you measure the brittleness by physical means you will show that you are also measuring sensory brittleness. But it does not always work out that way. You will not get an overall picture of texture by one physical test. You won't get it by any means except by a fairly complicated sensory assessment scheme. But, hopefully, as information builds up we will be able to identify more and more textural attributes that can be related to more clearly defined physical properties. The advantage of this is that hopefully the interpretation of results will be a little easier.

This was our approach with the biscuits. We spent months with the panels ascertaining what they considered to be the important textural attributes. We came up with crispness, brittleness and hardness as the ones they felt the most important and it was on the basis of this work that we proceeded with the instrumental tests. You always have to start with the sensory side because this is what you are measuring—the sensory properties.

Land: Do you regard the instrumental measures of texture, described as objective in your title, as being more free from bias (i.e. objective) than the sensory data on texture?

Brennan: No, we included in the paper details of our sensory methods as well. We regard them as being as objective in certain respects as the instrumental tests.

Jeffery: In sensory evaluation of texture did you use *texture profile* methods to assess overall texture?

Brennan: No, we used magnitude estimation procedures. The texture profile method is used more and more widely but there are still serious doubts as to the best way of going about it. We have used it for other purposes but we did not use it for this particular study. If we were looking for a more complete description of texture I think we would have to go for the profiling system.

Harper: Did you use the technique of principal component analysis in this work?

Brennan: No, it might be worth doing so.

Kearsley: Sample size is important in some instrumental methods of texture evaluation. Is sample size important in sensory methods of texture evaluation?

Brennan: It certainly is. It depends on the object you are talking about, on the type of food. A spoon size, for example, is important with liquids. Whether you give the panel a whole fruit or a piece of fruit obviously makes a considerable difference. Sensory tests are empirical to that extent. You have to standardise your procedure just as you have in any instrumental test.

Lee: Do you have any experience of assessing the texture of foods (which flow) by visual means?

Brennan: No, we have not done any detailed studies on this but obviously the information you get on looking at the product and handling it before you actually masticate it does contribute significantly to your assessment. We did some studies on apples where appearance did tell us a lot.

McCracken: You have indicated that sensory tests must be allied to instrumental texture measurement methods to get meaningful results from such methods. Biscuits are in a ready-to-eat form, whereas peas are subjected to, for example, tenderometer tests in their raw state as part of a QC/purchasing scheme. Are there added complications in the texture 'measurement' of raw food materials?

Brennan: When you are studying texture measurement obviously first of all you have to identify what the characteristics are you are looking for. Then you have got to set about finding the best way instrumentally of measuring those properties. The principle is the same for raw, processed or manufactured foods.

Hutchings: The difference between crispness and brittleness appears to be rather subtle. Does either of these come from a visual cue rather than a mechanical cue—can the panellists tell the difference between these attributes in the dark?

Brennan: Yes, we put them in the dark and different conditions of lighting. Under all types of conditions there were two distinct properties. Of course we started with discussions in which we gradually built up the terminology which we decided to use. They were not fed with the words—they came from them.

Knights: Has any work been done on the measurement of the forces produced by normal mastication of biscuits, since this represents the parameter which is required?

Brennan: We have not personally but there has been work done using strain gauges, etc. It is not very well defined work. We did a short study some time back, using electromyography (measuring the e.m.f. developed in the muscles during mastication) but we did not find anything very conclusive. It is a bit easier with liquid foods but difficult to establish the loads involved in biting foods.

Harries: As a contribution to the last question I would like to point out that a method of this type has been tried with meat. The chew count was at one time much used and there is a large literature on it.

Brennan: This is true and it features as one of the parameters in the profile method. I suppose chewing gum represents infinity, doesn't it, because it is never 'fit for swallowing'.

15

Aspects of Fish Texture

P. Howgate

Ministry of Agriculture, Fisheries & Food,
Torry Research Station, P.O. Box 31, 135 Abbey Road,
Aberdeen AB9 8DG, Scotland

ABSTRACT

Fish flesh is muscle tissue and basically it has a fibrous texture similar to that of mammalian and avian meats. It is, however, softer and more tender. To a large extent the differences can be accounted for by differences in morphology, protein composition and biochemistry. A wide variety of fish species, both vertebrate and invertebrate, are consumed as food around the world with an accompanying diversity of textures. These can range from the soft and tender texture of a fish like plaice to the firm, rubberiness of squid. Even within a species texture can vary depending on biological factors of which nutritional status is most important. The pH of fish muscle has an important influence on its texture.

Fish is generally not as stable to some processing procedures as are other meats and texture is often adversely affected. During frozen storage under unsuitable conditions the flesh becomes tough, dry and stringy. Dried fish does not readily resorb water and the rehydrated product is tough and fibrous.

A texture profile procedure has been used to study the texture of fish and fish products. The attributes of firmness, elasticity, fibrousness, toughness and succulence are scored on an intensity scale. Factor analysis demonstrates that most of the variance between samples can be accounted for by two new factors, one related to the mechanical properties of firmness, elasticity and toughness, the other to fibrousness and succulence.

249

INTRODUCTION

Fish is consumed mostly for its flesh though other organs such as gonads are less commonly eaten. The flesh is the muscle tissue of the animal hence its basic properties are similar to those of the other important flesh foods, meat and poultry. It is inevitable then in this review of fish texture that I shall be drawn into making comparisons with the texture of these other commodities. But before discussing the texture of fish in detail I would like to spend a little time in describing various features of the fish catching and processing industry and particularly in highlighting the ways fish and meat differ as food commodities.

Fish as Food

The world catch of aquatic animals, excluding whales, seals and other warm-blooded species, is about 70×10^6 tons of which 50 $\times 10^6$ tons are used directly for human food; the remainder is converted into animal feed.[1] In comparison the world production of meat and poultry is more than double that—about 115×10^6 tons. Thus, globally, aquatic animals are not as important a source of flesh food as are the other two commodities but these overall figures obscure a wide disparity in their relative importance among various communities. In many developing countries, particularly in South-East Asia, and in some advanced countries—Japan is an example—aquatic products are a major, if not the main, source of animal protein. In countries with high standards of living fish is nutritionally of lesser importance and often its role is as an alternative to meat and poultry in providing variety in the diet.

Probably a few hundred different species of aquatic animals, vertebrate and invertebrate, are consumed as food throughout the world though there does not appear to be a comprehensive list. In Britain alone nearly fifty species or groups of closely-related species are separately listed in official returns of marine catches.[2] This is in sharp contrast to the meat and poultry industries where only a few species are utilised to any extent. This situation arises from the fact that, on the whole, fish is caught in the wild state; so far as fishing is concerned man is still predominantly an opportunist hunter and gatherer. About 10% of the world catch of vertebrate species comes from fresh water and a substantial proportion of this is farmed or cultivated; some bivalve shellfish are also farmed. Even so, probably more than 95 % of the world production of aquatic food animals is caught in the wild state.

Virtually all the species harvested are suitable for human food—only a few are unpalatable or unwholesome—and the limit to what is used as food is set more by considerations of processability than of edibility. This means that the sensory properties of fish and fish products encompass a wide range.

About 90 % of the world catch consists of vertebrate species, sometimes referred to as fin-fish to distinguish them from the remaining 10 %, the invertebrate species. Though the latter are only a small proportion of the total they have a relatively higher economic importance as they include some of the luxury seafoods such as lobsters, crabs, squid, oysters and clams with high unit value. In this review though I shall be mainly concerned with the texture of vertebrate fish and unless it is evident from the context the word 'fish' will refer to this group.

Another consequence of fish being caught and not farmed is that the processor has very little control over its intrinsic quality. In practice, the only control that can be exercised is for the fisherman to be selective as to where and when he catches the fish. As a consequence fish and fish products even from a single species can be variable due to a number of biological factors many of which are seasonal. Nevertheless a fish fillet is very homogeneous in its properties and except for a very few instances, there is no equivalence in the fish processing industry to the butchering into cuts with different culinary properties as exists in the meat industry.

The Importance of Texture to the Acceptability of Fish

Cooked fish can exhibit quite a wide range of textural properties but generally it is soft, tender, juicy and somewhat fibrous. There have been few published surveys of the factors that influence the acceptability of fish but it seems that texture is not an important determinant compared with flavour and, possibly, appearance. Szczesniak[3] studied the awareness of adults to various food attributes including texture; fish was not amongst those foods eliciting a large number of texture responses whereas meat was. Rasekh *et al.*[4] concluded from an investigation of the sensory properties of canned tuna that consumer preference was weighted about 40 % each towards appearance and flavour and 20 % for texture. Connell and Howgate[5] also found that the hedonic rating of cod of various qualities was more influenced by flavour than texture.

This is not to say that texture by itself is never a limiting factor in consumer acceptability. The comment I have just made that texture is not an important factor in the acceptability of fish products applies to normal fish as it reaches the consumer. Certain biological factors are known to cause unusual textural conditions that would certainly be unacceptable to the consumer but such samples would be screened out during the normal quality control procedures in the factory. Also, some processing operations affect fish texture and if not properly controlled will result in an unacceptable product.

FACTORS INFLUENCING THE TEXTURE OF POST-RIGOR, UNPROCESSED MUSCLE

Fish is a perishable commodity and it is almost invariably stored in ice or at chill temperatures before sale or further processing and during distribution. This section deals with those intrinsic properties of fish that could influence the texture of fish as it commonly reaches the consumer, that is, after a few days in ice, when rigor has resolved but before appreciable bacterial spoilage has occurred. Processing may then have a further effect.

Structure

The structure of fish muscle has recently been reviewed. The trunk muscle is divided into segments, the myotomes, separated by sheets of connective tissue. The fibres extend across the width of a myotome and are inserted into the sheets of connective tissue. This segmental structure is well seen in cooked fish fillets and gives rise to its flaky appearance. The fibres are short, generally less than 20 mm long, depending to a large extent on the size of the fish. Their diameters are variable in the range 0·02–1·0 mm,[7] a little larger on average than those in meat.

The microscopical structure of the fibres is typical of striated, voluntary muscle and basically is not different from that in meat animals.[6] What small differences exist I do not think would account for the differences in texture between fish and meat.

Protein Composition

The protein content of fish is very variable but is around 16 % of the wet weight; the variations are the subject of a later section. The stroma fraction is about 3 % of the total protein in most species of fish though in some it can rise to 10 %.[8] The collagen of fish from temperate waters is very labile and at rates of heating encountered during normal cooking, gelatinises at around 35 °C;[9] collagen of fish from tropical waters is more stable. Connective tissue proteins have long been considered to have an important influence on the texture of meat (though I gather this view is not quite so strongly held now as it was)[10] but it is unlikely they make a very significant contribution to the texture of fish.

Biological Variation Within Species

There is a considerable within-species variation in texture that arises from many sources. Apart from variation among individuals within a group there are general differences among stocks from separate fishing grounds and there are seasonal effects that are cyclic within a year. A major reason for these effects seems to lie in differences in nutritional status. In temperate waters the availability of food varies with the season, relatively abundant from late spring to early autumn, scarce during the rest of the year. As food becomes scarce a fish is able to mobilise lipid reserves in the liver as fuel but when these are depleted tissue protein will be mobilised instead. In addition, towards the end of the winter, an adult fish will be building up gonads which can occur only at the expense of muscle tissue if food is not available. As a consequence of these factors fish in late winter and early spring are in an emaciated condition, thin and flabby, and the flesh has a low protein content and high water content. Fish in poor condition like this tend to have soft, almost sloppy textures compared with the firm, dry textures of well-fed fish.

The texture of fish flesh is known to be strongly influenced by its pH.[11-16] This factor alone probably accounts for almost all the variations in texture between individual fish within a species. The pH of the post-rigor muscle is dependent on the muscle glycogen content in the living animal. During the death struggle and subsequent rigor mortis, the glycogen is converted to lactic acid which accumulates in the tissue. The glycogen content is very variable and is affected by nutritional status hence the ultimate, post-rigor pH is also variable and shows a seasonal fluctuation.[13,16]

Fish with a low pH have a firm, dry, somewhat tough texture, those with a high pH are soft, juicy and very tender. A similar effect of pH on texture has been described for beef and mutton.[17,18] In beef the pH of post-rigor meat is about 5·5 compared with an average value of around 6·7 for cod. Cod flesh is softer and more tender than beef and it is conceivable that much of this difference is in fact due to the difference in pH. Unfortunately there does not seem to be on record the results of an experiment where a panel has assessed both meat and fish on the same texture scale. Connell and Howgate using a sensory scale ranging from 0 = soft to 5 = very tough found that a unit increase in pH was associated with a decrease of 1·8 units in toughness of cod and haddock. Bouton *et al.*[18] using a toughness scale ranging from 0 = very tender to 9 = very tough, i.e. about twice the length of that used by the former workers, found that a unit change in pH was associated with a change of approximately 4 units in texture score of beef. This similarity in regression coefficients after allowing for scale lengths is quite striking and suggests that the pH/texture relationships are basically similar. Of course, the large assumption has been made that the two panels are using the scale descriptions in the same absolute way and not relative to the material being tested.

Though pH has an important influence on texture it is unlikely to be the only one. Love *et al.*[16] have investigated the effects of some of the other biological factors. They studied fish from several fishing grounds caught at different seasons and measured protein content and water content as well as pH. These variables are highly intercorrelated as they are all affected by nutritional status. Low protein content which one would expect to give rise to a soft texture is associated with high water content and high pH. They used a multiple regression approach to resolve the separate effects of the variables on texture and found that the variation in pH accounted for most of the variance in toughness amongst the samples. After allowing for this there was a small effect of water content. They also found a small effect of size, the larger fish being tougher. Since size is related to age there is an obvious analogy here with the age effect in meat animals.

The conclusion that texture is only little influenced by depletion of tissue protein is true within a fairly narrow range of water contents. In some species the depletion is so severe that texture is considerably affected. Catfish and Greenland halibut are particularly prone to this condition in which the protein content can drop to less than 10 %. The flesh is translucent in appearance with a soft, jelly-like consistency—in fact such fish are referred to as being 'jellied'.[19] When cooked the texture is soft and mushy and the fibrous character is largely lost. Such fish are unpleasant to eat and when severely affected are quite revolting.

Biological Variation Among Species

Taking all species into account, vertebrate and invertebrate, aquatic animals present a wide range of textures. Cod is typical of vertebrate fish with a soft, tender, juicy and fairly-fibrous texture. Small flatfish like plaice and sole are soft, somewhat dry and with shorter fibres than cod; larger flatfish like halibut and turbot are firm, drier still and more fibrous. Some fish, tuna is an example, are quite firm and tough and their texture is more like meat than the generality of fish. Probably much of the difference amongst species can be attributed to the pH effect—it is known, for example, that halibut and tuna can have muscle pHs below 6·0—but protein content and connective tissue content must also exert their influences. Unfortunately, though the association between texture and composition and pH is known in a general way there is little quantitative evidence available to make a firm assessment.

Some species of fish like herring and mackerel can have large amounts of free triglyceride lipids in the flesh, perhaps as much as 30%. The concentration is dependent on season and as the lipid content increases the water content decreases, the sum of the two tending to remain approximately constant. When the lipid content is high the texture of such fish is softer than when it is low.

There are major differences in texture between vertebrates and invertebrates and among invertebrates as a class that can be attributed to structural factors. Thus the white meat of decapod crustacea like crabs and lobsters is generally very firm and fibrous compared with vertebrate species even though the protein content is about the same and the pH usually higher. The diameters of the muscle fibres in these species are larger than those in vertebrate fish, a feature that will contribute to the fibrous character. The microscopical structure of the fibres is very similar to that in vertebrate striated muscle though there is a greater variation in sarcomere length; some fibres have sarcomeres up to $12\,\mu$m long compared with $2\,\mu$m in vertebrates.[20] Whether or not this feature has an effect on texture must be a matter for speculation.

Squid muscle has a firm, smooth, slightly tough and rubbery texture which is welcomed in some communities and disliked in others. The muscle has a fibrous structure though this is not obvious to the eye in the raw state and not readily discernible in the cooked state. The contractile elements of the fibre consist of interdigitating thick and thin filaments similar to the situation in voluntary muscle but they are not arranged in sarcomeres delimited by Z-bands[6] as they are in cross-striated muscle. The relationship between structure and texture in this class of animal is rather obscure.

The soft parts of bivalve shellfish like clams, mussels and oysters and of gastropod molluscs like whelks are usually eaten entire but sometimes the muscular part is separated and consumed by itself. This muscle tissue is firm and somewhat rubbery. Structurally, it consists mainly of smooth muscle and contains the unusual protein, paramyosin. Once again, the relationship between structure and texture is obscure.

SOME EFFECTS OF HANDLING AND PROCESSING

Rigor Mortis

Fish are usually gutted soon after catching and stowed in melting ice. Under these conditions cod, for example, will go into rigor within 2–8 h and resolution will be complete within 2 days. Normally fish go through rigor 'on the bone' and there is no overall shortening of the muscle. However, if a fillet is cut off the fish before the onset of rigor and left unrestrained it will contract during rigor. The degree of shortening depends on the glycogen content of the muscle and also on the temperature. A fillet from a well-fed rested fish held at room temperature can contract by 40 % of its resting length. Such a fillet is firm to the touch and when cooked initially has a soft texture but the bolus formed after chewing a few times is tough and rubbery. If a pre-rigor fillet is cooked it suffers a powerful contracture which results in a dry, soft and crumbly texture. It is likely that the contraction has broken the fibres into short compacted segments.

A similar phenomenon is well known in the meat industry.[21] When a muscle is allowed to contract during rigor mortis it is tougher than its counterpart that has been restrained. The degree of toughening is inversely related to sarcomere length[10] though Bouton *et al.*[22] showed that the effect was considerably diminished at pH 6·5, the usual pH of fish flesh. Reminiscent of the effect of cooking pre-rigor fillets, when beef muscle contracts considerably the texture is softer than normal.[10]

The effect of rigor contraction on texture of fish has been known for a long time. A technique called 'crimping'[23] was practised in the 17th and 18th century and possibly later whereby newly caught fish were slashed through to the bone by several transverse cuts. Sometimes the fish were then soaked in water, a process that is now known to accelerate rigor in fillets. Since fish were not held in ice in those times a strong rigor contraction would ensue and the flesh between the cuts would contract. This is reported to give the fish a firm texture. Fish crimped in this way is often illustrated in drawings and paintings of fishmongers' shops of the 18th century. Some paintings also show flatfish restrained into a curve with head and tail tied together. Presumably the intention was for the fish to go into and pass through rigor in this state. One would then expect the inner side to be tough due to shortening and the outer to be comparatively tender. Love[24] carried out an experiment with cod where he allowed bent fish to go through rigor in ice, but a panel using a triangle test procedure could not detect a difference in texture between the inner and outer fillets. Perhaps if the experiment were repeated with rested fish at ambient temperatures an effect would be demonstrated.

Rigor contraction is a problem with fish frozen at sea. If the fillet is removed and frozen before the onset of rigor it will contract as it thaws. Such fillets have a tough and rubbery texture when cooked. If the fillets are frozen into a block and the block is thawed slowly, rigor occurs before thawing is complete and when the block still has structural rigidity. The fillets then do not contract and have a normal texture.

Icing

On further storage of fish after resolution of rigor mortis the texture softens. This is noticeable in raw fish which is firm and elastic to the touch when fresh but soft and plastic when stale. After cooking, stale fish is softer and more tender than fresh. During staling and particularly when bacterial spoilage is active, the pH rises as basic compounds like trimethylamine and ammonia are formed. For example, in cod and haddock, the pH can only rise by 0·5 units during storage for 14 days at 0 °C. This in itself will cause a marked softening without taking into account any possible proteolytic breakdown of structural proteins. In fact it is difficult to detect any proteolysis during storage up to the point where fish is still acceptable. There is considerable between-samples and within-sample variance in the free amino acid content of fish flesh and the results of free amino acid determinations to detect proteolysis have not been conclusive.

Storage in the Frozen State

Fish is less stable during frozen storage than meat. Because of this bulk cold stores intended for holding fish for long periods must be held at $-30\,°C$ whereas $-18\,°C$ is adequate for meat. At $-18\,°C$ most varieties of fish would be unacceptable within 3 months. Changes in appearance and flavour occur during frozen storage which adversely affect quality but texture changes are also important and can be a limiting factor in determining acceptability.

These textural changes can be detected in the raw state after thawing. Thus the flesh of a badly-stored fish is firm to the touch and if a fillet is held horizontally it will stand out somewhat stiffly whereas a fillet from a fish stored under good conditions will hang limply. Also the water holding capacity is reduced during storage under poor conditions and much fluid can be expressed from the fillet by manual pressure. Badly-stored fish after thawing and cooking has a firm, tough, dry and very fibrous texture.

These effects are progressive during storage and the rate of deterioration is very temperature dependent.[12,13] At temperatures around $-30\,°C$ the rate is very slow and the changes are hardly noticeable over the period of time that a processor would want to hold frozen stocks. Cowie and Little[25] have pointed out that for cod stored at $-29\,°C$ the effects of pH are much greater than those of storage.

Some slight firming of the texture of high pH fish could be an advantage. Kelly[26] found that the texture of unfrozen cod was most acceptable at pH $6·6$ but fell above and below that value. During storage at $-7\,°C$, samples at all pH values increased in toughness. Those at pH values below $6·6$ actually improved in texture up to the level equivalent to wet fish at pH $6·6$. It also follows from this that fish of low pH have a shorter potential shelf life in the frozen state than those of high pH if texture is the sole criterion of quality.

The increase in toughness and the other changes occurring during frozen storage are usually attributed to alterations in the myofibrillar proteins; the subject has been comprehensively reviewed recently.[27] There is no doubt that reactions associated with protein 'denaturation'—for example, loss of extractability, loss of enzyme activity and reduction in water-holding capacity—do accompany toughening in the frozen state but I do not believe there has yet been a convincing explanation of how these effects are linked with changes in rheological properties. Denaturation of itself does not cause toughening—after all, fish protein is denatured on cooking—and formation of protein cross-linkages have to be invoked to explain the mechanical properties of toughened muscle.

The microscopical structure of fish muscle is also affected by frozen storage under adverse conditions.[6,28] In particular the sarcoplasmic reticulum degrades and appears to act like a cement holding the individual myofibrils together. This phenomenon could contribute significantly to the textural change in frozen-stored fish.

Drying

Drying as a method of preserving fish for long-term storage has been practised since ancient times. In technologically-advanced countries it has given way to frozen storage but is still important in many developing countries. The traditional method is to expose the fish, often split in order to increase its surface area, to sun and wind. The more technologically-advanced process is to dry the fish in a current of warm air in a kiln. Freeze-drying has been investigated but is not used commercially at present.

Air-dried fish is hard and compact in the dried state. It does not rehydrate well and will resorb only about half the water lost during drying.[29] The cooked product is firm, tough and dry though still highly acceptable in many communities. Freeze-dried fish retains its original volume after drying and will resorb virtually all the water lost during dehydration though much of this is only loosely held and can be easily expressed on squeezing.[30] Its texture is rather firm, tough and dry but not to the same extent as air-dried fish.

The sensory properties of reconstituted dried fish have not been studied to any great extent and little is known in a quantitative way of the factors that influence them. It is known that the pH of the reconstituting medium has an effect on the swelling of the flesh and the uptake of water. The Norwegian product 'lütefisk' is prepared by soaking dried fish in dilute alkali. It fully rehydrates to a firm but gelatinous product having a soft, tender texture when cooked. One sample that I have tasted was extremely soft and gelatinous. It had a pH of 10·3 and a water content of 94 %! The proteins of fish flesh are very much altered by dehydration and lose their extractability, enzyme activity and water binding properties.[29-32] The changes resemble those of frozen fish stored under adverse conditions but the damage is even more extreme. Connell[30,32] has discussed these protein changes and the role they play in modifying texture.

Mincing

Fish is commonly filleted and the fillets are sold to the consumer or converted into other consumer products like fish fingers or fish portions. Somewhere in the region of 30–40 % of the original weight of fish can be obtained as a fillet but an additional 10–15 % of flesh is left on the skeleton or in the trimmings. There has been a move in the fish processing industry towards the recovery of this flesh by using bone separators originally developed for the meat and poultry industry. Some of these separators recover the meat in a finely divided form almost like a puree but the one most commonly used in Europe is the machine made by Baader. In this machine the material being treated—skeleton, trimmings, dressed carcase—is nipped between a revolving perforated drum and a moving rubber belt. The flesh is squeezed through the perforations and is recovered, the bones and skin being rejected. The product retains much of the fibrous texture of the original flesh and looks like mince. There are some textural problems associated with this process.[33]

If skeletons are used as the raw material the cooked mince has a soft, gelatinous texture. It is likely that this is due to the presence of a high proportion of gelatine arising from the large amount of connective tissue scraped off the skeleton. If fillets are passed through the machine the mince is slightly firmer, tougher and drier than the original intact flesh. This difference is noticeable immediately after preparation without any intermediate storage.

MEASUREMENT OF TEXTURE

Sensory Methods

The texture of fish and fish products is often measured by scalar methods though other tests are used such as just-noticeable difference. The most common scales have been based on the continua tender–tough, soft–firm and dry–juicy. Though these scales have proved useful in quantifying the effects of intrinsic factors like pH and of processing methods like frozen storage they do not give a complete picture of the texture of a product. For example, a fish with a low pH but not frozen may have the same sensory score on a toughness scale as a fish of high pH which has suffered some frozen storage deterioration. An experienced assessor though, can distinguish between their textures from other clues. To overcome this problem additional scales for textural characteristics must be used to form a texture profile of a product.

Harries *et al.*[34] have described a texture profile for beef, Frijters[35] one for chicken and Webb *et al.*[36] one for shrimp. Sorensen[37] used a texture profile approach in his study of the texture of minced cod flesh.

Table 1 shows the profile scheme I have used to investigate the texture of fish and fish products. The scheme is provisional and will certainly be amended in the light of experience.

Like the profile of Harries *et al.*[34] it distinguishes the initial impression of texture on the first few bites from the characteristics after chewing. The words for the texture variables and those used for defining the extremes of the scales are taken from the glossary compiled by Jowitt.[38]

A small panel of 4 assessors was trained to evaluate the texture of fish and fish products with this profile. Three sets of products were examined. Set 1 consisted of 17 different species of fish caught in the North Sea off Aberdeen. They were frozen after 2–3 days in ice and held at $-30\,°C$ for up to 4 months until they could be evaluated by the panel. At this temperature storage effects are negligible and the texture would be typical of good quality, post-rigor fish. Set 2 was part of a project on the production of minced flesh and consisted of mince obtained by extruding cod fillet through a plate with holes of 3, 5 or 7 mm. Untreated cod fillet was included as a control. Set 3 was designed to compare the effects of frozen storage and consisted of cod and haddock frozen and stored under a variety of conditions to give a range of textural properties.

The results of profile analysis are not simple to evaluate and multivariate methods are often used to reduce the data. Harries *et al.*[34] and Frijters[35] used principal component analysis; I have used the closely related method of factor analysis. The analysis was carried out on an IBM 1130 computer using a library program.

One of the aims of principal component and factor analysis is to reduce the original number of variables to a smaller number of components or factors without too much distortion of the relationship between the original variables or too much loss of information. Harries *et al.*[34] found that two new components adequately explained most of the variation between samples of beef,

TABLE 1
Provisional texture profile for fish products

Initial characteristics
Response to the properties of the material on the first few bites.

Wetness: The release of water on compression. This is the initial
response and is to be distinguished from succulence.
0—no water released but not necessarily dry
5—wet, sample releases water very readily

Firmness: The force required to bite into the material
0—very soft, very easily compressed
5—firm, high resistance to compression

Springiness: The ability of the material to return to its original
shape after deformation.
0—completely plastic, retains its deformed state
5—springy, returns to its original shape

Secondary characteristics
Response to the properties of the material after chewing a few times.

Fibrousness: Property of separating into filamentous structural
elements.
0—not fibrous
1—short fibres, almost mealy
5—long fibres

Toughness: Resistance to breakdown on chewing to a state
suitable for swallowing.
0—very tender, very easily broken down
10—very tough, needs chewing for a long time

Succulence: The sensation of juiciness in the mouth.
0—very dry, tends to reduce the moisture in the mouth
5—succulent, juicy, tends to increase the moisture
in the mouth

---

while Frijters' data required 3 components. Table 2 shows the results of factor analysis on the 3 sets of fish data. In each case the original 6 variables are reduced to two new factors while still accounting for a very high proportion of the original variance. It must be emphasised that the new factors are none of the original variables and factors in one set are not identical with factors in another. Table 2 lists the loadings of the original variables on the new factors, that is, the correlations between them, after orthogonal rotation. There is an implicit assumption behind the use of factor analysis that the original set of variables is a more complex expression of a simpler underlying structure and the analysis is an attempt to extract this structure. It appears from the results shown in the table that there is a simpler structure in each case but it is not the same for each set of products.

The variables firmness, springiness and toughness are highly correlated with factor 1 in all 3 sets of data. One intuitively feels that these 3 parameters are really manifestations of a single structural property and the panel is expressing what is really a single stimulus in

TABLE 2

Loadings of original six variables on two new factors following factor analysis of texture profile data from three sets of data

	Data set[a]					
	1 Factor		2 Factor		3 Factor	
	1	2	1	2	1	2
Wetness	−0·49	0·65	−0·10	−0·33	−0·05	0·71
Firmness	−0·94	0·19	−0·88	−0·36	−0·98	0·09
Springiness	−0·93	−0·03	−0·70	−0·04	−0·85	0·28
Fibrousness	−0·83	−0·36	−0·05	0·84	−0·65	0·57
Toughness	−0·97	−0·16	−0·85	0·15	−0·93	0·30
Succulence	0·01	−0·43	0·55	0·31	0·72	0·38
Cumulative % of total variance	87	99	70	88	77	97

[a] Set 1: 17 different species of fish.
  Set 2: extruded cod mince.
  Set 3: frozen-stored cod and haddock.

different ways. If this is so then the sensory scores for the variables will be highly intercorrelated and will be loaded onto the same factor. This factor can then be considered a 'mechanical' factor. Both Harries and co-workers and Frijters found that their factor 1, the one accounting for most of the variance, was related to mechanical variables. Factor 2 does not exhibit such a pronounced single character but there is a tendency for it to be related to the succulence, wetness and fibrousness variables. As pointed out earlier, frozen fish loses its water-holding capacity and fluid is more readily expressed under pressure. This effect is measured by the wetness variable which in the case of data from set 3—frozen stored fish—has a wide range of values. This variable is distinguishing between the various samples independently of the mechanical variables and loads strongly on factor 2 only.

Similarly, fibrousness as might be expected, discriminates amongst the minced samples—data set 2—independently of the mechanical variables, and loads onto the second factor only.

Other patterns can be extracted from the results but I am reluctant to attach too much significance to them in explaining basic features of the texture of these products. I am not sure that the profile I have used adequately distinguishes between and defines the critical sensory attributes that discriminate amongst the textures of a wide range of fish products. For example I do not consider that only one variable, fibrousness, fully describes the particle character and structure of fish products; very likely a cohesiveness factor is required as well.

In spite of these reservations the results do indicate that the texture profile method is potentially capable of providing a deeper insight into the texture of fish.

Non-sensory Methods

In contrast to the situation in the meat industry there are few reports of the use of instrumental methods for measuring the texture of fish. In order to measure the texture of crab products Dassow et al.[39] built an instrument which is similar to the Kramer shear press in its operation. Sutton and Main[40] and Main et al.[41] have described a penetrometer-type instrument for assessing the toughness of cooked fish. The force required to press a plunger a fixed distance into a block of fish is measured. They report that it correlates well with sensory measures of toughness.

These two machines were designed specifically for fish products; other workers have used universal testing machines. Dyer and Hiltz[42] measured the compressibility of scallop muscle with an Instron instrument but found that the values did not correlate well with sensory scores. Bosund and Beckemann[15] however, using the Kramer shear press in the Instron obtained good correlation between maximum force and sensory scores for toughness.

Love and Muslemuddin[43] have designed a test for toughness of frozen fish in which a small sample of fibres is blended under standard conditions and the transmittance of the resulting suspension measured. As the fibres become tougher during storage they are more difficult to break down and the suspension is clearer hence an increase in transmittance is associated with increased toughness. This test does measure some rheological property of the fibres but is only indirectly related to texture as assessed by sensory methods.

SUMMARY AND DISCUSSION

Considering all types of normal, post-rigor fish that has not suffered any processing damage, the major determinant of toughness is pH. It is not difficult to see the reason for this. As the pH of a protein deviates from the isoelectric point, about pH 5·6 for myofibrillar proteins, the charge on the molecule increases. The filaments will therefore carry an increased charge and they would be expected to repel each other with increased force. This should tend to loosen the structure and soften the texture. Rome[44] measured the inter-filament spacing of glycerinated muscle fibres by X-ray diffraction and found that the interfilament spacing did increase with pH, supporting this idea, but the findings do not seem to have been confirmed in untreated muscle. Other biological factors do affect texture but these effects are small compared with pH unless the muscle tissue has been severely depleted by starvation.

The texture of fish is modified by normal processing methods like drying, frozen storage and mincing. The reactions leading to these changes are not clearly understood. It is known that the constituent proteins are altered in a number of ways and that there are changes in the structure but the relative importances of these to the textural properties of fish products is still a matter for debate.

Some of the factors that are known to influence meat texture such as pH and rigor-mortis contraction are also known to influence fish texture. I believe a closer collaboration between meat scientists and their counterparts in the field of fisheries technology would be beneficial to both sides. Far more is known about the texture of meat and the factors that affect it than is known about the texture of fish—a glance at the contents of food science and related journals will reveal this—but I am sure there are aspects of the latter that are relevant to an understanding of the former. It would be particularly interesting to have a texture profile panel assess both fish and meat to determine if the textures of both commodities lie on the same continua and differ only quantitatively or whether there is a distinct qualitative difference. I believe the former is more likely.

REFERENCES

1. FAO (1976). *The State of Food and Agriculture* 1975. FAO, Rome.
2. Ministry of Agriculture, Fisheries and Food (1976). *Sea Fisheries Statistics*, HMSO, London.

3. Szczesniak, A. S. (1971). J. Texture Studies, 2, p. 196.
4. Rasekh, J., Kramer, A. and Finch, R. (1970). J. Fd Sci., 35, p. 417.
5. Connell, J. J. and Howgate, P. F. (1971). In: Fish Inspection and Quality Control, ed. R. Kreuzer, Fishing News (Books) Ltd, London, p. 155.
6. Howgate, P. (in preparation). In: Microscopy of Food, ed. J. C. Vaughan, Academic Press, London.
7. Love, R. M. (1958). J. Sci. Fd. Agric., 4, p. 195.
8. Hamoir, G. (1955). Adv. Protein Chem., 10, p. 227.
9. Aitken, A. and Connell, J. J. (in preparation). In: Physical and Chemical Effects of Heat on Foodstuffs, ed. R. J. Priestley, Applied Science Publishers, London.
10. Harris, P. V. (1976). J. Texture Studies, 7, p. 49.
11. Kelly, K. O., Jones, N. R., Love, R. M. and Olley, J. (1966). J. Fd. Technol., 1, p. 9.
12. Connell, J. J. and Howgate, P. (1968). J. Sci. Fd. Agric., 19, p. 342.
13. Connell, J. J. and Howgate, P. (1969). J. Sci. Fd. Agric., 20, p. 469.
14. Ahmed, E. M., Koburger, J. A. and Mendenhall, V. T. (1972). J. Texture Studies, 3, p. 186.
15. Bosund, I. and Beckemann, M. (1972). Bull. Int. Inst. Refrigeration, Annexe, 1972–2, p. 29.
16. Love, R. M., Robertson, I., Smith, G. L. and Whittle, K. J. (1974). J. Texture Studies, 3, p. 186.
17. Bouton, P. E., Harris, P. V. and Shorthose, W. R. (1971). J. Fd Sci., 36, p. 435.
18. Bouton, P. E., Carroll, F. D., Fisher, A. L., Harris, P. V. and Shorthose, W. R. (1973). J. Fd. Sci., 38, p. 816.
19. Connell, J. J. (1975). Control of Fish Quality. Fishing News (Books) Ltd, London.
20. Atwood, A. L. (1972). In: Structure and Function of Muscle, ed. G. H. Bourne, 2nd edn., p. 421. Academic Press, London and New York.
21. Newbold, R. P. and Harris, P. V. (1972). J. Fd. Sci., 37, p. 337.
22. Bouton, P. E., Carroll, F. D., Harris, P. V. and Shorthose, W. R. (1973). J. Fd Sci., 38, p. 404.
23. In The Shorter Oxford English Dictionary (1944), ed. C. T. Onions, 3rd edn. Oxford University Press, London.
24. Love, R. M. (1966). J. Fd. Technol., 1, p. 137.
25. Cowie, W. P. and Little, W. T. (1966). J. Fd. Technol., 1, p. 335.
26. Kelly, T. R. (1969). J. Fd Technol., 4, p. 95.
27. Sikorski, Z., Olley, J. and Kostuch, S. (1976). CRC Crit. Rev. Fd Sci. Nutr., 8, p. 97.
28. Love, R. M. (1968). In: Rheology and Texture of Foodstuffs. Monograph 27, p. 120. Society of Chemical Industry, London.
29. Kanna, K., Tanaka, T., Kakuda, K. and Shimizu, T. (1971). Bull. Tokai Reg. Fish. Res. Lab., No. 68, p. 51.
30. Connell, J. J. (1962). In: Freeze-Drying of Foods, ed. F. R. Fisher, National Academy of Sciences–National Research Council, Washington, USA, p. 50.
31. Connell, J. J. (1957). J. Sci. Fd. Agric., 8, p. 526.

32. Connell, J. J. (1958). In: *Fundamental Aspects of the Dehydration of Foodstuffs.* Society of Chemical Industry, London, p. 167.
33. Howgate, P. (1976). In: Proc. Conf. *The Production and Utilisation of Mechanically Recovered Fish Flesh (Minced Fish),* ed. J. N. Keay, Torry Research Station, Aberdeen, Scotland, p. 49.
34. Harries, J. M., Rhodes, D. N. and Chrystall, B. B. (1972). *J. Texture Studies,* **3**, p. 101.
35. Frijters, J. E. R. (1976). *Poultry Sci.,* **55**, p. 229.
36. Webb, N. B., Howell, A. J., Barbour, B. C., Monroe, R. and Hamann, D. D. (1975). *J. Fd. Sci.,* **40**, p. 322.
37. Sorensen, T. (1976). In: Proc. Conf. *The Production and Utilisation of Mechanically Recovered Fish Flesh (Minced Flesh),* ed. J. N. Keay, Torry Research Station, Aberdeen, Scotland, p. 56.
38. Jowitt, R. (1974). *J. Texture Studies,* **5**, p. 351.
39. Dassow, J. A., McKee, L. G. and Nelson, R. W. (1962). *Fd. Technol.,* **16**(3), p. 108.
40. Sutton, A. H. and Main, G. (1967). In: *Freezing and Irradiation of Fish.* Fishing News (Books) Ltd, London, p. 371.
41. Main, G., Ross, R. I. and Sutton, A. H. (1972). *Lab. Practice,* **21**, p. 185.
42. Dyer, W. J. and Hiltz, D. F. (1974). *Bull. Jap. Soc. Sci. Fish.,* **40**, p. 235.
43. Love, R. M. and Muslemuddin, M. (1972). *J. Sci. Fd Agric.,* **23**, p. 1239.
44. Rome, E. (1967). *J. Molec. Biol.,* **29**, p. 591.

DISCUSSION

McCracken: Are the fish used in compiling the data in Section 1 frozen-at-sea fish or fish kept in ice? Would you expect different results depending on the treatment given?

Howgate: The treatment of the fish used in experiment 1 is described in more detail in the full text of the paper. The important point is that the samples represent good quality fish, not affected to any noticeable extent by processing. Differences amongst the samples can be attributed to species effects. Processing does affect texture but as the factor analysis loadings shown in the table [Table 2] demonstrate, the various textural attributes are affected to different extents depending on the type of processing.

Palmer: Concerning the last slide on factor analysis of fish texture, what does percentage variance refer to? Different results obtained by the panel on (i) cooked fish and (ii) minced fish are to be expected because the texture has been altered by the mincing.

Howgate: Strictly speaking, in the jargon of factor analysis, it is the per cent of the trace accounted for by each factor. It represents the .

percentage of the total variance amongst the samples that can be accounted for by each new factor. All the samples are cooked before presentation to the panel. Data set 1 is derived from fish that had not been processed other than holding for a few days in ice and storage at $-30\,°C$ for a few weeks, conditions I would expect to have little effect on texture. Mincing does affect texture and this is seen in the factor loadings shown in the table. In the first data set fibrousness is not very variable among the samples and does not differentiate amongst them. In fish minced under different conditions there is a much wider range in the fibrous attribute and this does discriminate amongst the various treatments, independently of other variables.

Palmer: Is there a difference between rigor effects on fish (cod) compared to crustaceans (prawns) because the latter is successfully commercially freeze-dried in comparison with the former?

Howgate: The texture of cod is very much affected by dehydration, even under good conditions. I have no personal experience of dried prawns but I do know they are used in some dehydrated meals. Why they should be more resistant to the deleterious effects of drying I do not know. We do not know the basic causes of toughening of dried fish. Prawns generally have a firmer, tougher texture than cod and there must be some fundamental difference in structure or protein properties between the two species to account for this. It is possible that these differences are also related to stability and to the effects of dehydration. I do not think differences in rigor effects have a bearing on this phenomenon

Sanni: The spoilage of fresh fish has been associated with the production of a dull appearance and texture. How would you consider the application of texture to the measurement of fish spoilage?

Howgate: As fish spoils the flesh becomes less translucent and appears dull. Why this should be I do not know. I can hypothesise that the leaching of the solutes from the flesh occurring during storage in melting ice will alter refractive properties of the fibres and cause dulling but I have no experimental evidence to support this.

The texture of fish becomes softer and more tender, as assessed in the mouth, during spoilage, but this property cannot be used as a basis for a test of freshness. The great variation in initial texture of fish would preclude precise measurements of changes occurring during storage. The softening of the raw flesh can be detected by touch and is included in some systems of assessing freshness of raw fish.

Frijters: An addition made to the remark that the relationships between textural variables are connected in the material and not in the sensation. If the perceptual process is considered as an S-O-R system at any three levels interaction between continua can occur, so if at the S level the correlationship between variables is broken up it supports the view that they go together in the material (s) and not in the perception (o).

Moskowitz: The recognition of a relation between pH and tenderness that you made, and the discontinuity between meat and fish points out the importance of *equations* and *functions* relating sensory and physical measurements. For too many years researchers have sought *only* correlations, not equations, relating the two domains.

16

Optimisation of Texture in Novel Protein Foods

L. G. Plaskett†

Biotechnical Processes Ltd, High Wycombe, Bucks., England

ABSTRACT

Slower-than-expected commercial development of meat analogues based upon textured vegetable protein can be attributed partly to marketing policies that are insufficiently venturesome and partly to a technical inability to produce top class products at an acceptable cost.

The advantages and disadvantages of protein spinning are discussed in relation to other protein texturising processes, especially those that are able to generate true fibres. Spinning has an ability to produce long, regular and completely aligned fibres that have unique advantages when assembling sizeable blocks of product to resemble meat: on the other hand the physical properties of the fibres, such as response to stretch and break-load, are markedly different from those of meat fibres; such differences adversely affect texture and eating quality unless compensated by other components of the finished analogues.

Nonetheless, the conclusion is drawn that spinning will probably be the method of choice for high quality meat analogue products, subject to achieving some important process economies. Based upon some recent work on protein spinning techniques, the prospects of achieving quite major process economies are considered to be good.

INTRODUCTION: WHY DEVELOP TEXTURED PROTEINS?

It is not always clear to the public, nor to scientists and technologists outside the food industry, why we seek to develop novel protein foods

† *Present address: Hillsborough House, Ashley, Nr. Tiverton, Devon EX16 5PA, England.*

271

based upon vegetable proteins. The reasons are to be found in the high and escalating costs of the familiar, naturally textured, animal food products such as meat, fish and cheese, and with the relatively-unattractive texture, or the lack of texture, associated with the vegetable-based alternatives.

In this field one can easily enter an argument as to whether animal food products, in particular meat, are in short supply or in surplus relative to market demand. I would like to dismiss this question, however, on the grounds that the volume of meat sales is constrained by price and that a much greater potential demand exists for meat if the price could be lower. In agricultural and commodity circles one certainly hears speak of both 'shortage' and 'surplus' in connection with meat; however, in this country the fluctuations, either in demand or supply, that cause these fluctuations are normally quite minor. Of far greater importance to the meat trade in the long term are, I suggest, the practical and biological limitations that constrain the overall supply of meat at present and may be expected to continue to do so to a large degree in future.

Texturised novel protein foods, insofar as they act as extenders or substitutes for meat, will at first tend to fill a volume of demand which is in excess of the meat trade's present sales volume; in short, as the volume of texturised novel protein foods increases, they are satisfying a latent demand which cannot be satisfied by meat itself at the present price levels. The same pattern may emerge in time in relation to fish and dairy products.

So long as this pattern remains, the meat trade and livestock farmers have little to fear from the introduction of novel protein foods!

In the longer term, however, the biological constraints that limit the volume of meat production may be instrumental in pricing meat beyond the pocket of the average consumer (or beyond his pocket for six days a week). If and when this happens, manufacturers of texturised protein foods must be ready to take over a role as suppliers of succulent, savoury, chewable, fibrous, high-protein foods to act as the principal component of a main meal.

It is towards this objective that the protein spinning technology discussed in this paper is aimed. It is an objective that calls for the texture of novel protein foods to be optimised: to the housewife the quality of meat itself is an emotive subject and she cannot be expected to accept an artificial substitute unless it meets the highest quality criteria.

BIOLOGICAL LIMITS TO MEAT PRODUCTION

These limits are not absolute. However, sheep and beef animals can only graze a limited amount of protein and energy from a given area of grass, while pigs and poultry call for concentrates that must be derived from arable farming. The limits are those prescribed by the farmers yield of feeds from the land and by the efficiency with which the farm animals can convert the feed to marketable meat. The yields of feed from the land may well be subject to slow improvement. However, they are currently being restricted by the high costs of fertiliser and imports are restricted by the limited availability and high costs of feed from outside Europe.

Regarding efficiency of utilisation by farm animals, Fig. 1 shows that these are unimpressive, inefficiency of conversion being the main weakness of a food economy based upon animal produce. The beef animal is the least efficient of all. In short, from any given vegetable food source it may be possible to feed from four to twenty times as many people by feeding the vegetable food direct than by passing it through the metabolism of an animal beforehand.

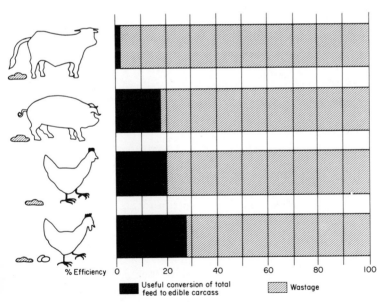

FIG. 1.   Wastage of feed by farm animals. Shaded areas indicate percentage of feed protein retained as edible protein in animal products.

Given the consumer liking for meat this inefficiency is not fatal to the future of the farm animal: it merely imposes high price and the future prospect of diminishing availability.

DEFINING A TEXTURED NOVEL PROTEIN FOOD

This is not an easy definition. It is usually implied, however, that a principal ingredient of such a food is protein that has been extracted from the original agricultural product from which it is derived, or that it has at least been refined, like soya flour or soya concentrate, by removal of other components. Secondly, it is a finished food item, ready to eat or incorporate into a composite dish.

Meat analogues are textured novel foods *par excellence* and are the main topic in this paper. In cheese analogues, the texture features are minimal and fish analogues are not yet well known.

Extruded soya flour used for extension of meat, which represents the bulk of texturised protein currently sold, is also excluded from this discussion on the grounds that it does not represent a food able to be eaten and enjoyed in its own right; its role is that of a food ingredient. Meat analogues comprise 100% or almost 100% of non-meat ingredients and do not require to be mixed with meat prior to consumption.

This is the class of product that calls for optimisation of texture.

COMMERCIAL DEVELOPMENT AND MARKETING POLICIES

As already mentioned, most texturised proteins sold are in the form of dehydrated minces or small chunks to which texture has been imparted by simple and inexpensive processes like thermoplastic extrusion. The customers are food manufacturers and caterers. They are used almost entirely for extending meat; typically their very modest textural properties, which are often spongy, and definite beany flavour limit the level of inclusion in meat to about 20% on a dry matter basis, although individual products vary widely. Obviously the role for such material is that of a cost-reducer which does not add, of itself, any specially desirable properties. The dryness of the product and smallness of the pieces renders it easily handled by users and durable in storage. A new type of demand has had to be created for this material and users familiarised with its peculiarities in application.

An onlooker to this market picture must surely find the course of its development to date quite unusual, even puzzling. The market for dehydrated meat is almost negligible and very little fresh or frozen meat is sold in minced or chunked form. Why should a substitute product be expected to succeed when offered in a form that is quite unrelated to the market pattern of the genuine product? Clearly a specialised market has been created, based upon convenience and often upon extreme cheapness, to caterers and manufacturers; the very nature of its extender role and the limited finished product range into which it can be incorporated severely restricts the actual and potential in this market sector.

The view is offered here that perhaps the market development of textured proteins, which a decade ago was thought likely to be far more rapid, has actually been hindered or arrested by the marketing stance adopted by producers in the early years. One would certainly have expected a time to arrive when technological progress in texturising permitted a more direct and open competition with meat than has in fact been realised. A principal thesis of this paper is that technology to enable a start to be made in this direction has been available for some years yet, unaccountably, with a few exceptions producers have chosen to approach the market in the same restricted way.

The demand for meat has never been adversely affected by its moistness, its lack of good keeping properties or by offering it in large sized pieces that require cutting or slicing by the user. Present technology could produce meat analogues having these same characteristics. There have been economic barriers to doing all this at low cost and I shall return to this subject later.

In conclusion, the consumer appreciates the fresh moistness of meat, dehydration as used at present does, in our experience, downgrade the quality of textured proteins; consumers also appreciate the opportunity to cut up and use meat as they wish. Optimising the texture of meat analogues therefore involves giving the consumer moist, large pieces of succulent product which can be a worthy starting material for the cook's artistry. That is a large demand in terms of both technology and marketing but I suggest that it is achievable. It is also suggested that a latent demand already exists, awaiting the imaginative marketeer; a great many people throughout the population lack the means to buy meat at all times when they would like to have it.

OPTIMISATION OF TEXTURE AND PRODUCTS

With the present market for texturised proteins so confined within one channel of development, much of it is unexplored and it would be presumptuous to define too precisely the nature of optimised texture and products. Table 1 summarises my company's views concerning an optimised product for the near future. Some of these features have already been explained or are obvious. One question deserving special comment is the degree of resemblance to meat or to a particular meat.

Our view is that really close resemblance to a particular meat is an unattainable goal with the present state of knowledge. A degree of resemblance can be attained; however, the frank attempt to copy a familiar meat predisposes consumers to criticise defects in the imitation. The best textured protein foods have appeal in their own right and may fairly be presented as meat substitutes without being direct copies of beef, pork, etc.

Finally, how meat-like should the product be? Our experience from panel tasting is that products which are fibrous, chewy and savoury with some meat-like flavour may be very well accepted, even though they are not rated as the most meat-like. Meat resemblance is hard to

TABLE 1
Criteria for development of meat analogues in accord with the definition given in this paper

Products should be:

(i)   Proteinaceous, some 30–60 % of the dry matter being protein.
(ii)   Capable of taking the place of meat in a main dish.
(iii)   Resembling meat in appearance and in being chewy and fibrous.
(iv)   Not formulated to resemble any particular meat.
(v)   Served in forms reminiscent of meat, e.g. large chunks, slices, steaks, burgers or blocks for slicing.
(vi)   Savoury in flavour, not necessarily entirely meat-like.
(vii)   Optimised for overall organoleptic acceptance rather than meat-resemblance.

FIG. 2.

define. Both fibrousness and chewiness are essential to it, yet savoury products with these qualities may not be thought meat-like. Clearly, a degree of meat-resemblance is essential; however, it is easier to produce very high levels of acceptability than very high levels of meat resemblance; fibrousness is very important and the fibres should be more or less aligned. It is a pity, therefore, that in many spun products the fibres are chopped and then randomised during mixing with other ingredients.

Provided that the food is entirely suited to consumption in meat-like situations, this makes it best policy to go for maximum acceptability.

Some moist, sliceable, highly acceptable products developed by Biotechnical Processes Ltd along these guidelines are illustrated in Fig. 2. They are produced in strongly coloured, strong-tasting versions and other versions light in colour and more delicate in taste.

THE SPINNING PROCESS

Spinning of proteins is under active development by Biotechnical Processes Ltd, and is regarded by the company as the method of choice. So much depends, in relation to meat resemblance, upon discrete and aligned true fibres, that we find no other method attractive. Certainly, by using prior art methods there are important economic penalties and we have been striving to overcome these.

The method, as it is applied to edible protein, arose directly from processes for producing proteinaceous textile fibres from such materials as zein, groundnut protein or casein.[2,3] From the mechanical point of view it is not unlike processes for making other manmade textile fibres.

Typically a protein preparation is dissolved in alkaline solution to form a viscous fluid known as a 'dope'. This then passed under pressure of a few atmospheres through a specially manufactured metal die known as a spinneret, perforated by several thousand very small holes of between, say, 0·05 mm to 0·5 mm diameter, into a bath of acid in which the fibres are formed by coagulation. The numerous fibres need to be drawn away from the spinneret and in practice this is done by passing the fibre bundle around a set of rollers which keeps it taut and removes the fibres from the bath continuously. The name 'spinning' is something of a misnomer for what is really a low-temperature wet extrusion process. However, in protein texturising parlance the name 'extrusion' is reserved for extrusion of semi-solid materials and in particular thermoplastic extrusion at high temperature and pressure.

The acid used for coagulation must be relatively weak, so that at the operating pH of, say, 2 to 4, it and its salts are present in high enough concentration to provide significant buffering capacity in the bath. Acetic, lactic and phosphoric acids are most commonly used.

The fibres first formed are passed through a further bath in which they are subjected to stretching and heating in order to toughen them. Some acid from the coagulation stage fails to be washed out in the stretch bath and must be neutralised by passing the fibres into another bath containing a slightly alkaline solution.

Afterwards, the fibres are washed with water in a fourth bath. Sets of driven rolls are necessary between the baths to advance the fibre to the next stage.

Subsequent handling of the fibre depends upon its end-use. It may be chopped up as it emerges from the wash bath or else subjected to passage through baths of flavour, fat binding agents, etc. for impregnation with these materials before being utilised in making up meat analogues.

This basic process was the subject of three patents by Boyer between 1953 and 1956 and for the most part it has not been modified much since then. Most developments have been concerned with such detail as additional ingredients in the dope, the method and equipment for dope preparation, the precise method of washing, raw materials for spinning and applications for spun fibre, including techniques for building up analogues from it. In particular there has been much pre-occupation with the problem of impregnating the fibres with the flavouring, binding and fat additives necessary for a good organoleptic result: the difficulty has been that the fibres adhere strongly together, making a rather compact tow into which additives cannot readily penetrate. Several patents assigned to General Mills Inc. reflect great attention paid to opening up or kneeding these tows so that additives can penetrate adequately.[4,5] Worthington Foods Inc. took special measures to deal with a related problem, that of leaching from the fibres the unwanted process aid chemicals.[6]

General Mills Inc. investigators also devoted great attention to dope mixing, which poses problems on account of the way in which dope viscosity changes with time,[7–9] and tends to develop heterogeneously viscous and non-viscous areas. The General Mills answer was a smear mixing process, one stage of which was conducted in a helical screw device.

The most extensive modification of the basic process—perhaps the only really fundamental change since Boyer's work—is that of Tombs.[10] In this version, known as mesophase spinning, the protein dope is a more or less neutral solution which, on passing the spinneret,

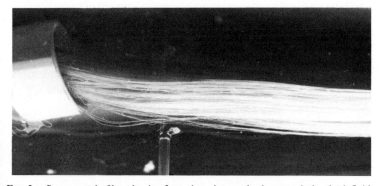

FIG. 3. Spun protein fibres issuing from the spinneret in the coagulation bath fluid.

FIG. 4. Spun fibre tow passes out of the coagulation bath on its way to the stretch bath, passing over Godet rolls.

is coagulated by heat. Such a process is inevitably very fastidious with regard to the solubility properties of the protein raw material; however, it offers certain advantages concerning consumption of chemicals and the ease with which additives may be incorporated.

A useful general account of spinning is given by Rosenfield and Hartman,[33] including some detail of the ways in which fibre is utilised in finished products. Figures 3 and 4 illustrate aspects of the spinning process.

COMPETING PROCESSES TO SPINNING

Extrusion

Extrusion-cooking (thermoplastic extrusion) is by far the most widely applied technique for texturisation of protein. Although no breakdown is available of the amounts of textured protein manufactured by the different techniques, a fair estimate would be that not less than 80–90 % of all textured protein is extruded. Its main applications are in producing meat extenders for human food use and for pet foods.

The commonest starting material is soya flour and, whichever protein source is used, extrusion is nearly always satisfactory using a less purified and therefore less expensive protein preparation than that required for spinning. This advantage and the very simple nature of the extrusion process has led to extremely competitive pricing for extruded products and has been a major factor in their commercial success.

The process itself is similar to that used for extrusion of expanded plastic products and the apparatus is also similar. The basic process was first described by Arnold *et al.*[11] A protein-containing raw material is mixed with water to give a 'dough' containing from 10 % to 60 % moisture and is then forced, by means of a compression screw operating within a heated barrel at from 200 to 400 °F and at least 1000 p.s.i. through an orifice. The sudden release of pressure within the material then leads to an expansion of its structure so that it contains numerous open and empty areas or 'cells'; the material produced consists, in fact, of a network of interlaced, interconnected ribbons or sheets of varying thickness and width. The empty cells have greater length than diameter and are more or less orientated in the direction of extrusion. It is usual to cut the product at the extrusion orifice with a rotating knife.

The apparatus has an entry-point for raw material into the barrel. The barrel is steam-jacketed, though the first part may be jacketed with water instead of steam if it is desired to feed ingredients into the extruder unmixed: the water jacket then prevents premature over-heating of only partially mixed ingredients. As the dough is moved towards the die, the screw and the heating jacket together produce the necessary increase in temperature and pressure.

After passing the restricted orifice at the end of the barrel the material may be made to pass either through a tube[12] before being passed out to the atmosphere, or through a second die-plate.[13]

High temperature and pressure are essential features of the process as it has now become generally accepted. It is apparent, for example, from the patent of Arnold *et al.*[11] that 'a pressure-heated plastic mass' is definitely required both for proper behaviour within the extruder and for generating the desired open-cell structure upon emerging from the die. A prior patent[14] does describe extrusion of a proteinaceous dough, but without high temperature and pressure, through a macaroni press, but the product lacked open-celled structure and required drying.

Later developments of extrusion have related mostly to use of various additives to the dough, such as sulphur compounds or elemental sulphur,[13] hypophosphites,[15] sodium hydroxide,[12] etc. and to the use of protein concentrates rather than soya flour.[15]

Non-Spinning, Non-Extrusion Processes

There are various texturising methods apart from spinning and extruding, commencing with work in 1906,[16] utilising the chewy quality of wheat gluten to produce so-called 'vegetable drops'. The naturally chewy character of gluten has been exploited many times since then in preparing meat analogue type products.[14,17]

A significant further development in the early 1950s was the production of chewy gels from other proteins, such as groundnut or soya. After some purification of the protein, a paste of it was prepared with water and the pH adjusted to a value near neutrality to render the protein susceptible to gelation.[18] The gel was shaped in a variety of ways, for example, by extrusion through a macaroni extruder and subsequently heat setting or, alternatively, heat setting a sizeable mass of the gel and then comminuting it and fabricating meat-like products from the pieces, with added binding agents to hold them together as a heterogeneous product.

In such a process very little texture is really being given to the product: a gel is a homogeneous mass of chewy protein: the products only have structure or texture insofar as the gel has been shaped, subdivided and interspersed with material having different properties.

Another process is that known as shredding.[19] It consists of injecting steam into a slurry of protein whilst it is being agitated by rotating blades. Apparently this is best done in an autoclave so that the temperature can be increased rapidly; the moisture content of the slurry is from 50–80%. This process does not appear to have been developed very far or commercialised but the principle remains interesting for the way in which it foreshowed later successful processes of General Mills Inc. and Ralston Purina involving heating protein slurries and/or the use of steam.

A third process is that known as 'puffing' and exemplified by a patent by McAnelly.[20] It consists of subjecting protein materials to heat and pressure whilst they are moist, followed by fairly sudden release of the pressure so as to release vapours and impart an expanded porous structure. This is obviously closely related to thermoplastic extrusion, in which expansion of the product upon exit from the extruder is a major feature. The main difference is that the protein is not being urged forwards through an orifice at the moment of expansion and consequently the open 'cells' in the product are not elongated or orientated. Another difference is that for practical reasons lower temperatures and pressures are likely to be employed. Palmer[21] devised a variation in which the surface of the material to be treated was sealed by heat setting prior to puffing to inhibit the escape of internally generated vapours. Another variation is that of Boyer *et al.*[22] in which the heat for expansion is generated internally by means of radiant energy, such as microwaves.

A further process is that of Liepa[23] in which a proteinaceous dough is rolled into sheets and the sheets are cut into thin strands which are then stabilised by autoclaving. A variation on this theme is a patent by the Battelle Development Corporation in which the rolled sheet is afterwards folded to give texture.[24]

Up until a few years ago this whole group of non-extrusion, non-spinning processes were a set of interesting but largely unexploited technologies. This has been changed by the introduction of important new processes from General Mills Inc. and Ralston Purina.

First came that of Frederiksen[25] and of Hoer,[26] both assigned to Ralston Purina. Protein in slurry form is put into a reactive condition by treating at alkaline pH and subsequently adjusting to slightly acid pH: the slurry is then passed through a heat exchanger under high temperature and pressure, when protein filaments are formed.

A process invented by Dunning *et al.*[27] and assigned to General Mills Inc. consists of introducing fine, dry, particulate protein into one end of a tube (elongated treatment chamber) and blowing the protein along the tube with high pressure steam: the apparatus used for delivering the dry protein into a stream of pressurised steam shows much mechanical engineering complexity and ingenuity. However, the process was modified in a further patent by Strommer[28] in which protein was moistened before delivery into the steam jet by passing through an extruder without application of heat or pressure.

ADVANTAGES AND DISADVANTAGES OF SPINNING

The principal advantage of spinning resides in its ability to produce strong, discrete fibres that are long and are aligned together in the same way that fibres are aligned in meat. The process has few other advantages but this unique characteristic accords it an outstanding place in meat analogue technology.

The 'heated protein slurry' process of Ralston Purina clearly produces true fibres but so far as we know they are relatively short and unaligned. Other non-spinning, non-extrusion processes like shredding apparently produce some fibrous characteristics but without fibre orientation or, at best, with fibres irregular in size and only partly aligned.

The disadvantages of spinning when carried out as described above, relative to other processes, are:

(i)   significant complexity of process and apparatus;
(ii)   consumption of process aid chemicals;
(iii) effluent consequent upon (ii);
(iv)   difficulty of removing process aid chemicals from the fibres and of impregnating the fibres with flavours and additives;
(v)   some wastage of raw material;
(vi)   the requirement for a protein isolate of high purity.

The history of spinning development also reveals some difficulty in binding the fibres together in finished products. All these disadvantages carry their economic penalties and doubtless largely explain the very slow commercialisation of spun products.

Consequently we regarded spinning as the method of choice for texturisation but with a high priority accorded to solving its present technical and cost disadvantages.

Finally, spinning shares one disadvantage in common with all texturisation processes, that the physical properties of the texturised product are not those of meat. In the case of spun fibre, its load/elongation curve, its breaking load and its response to repeated stresses (as in chewing) all differ quantitatively from the properties of meat fibres.[29,30] Perhaps the greatest difference, apart from breaking strength, is the very much greater extension before breaking that is exhibited by spun protein fibres. Therefore, the fibres by themselves are not capable of yielding a very meat-like texture, even when binding agents are used to make them adhere together. Other inter-fibre components must be selected to compensate for the effects of those properties of the fibres themselves that are unwanted and unmeat-like. Many patents cover characteristics of the inter-fibre material[31,32] and in general each producer who uses spinning develops his own approach to compensating for these physical properties.

PROCESS ECONOMIES IN SPINNING

The great desirability of spun fibre, or even the necessity for it, if the texture of novel protein foods is to be optimised, is a tremendous incentive towards solving the remaining technical barriers to manufacturing it economically. That has been our goal in Biotechnical Processes Ltd for the past two and a half years. The results are written up in the form of patent applications not yet published but the estimated economic effects of the changes made to the basic process can be presented here.

Firstly, in the manufacture of the fibre itself, the usual selection of process-aid chemicals results in several causes of high cost. The need to continuously replenish the chemicals themselves, then consequently deal with them as components of an effluent, adds a great deal of cost. To leach unwanted chemicals from the fibres and then impregnate the fibres with desired additives is difficult to achieve successfully,

TABLE 2

Projected process costs for conversion of any spinnable protein source into fibre.[a] Costs are for producing 100 kg dry weight of flavoured spun fibre by two processes

Item	Costs by prior art process	Costs by new process
Utilities	£30·00	£35·00
Labour and supervision	£57·50	£52·50
Maintenance	£12·50	£12·50
Process aid chemicals	£82·50	£8·25
Depreciation	£25·00	£22·50
General overheads and management	£61·00	£61·00
Effluent disposal	£10·00	£1·00
Losses of protein raw material	£51·45	—
Total process costs	£329·95	£192·75

[a] These details represent our best estimates under UK economic conditions, March 1976.

complicates the process and wastes chemicals and ingredients. It is also responsible for some losses of protein raw material.

All these causes of excess cost have been tackled in our programme and have been either eliminated or reduced. The estimated effects upon the production of spun fibre are summarised in Table 2, indicating a 41·5 % reduction. At this stage the product consists of fibre alone, which has not yet been formed into finished meat analogues and the costs estimated in the table are the process costs for conversion to fibre, without the costs of the protein raw material itself.

TABLE 3

Projected costs[a] of finished meat analogue products.[b] Costs are for fibre and ingredients for 1000 kg dry weight of finished meat analogue based upon spun fibre by two processes

Item	Costs by prior art process with soya isolate	Costs by new process
Weight of fibre needed	500 kg	200 kg
Protein raw material cost for fibre	£441·00	£68·60
Flavouring cost for fibre	£10·60	£4·24
Process costs for fibre	£164·98	£38·55
Flavoured inter-fibre material at say, £350 per 1000 kg	£175·00	£280·00
Total costs of fibre and other ingredients	£791·58	£391·39

[a] The costs of combining fibre with other ingredients to give a particular analogue composition are so variable that they have not been included here.
[b] These details represent our best estimates under UK economic conditions, March, 1976.

This is taken into account in Table 3 because the newly developed processes can employ cheaper protein sources (usually blends of different vegetable proteins) than the soya isolate conventionally employed. This is achieved by allowing the purity of the protein to drop from around 95 % to closer to 80 % protein.

The Table 3 figures also take into account that the products we now make use less fibre per unit weight of finished analogue. This is accomplished by positioning and orientating the fibres within the product so as to derive maximum textural effect from a limited proportion. Since fibre is an expensive ingredient this also reduces costs and the total estimated costs for finished fibre at the base of

Table 3 shows a 50·5 % reduction compared with the best known prior art methods.

CONCLUSIONS

Unfortunately, technical detail of these process modifications cannot yet be made public. However, the sources of the estimated cost savings have been indicated: the scale of cost reduction is clearly of a magnitude that could alter fundamentally the competitive relationship between spun and non-spun texturised novel protein foods. This prospect is opened up by assiduously minimising the costs at each step in their production and by eliminating possible cause of plant complexity or materials wastage.

REFERENCES

1. Marks, H. F. (1971). In: *Conference on New Protein Foods* organised by Agricultural Development Association in conjunction with the University of Reading.
2. Caldwell, W. A. and Winton, E. R. (1947). British Patent 593 564.
3. Boyer, R. A. (1953). British Patent 699 692.
4. Dechaine, R. C. and Callaghan, R. W. (1966). British Patent 1 047 965.
5. Page, J. A. and Bauer, W. G. (1969). British Patent 1 152 327.
6. Worthington Foods Inc. (1972). British Patent 1 298 437.
7. Thompson, R. H. K. (1946). In: *Proceedings of the Symposium on Protein Fibres*, Society of Dyers and Colourists, p. 173.
8. Westeen, R. W. and Kuramoto, S. (1955). British Patent 987 348.
9. General Mills Inc. (1968). British Patent 1 132 987.
10. Tombs, M. P. (1972). British Patent 1 265 661.
11. Arnold, A. F. *et al.* (1966). British Patent 1 049 848.
12. Flier, R. J. (1968). British Patent 1 105 904.
13. Jenkins, S. L. (1970). US Patent 3 946 858.
14. MacAllister, R. V. and Finucane, T. P. (1963). US Patent 3 102 031.
15. Calvert, F. E. and Atkinson, W. T. (1970). US Patent 3 498 794.
16. Kellogg, J. H. (1906). US Patent 869 371.
17. Kjelson (1965). US Patent 3 197 310.
18. Anson, M. L. and Pader, M. (1956). British Patent 746 859.
19. Rusoff, I. I., Ohan, W. J. and Long, C. L. (1962). US Patent 3 047 395.
20. McAnelly, J. K. (1964). US Patent 3 142 571.
21. Palmer, H. C. (1972). US Patent 3 645 747.
22. Boyer, R. A., Schultz, A. A., Oborsh, E. V. and Brown, A. V. (1972). US Patent 3 662 673.

23. Liepa, A. L. (1973). British Patent 1 335 596.
24. Battelle Development Corporation (1974). British Patent 1 433 278.
25. Frederiksen, C. W. (1972). US Patent 3 662 671.
26. Hoer, R. A. (1972). US Patent 3 662 672.
27. Dunning, H. N., Strommer, P. K. and van Hulle, G. J. (1972). US Patent 3 707 380.
28. Strommer, P. K. (1973). US Patent 3 778 522.
29. Cumming, D. B., Stanley, D. W. and de Man, J. M. (1972). *Can. Inst. Food Sci. Technol. J.*, **5**, p. 118.
30. Iles, B. C. and Elson, C. R. (1973). Textured protein products—A textural investigation, *Technical Circular* No. 532, BFMIRA, Leatherhead.
31. General Mills Inc. (1964). British Patent 977 238.
32. Anson, M. L. and Pader, M. (1957). US Patent 2 813 025.
33. Rosenfield, D. and Hartman, W. E. (1973). *Proceedings of the World Soy Protein Conference*, Munich, published in *J. Am. Oil Chemists Soc.*, (1974), **51**.

DISCUSSION

Questioner: Are the properties of the extruded proteins unchanged?

Plaskett: Yes, the properties are the same. From a physical and textural point of view the properties of the fibre are completely unchanged but there are some advantages in terms of flavour adhesion and retention.

Jeffery: How much cross linking is (a) desirable and (b) able to be induced in the protein spinning process?

Plaskett: By 'cross-linking' are you referring to intermolecular cross-linking between protein chains or to simple adhesion between fibres?

Jeffery: Simple adhesion between fibres.

Plaskett: Inducing adhesion between the fibres is usually termed 'binding'; various binder systems have been developed by many different workers and they generally fall either into the class of carbohydrate-based systems or into the class of protein-based systems, which depend upon gelling of the protein by heat. Effective binding in this way is definitely desirable, to stop the product from being merely a mass of independent fibres. Most of the binding systems known have quite limited performance; they are not as effective as one would like. It is one of the defects of most spun products that the fibres themselves are very strong and the forces holding them together are too weak.

We have been able to make some important progress in this area and the details will be published in our patent specifications.

Inducing the fibres to adhere together during spinning is possible. It is a question of formulating the dope to produce this effect. However, it is not desirable, in our view, to do this because washing and impregnating the fibres is then extremely difficult and the congealed mass of fibres is not very flexible in use.

Palmer: Does the process described claim to reduce the two main defects of the extruded product, viz. (a) beany off-flavour and (b) lack of succulence?

Plaskett: Our process by itself does not do anything to reduce bean flavour, but we have produced this effect in our products by using blends of protein that are wholly or mainly derived from non-soya proteins and which have bland flavours. Regarding succulence, I would not like you to think this was what I had in mind when I criticised the dryness of existing products. I was referring to the common practice of marketing the products in dehydrated form for subsequent re-hydration. That is a matter of choice for the manufacturer. However, if you mean that most existing extruded products are still not very succulent after re-hydration, I agree. Indeed, our products do correct this defect because they hold water and fat within a matrix; the water and fat are not so easily pressed out from the product as they are from the sponge-like structure of most extruded proteins.

Rolfe: In the last table of data presented by Dr Plaskett the composition of the two meat analogues is quoted as 500 kg or 200 kg of protein per 1000 kg dry solids of the meat analogue. Is this information correct? 200 kg of protein per 1000 kg of hydrated meat analogue would approximate to the composition of meat, but if the information is correct and only 20 % of the solids in the meat analogue are protein then the nutritive value is very much below that of meat. Also relative cost of nutrients purchased is a valid means of comparison between meat and meat analogues, and using such a yardstick how does the 20 % protein analogue compare in price with meat? The latter point on relative costs was not raised but I suspect Dr Plaskett would like to deal with this point.

Plaskett: This is all on a dry weight basis.

17

The Importance of Texture in Chocolate Confectionery

J. BEESLEY

*Confectionery Group Quality Control, Cadbury Limited,
Birmingham, England*

ABSTRACT

Within the confectionery industry there are numerous techniques available to control the solubility of sucrose by the manipulation of well-known physico-chemical relationships. The control of size and distribution of sucrose crystals by this means gives rise to a range of possible textures in confections which vary from hard/smooth to soft/elastic.

There are other products whose textures are dictated by moisture content and the ratio of milk solids to total fat where the control of sucrose crystallisation is less important, the choice of ingredients for these confections being directly related to the type of texture required and the conditions under which the product will be packed and sold.

Another range of products relies on the gelling abilities of various compounds to produce the desired texture, and sucrose in this case is used solely as a sweetener and filler.

In the production of milk chocolate the manufacturer is not only concerned with the control of sucrose particle size, but also with the particle size distribution of fibrous cocoa material and chocolate crumb aggregates which are produced during manufacture.

The measurement and control of particle size distribution and texture of confectionery products is carried out using a range of scientific devices; however, the final arbiter as to whether the producer has achieved the correct mix of texture quality and flavour availability is the consumer. Failure by the manufacturer to recognise how discriminating the consumer can be in identifying texture changes may eventually lead to purchasing resistance.

INTRODUCTION

The textural properties of chocolate confections are greatly influenced by their internal structure. However, it is important to remember that the word texture is a blanket term or a composite of many properties (including touch, sight and hearing) each of which interact in a pattern of multiple responses, together with other senses which require individual evaluation.[1] Once we accept a chocolate visually and we begin to consume it, we bring into play the senses of taste and smell. Sensory perception of texture depends on the deformation of the product resulting from the application of pressure and/or on the surface properties, such as roughness, smoothness or stickiness estimated by the sense of touch. While a consumer may develop an idea of the texture when he handles the product, texture is best indicated by contact sensations in the mouth.

Cakebread[2] has shown that the rate at which the consumer appreciates flavour may be conditioned by texture, density, solubility and the presence of flavour enhancers. Table 1 shows the relationship between density, flavour release and texture for certain types of confectionery.

Procedures for the sensory evaluation of textural properties by specialist and general consumer panels[3] are well established. The methodology[4] along with the scoring procedures which can be used when comparing two or more samples has also been thoroughly researched; however, it is worth remembering that the olfactory threshold for humans deteriorates with age. Hinchcliffe[5,6] demonstrated that the acuity of the sense of taste declines logarithmically with age. The rate of deterioration, which was the same for both sucrose and sodium chloride, corresponded with a 50 % loss of taste sensitivity in 29 years using 20 years as the base starting point.

Thus we can see that texture has a great deal to do with the acceptability of a product, and this applies particularly to chocolate confectionery. Although texture itself does not create a flavour sensation, it affects the rate at which a flavour is made available. When a hard caramel[7] is eaten it dissolves slowly from the surface inwards, and the flavouring substances are steadily released over a period. With fondants, pastes, chocolate and other soft chocolate confectionery the whole unit is softened rapidly in the mouth and a lot of flavour is available quickly. The type and quantity of flavours to be added must be related to these factors. Crisp, aerated confections provide a

TABLE 1

The relationship between various parameters for nine types of confectioneries

Type of sweet	Approximate specific gravity	Flavour release effects	Texture
Boiled sweets	1·54	Slow start then steady release	Hard, smooth
Butterscotches, brittles	1·50	Fairly rapid flavour surrender	Hard, frangible glass
Toffees, caramels	1·45–1·48	Hard toffee similar to boiled sweet. Soft toffee—slow release at start—speeding up on chewing	Hard, chewy to firm
Fudges	1·39–1·43	Rapid release	Smooth, grained
Fondants	1·44–1·48	Very rapid release	Smooth, grained
Nougats	1·30–1·34	(a) Slow release at first—speeding up on chewing	Hard, brittle aerated
		(b) Slow release at first—then very rapid release	Firm, grained, aerated
Jellies	1·38–1·40	Slow release when sucked—increases with chewing	Smooth, elastic
Gums	1·40–1·42	Release slower than jellies	Smooth, tough
Marshmallows	0·5–0·6	Steady release on chewing/dissolving	Soft, elastic

different texture, and with these particularly their acceptability is often more related to the texture than the taste. However attractive a taste these products have, loss of crispness destroys their palatability. Other textures are detrimental to taste—chocolate which is badly refined is gritty; over-refining, however, produces a product which may be slimy to the palate. The latter effect is much more noticeable in milk chocolate than in dark.

Earlier in this paper a brief reference was made to the sensory evaluation of textural properties, and it is worth while expanding this subject to incorporate some quantifiable data on what constitutes smoothness and roughness in chocolate confectionery terms. It would be an extremely laborious task to cover the whole range of possible chocolate confectionery products, and a variety of product types have been selected as possible bench marks against which other confections may be evaluated. The product types selected are milk chocolate, fondant cremes, gums, jellies and caramel.

MILK CHOCOLATE

There are four critical points in the production of milk chocolate which will determine the texture and particle size distribution in the finished product, and these occur no matter which milk chocolate production process is selected. They are:

1. The cocoa nib grinding process.
2. Aggregates of milk solids, sugar and cocoa liquor which have been formed during the crumb process by the final crystallisation and drying processes.
3. The chocolate refining and conching processes.
4. The chocolate tempering process.

The main milk chocolate processes now in use throughout the world are:

(a) The chocolate crumb process where pasteurised milk is evaporated under vacuum to approximately 50% solids, and sugar is then added, dissolved and the resultant mix condensed to about 90% solids. Cocoa liquor is then added, and the resultant magma is dried under vacuum to 1% moisture. After the addition of cocoa butter and lecithin extenders the mixture is refined, conched and sieved before becoming available for moulding or other uses.

(b) The milk powder process where the milk solids are incorporated using spray or roller dried milk powder, and the process then follows along similar lines to (a).

(c) The block milk process where sweetened condensed milk at approximately 8% water content and 45% sucrose is used directly as an ingredient or as a source of milk in the crumb process.

The particulate matter in milk chocolate is made up of cocoa material, sugar or milk crumb aggregates, and each of these produces a different sensation on the palate. Large sugar crystals are obviously gritty but disperse. Cocoa particles give a persistent sensation of roughness, whereas crumb aggregates soften and disperse in the mouth after a short time.

Cocoa Liquor Production

The particle-size distribution of the cocoa material is determined early in the chocolate process when the cocoa bean, after cleaning, is roasted to enhance its flavour, winnowed to remove the shell, then milled and ground to reduce the particle size of the cellular structure in the cocoa nib.

There are numerous devices available for milling cocoa nibs. All of them involve processes which rupture the cell walls of the nib releasing cocoa fat, which is liquefied by the frictional heat produced. As grinding continues, the particle size of the fibrous material reduces and the paste becomes more fluid.

Cocoa liquor going forward for the manufacture of chocolate crumb should be capable of passing through a 100 μm sieve. In modern factories this is achieved by using micro-pulverisers to initially reduce particle size before passing the liquor through high output horizontal disc mills. C. L. Hinton[8] has claimed that the limit for the detection of particles by the tongue is 25 μm. We will see later that chocolate is composed of a mixture of particle sizes which can vary from 3–100 μm—even a small proportion of large particles can produce a gritty effect on the palate. It is the distribution of particle sizes in a sample of chocolate which is more important for comparative texture purposes than the average size of the particles. It is important, therefore, that analytical methods used in the control of processes used to reduce particle size for textural related purposes take account of this fact.

Cocoa, Milk Solids, Sugar Agglomerates

The development of the chocolate crumb process[9] revolutionised the manufacture of milk chocolate, and in those countries which have adopted its use sales of milk chocolate have greatly increased. During the crumb making process the particle size of the crumb aggregates is controlled by passing the condensed evaporated sugar/milk mixture through a small crystalliser and then to a kneader where the cocoa liquor is added. The mixture of liquor and crystallising condensed milk makes a very stiff magma and this continues to crystallise during kneading. For good control the average of the larger particles would be of the order of 50 μm. If during the manufacture of crumb the crystallisation has proceeded too slowly, the sugar crystals will have grown too large and aggregates containing these large crystals will be formed. These make grinding, the next stage in the process, more difficult and output will be reduced.

Refining of Chocolate Paste

Refining involves the crushing, abrasion, attrition and shearing of cocoa and sugar fragments to produce a product which has the desired particle size. Over refining may be costly, the final size reduction requiring considerable amounts of power, and may produce a chocolate which is clinging and generally unpleasant to the palate. The variable factors in any refining process are the feed rate and the degree of particle size reduction that is desired. During refining the particle size falls and the total surface area of the particles rises; increases in surface area in chocolate particles require the addition of more cocoa butter to maintain the same flow properties. Comparisons between chocolate samples with similar compositions show that the smaller the particle size the greater the viscosity. During refining a considerable amount of frictional heat is generated, progressively with smaller particle sizes, and an efficient internal water cooling system should operate within the grinding rollers. Changes in chocolate flavour will occur if the refining temperatures are allowed to become excessively high. Refining is usually followed by a conching process, where the primary aim is one of flavour development by the removal of volatile acidic components remaining after the cocoa bean fermentation process. Other benefits which improve chocolate texture are the removal of moisture from the product, a smoothing of any sharp edges remaining on sugar crystals, changes in viscosity and a thorough mixing which breaks up the aggregates of sugar, milk solids and cocoa particles.

Tempering of Chocolate

Tempering[10] is a method of inducing cocoa butter to seed or crystallise in a stable form to produce a product with a good shelf-life, permanent colour and gloss. Poorly tempered chocolate frequently gives rise to fat bloom due to the development of crystals of unstable fat on the surface of the chocolate. In particular the type and amount of fat has a major effect on the behaviour of the liquid chocolate and the ratio of soft to hard fats will not only affect the tempering conditions, but will also have a pronounced effect on the texture of the finished chocolate.

OTHER CONFECTIONS

The present day confectionery industry has as its major ingredient sucrose, and it is certain properties of this chemical that have resulted in the production of two main groups of confection, these being:

(a)   the hard boilings, toffee and caramel;
(b)   fondants and pastes.

The graining of caramel using fondant produces another confection, fudge.

FONDANT

The manipulation of concentrated sucrose solutions[11] under various temperature conditions, plus the addition of other ingredients, produces a whole variety of possible textures. Sugar solutions, when concentrated by boiling, form supersaturated solutions, and these, on cooling, produce a product with an amorphous structure. If the cooling is accompanied by agitation or beating, a mass of minute sugar crystals suspended in syrup is formed. Sugar has a limited solubility in water at normal temperatures (approximately 67%) and this will produce graining or recrystallisation in hard boilings and coarse texture in fondants; it also leaves these products susceptible to microbiological spoilage.[12] The addition of invert sugar or preferably glucose syrup increases the concentration of the syrup phase in fondants, making the product resistant to microbial attack and encourages the formation of fine sugar crystals. In hard boilings, glucose and invert sugars retard graining. To ensure that microbiological problems do not occur it is essential that the fondant creme has a syrup phase with a soluble solids concentration of not less than 75% at normal temperatures. Fondant is prepared by dissolving the sugar with invert or glucose present in water and evaporating until a supersaturated solution containing approximately 12% water is achieved. This solution is cooled with violent mixing or beating, and the sucrose then recrystallises in the form of fine sugar crystals. Examination of the fondant under the microscope should show an even distribution of sugar crystals, the larger ones ranging between 10–15 μm. The presence of a proportion of larger crystals or uneven size distribution indicates inefficient operation of the mixer or cooler. Occasionally small amounts of colloidal matter such as gelatin, egg or starch are added to further retard crystallisation. If rework syrup is being used in the recipe this will often include small amounts of these materials.

The fondant is then 'remelted' in order to bring the material into a fluid condition for mixing with flavours, colours and other ingredients, and to enable it to be deposited into moulds or chocolate shells.

The traditional method is to heat the fondant to between 135–150 °F with the addition of a syrup mixture at 75 % solids, made with a sucrose/glucose ratio similar to the original fondant. When a fondant is remelted and subsequently cooled, during use a crystal size increase occurs due to the growth of crystals of sucrose from the syrup phase and an increase in the size of crystals already there. This increase in number and size of crystals gives the moulded fondant a certain amount of rigidity and body, and the process control during this stage of manufacture will dictate the texture of the final product. Remelting temperatures over 150 °F will result in an appreciable increase in the syrup phase, and when this crystallises it will tend to give coarse crystals. Rougher, short fudge-like texture may be obtained by taking the temperature up as high as 165 °F carrying out the final stages of remelting through a hot nozzle.

The crystal size of a good assortment creme should range between 20–30 μm. Any significant proportion of crystals above 30 μm will make the creme taste rough.

GUMS, JELLIES AND PASTILLES

Gums,[13] jellies and pastilles constitute a large class of low boiled confectionery which usually contain about 20 % moisture. The texture of these products, which ranges from jammy to rubbery, is obtained by the use of various water binding gelling agents, these principally being gum arabic, starch, gelatin, agar and pectin. Most processes start with a boiled solution of sucrose/glucose to which the gelling agent is added. This mixture is then cooked and deposited into starch moulds, although in modern continuous plants depositing directly into moulds is now possible.

Hard gums are normally prepared from gum arabic as the sole gelling agent, this representing 50% of the total solid matter present. The texture produced is hard and short. If a softer eating product is required then the level of gum arabic is reduced and another gelling agent, such as gelatin, is used; these products are usually called pastilles.

Jellies which frequently use a mixture of gelling agents, e.g. gelatin and thin boiling starch, have a texture which ranges from rubbery through to almost jam-like; the texture may be improved to give a shorter bite by increasing the percentage of thin boiling starch.

A derivative of this type of confectionery is Turkish Delight, and traditionally this is produced from a boiled mixture of sugars and a starch based gelling agent, which, after cooling, is poured onto a slab, cut and then dusted with icing sugar. Many modifications are possible using starch and pectin or starch agar and gelatin. Turkish Delight produced in this way is usually deposited into starch moulds, and after drying and tipping out enrobed with chocolate. Nearly all the problems associated with the texture of this product arise because of incorrect treatment of the starch. It is essential that during manufacture the starch is completely broken down and gelatinised; failure to obtain complete gelatinisation will result in a spongy texture, complete gelatinisation gives maximum body to the product.

CARAMEL

Caramel is composed of a number of possible ingredients, including sucrose and brown sugars, glucose syrups, invert, honey, malt or maple syrups, starch, milk products, vegetable oils, emulsifiers, salt and flavours blended in various proportions and processed so as to have desired physical properties. A number of inter-relating factors must be considered when balancing the proportions of ingredients in a caramel recipe, the more important of these factors being:

(a) the desired texture of the confection;
(b) flavour characteristics of the product;
(c) grain (crystallisation) prevention;
(d) colour;
(e) flow characteristics;
(f) protection from moisture transfer or absorption.

The greatest single factor affecting the texture and chew of the finished product is moisture content. This will vary depending on the cooking temperature and residence time in the cooker, and the amount of fat which has been included in the recipe.

The presence of milk solids also has a pronounced effect on the texture, and this will also have a bearing on the flavour and colour. In general, the higher the level of milk solids present the harder will be the caramel.

The choice of fat to be used will depend on the ultimate market the product is destined for, but here again the fat content and use or non-use of emulsifiers will have a pronounced affect on the resultant texture of the confection. The ratio of sucrose and lactose to the total glucose and invert sugar solids has some affect on the final texture, but will have prime significance in the keeping quality of the finished product.

CONCLUSION

In conclusion, within the confectionery industry there are numerous techniques available to control the solubility of sucrose, and by doing so a whole range of possible textures become available. The keeping life of the finished product will be influenced by numerous factors including water activity, equilibrium relative humidity and the atmosphere the product is subjected to during storage.

The choice of a suitable wrapping material either as a moisture barrier or with moisture transfer properties will be dictated by the ERH of the product, and the relative humidity of the storage and distribution conditions which the product will have to accommodate.

Numerous methods are available for texture[14] and particle size measurement and the choice of instrument to be used will obviously depend on the product in question.

Whilst instrumental measurements are aimed at displacing traditional forms of sensory evaluation, there is no substitute for man and the sensory evaluation he performs. Failure by the manufacturer to recognise how discriminating the consumer can be in identifying texture changes may eventually lead to purchasing resistance.

REFERENCES

1. Yeatman, J. N. (1972). *Food Technol.*, **26,** p. 141.
2. Cakebread, S. H. (1971). *Confect. Prod.*, **37,** p. 168.

3. Abbot, J. A. (1972). *Food Technol.*, **26,** p. 42.
4. Larmond, E. (1970). *Methods of Sensory Evaluations of Food*, **1284,** Canada, Dept. Agr. Pub.
5. Hinchcliffe, R. (1958). *Acta Oto-Largugol.*, **49,** p. 453.
6. Hinchcliffe, R. (1962). *J. Gerontol.*, **17,** p. 45.
7. Weckel, K. G. and Steinke, J. (1973). *The Manufacturing Confectioner*, **55,** p. 24.
8. Hinton, C. L. (1958). 12th Pennsylvanian Manufacturing Confectioners Association Conference.
9. Minifie, B. W. (1970). *Chocolate, Cocoa and Confectionery*, Churchill, London, p. 91.
10. Cook, L. R. (1975). *Candy and Snack Industry*, **40,** p. 32.
11. Cakebread, S. H. (1972). *Confect. Prod.*, **38,** p. 78.
12. Mansvelt, J. W. (1973). *Confect. Prod.*, **39,** p. 542.
13. Lees, R. and Jackson, B. (1973). *Sugar Confectionery and Chocolate Manufacture*, Leonard Hill, London, p. 226.
14. Szczesniak, A. S. (1972). *Food Technol.*, **26,** p. 50.

DISCUSSION

Bartoshuk: The two samples of chocolates appear to me to differ much more in sourness than sweetness. Since the only difference between them has to do with sugar crystal size, some kind of interaction must be occurring. Possibly the greater sweetness of the chocolate with the larger crystal size is suppressing the sourness produced by the tangerine flavour.

Beesley: The sourness can only be related to the flavour which, after addition to the fondant, gives the chocolate centre a pH of 4·0. Any difference in sweetness is probably related to the difference in crystal size between the two fondants used, the chocolate centre containing sucrose of relatively small crystal size dissolving faster in the mouth than the larger crystals in the second sample. This would apparently make the first sample sweeter than the second.

18

Sensory Properties of Foods Which Flow

P. Sherman

*Queen Elizabeth College (University of London),
London, England*

ABSTRACT

*Word association tests indicate that a large number of terms are
required to describe the textural properties of foods. If attention is
restricted to fluid foods, however, only a small number of these terms
are involved, for example, viscosity (thick–thin), spreadability,
creamy, gummy and slimy. Recent studies using consumer panels and
instrumental test methods have intimated the criteria used to sensorily
evaluate these properties and whether they are identified in-
stantaneously or after a time lag. Some of the pertinent studies will be
reviewed, with particular reference to the evaluation of viscosity,
spreadability and creaminess. Furthermore, by comparing panellists'
evaluations of these properties with instrumental measurements
performed under conditions closely simulating those to which the foods
are subjected during panellists' evaluations, a deeper understanding
has been achieved of the mechanics of sensory evaluation. During the
evaluation of some textural properties, as for example viscosity or
stickiness, at least two independent mechanisms are operating and the
panellists' evaluations are based on the total effect resulting therefrom.
Only one of these mechanisms relates directly to the textural property
under evaluation. If the secondary mechanism contributes significantly
to the overall effect identified sensorily, then the question arises as to
whether panellists, or consumers, can reliably evaluate these textural
properties.*

INTRODUCTION

Word-association tests carried out with food technologists and general consumers using foods associated with typical menus indicate that a large number of terms are used to describe the textural properties of foods.[1,2] This number reduces to a much smaller number, however, if attention is restricted to fluid foods. Typical examples are creamy, smooth, sticky, gooey, gluey, greasy, thick and runny. During recent years investigations have been made into the criteria whereby consumers evaluate some of these characteristics sensorily, in particular the associated mechanical conditions, and how these evaluations can be simulated instrumentally. This paper will review some of these studies with reference to the evaluations of viscosity (thick–thin), stickiness, creaminess and spreadability. These characteristics probably have the greatest influence on the consumers' overall evaluation of a fluid food's consistency.

VISCOSITY

Evaluation in the Mouth

Panel studies indicate that viscosity evaluation in the mouth is based on the food's flow characteristics in the narrow channel formed by the tongue's surface and the hard palate.[3,4] The evaluation is made as soon as the food is introduced into the mouth, so it is unlikely that the food's structure is modified by mixing with saliva at this time. This latter observation is important to the design of instrumental tests which reproduce the sensory evaluation.

The mechanical conditions operating in the mouth at the time when viscosity is evaluated can be determined by comparing panellists' responses with the viscometric flow characteristics of the food under examination. Figure 1 illustrates the principles involved when comparing four samples A, B, C and D. Samples A, B, and C are non-Newtonian foods, that is, they are not simple fluids with viscosities which remain constant irrespective of the shear rates to which they are subjected. Like most fluid foods their viscosities decrease as the shear rate increases because they are dispersions or emulsions and their internal structures break down to an increasing extent. Sample D, on the other hand, is a simple Newtonian fluid such as a dilute sugar solution. A restriction has to be applied in selecting the samples in

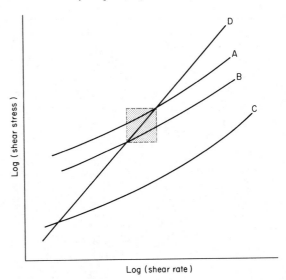

FIG. 1. Flow curves for a Newtonian and three non-Newtonian food commodities.

that their viscosities should not appear visually to be very different, otherwise this could influence the subsequent sensory evaluations. The four samples are presented to a group of panellists and they are asked to examine the samples in the normal way and indicate which of the samples A, B and C appear to have the same viscosity in the mouth as Sample D. At the same time the flow properties of all four samples are examined with a suitable viscometer which offers a wide range of shear rates and shear stresses. With the example illustrated in Fig. 1 the panellists' responses indicated that samples A and B appeared to have the same viscosity in the mouth as sample D. The double logarithmic plot of the viscometric data for the four samples indicates that the only shear rate–shear stress conditions for which this response is valid are those within the shaded rectangle.

This test procedure is now repeated with additional groups of samples. All samples within any one group must appear visually to be very similar in viscosity, but the samples are selected so that there are substantial differences in viscosity between the groups. The concentration of the sugar solution representing the comparison standard within each sample group has to be adjusted so that it also appears visually to be of similar viscosity to the other samples in the group.

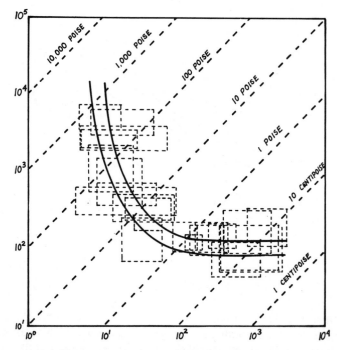

Fig. 2. Shear stress and shear rate bounds associated with the oral evaluation of viscosity.[4] Ordinate: shear stress (dyne cm^{-2}). Abscissa: shear rate (s^{-1}).

Figure 2 shows the results of a typical series of tests with the shear stress–shear rate conditions operating in the sample group evaluations reproduced collectively.[4] The two continuous lines, which form the superimposed master curve, represent the overall shear rate–shear stress limits. The broken straight lines represent the shear rate–shear stress plots for Newtonian fluids ranging in viscosity from 0·01 to 10 000 poise.

The master curve in Fig. 2 is also given in Fig. 3, and superimposed on it are the viscometrically derived shear rate–shear stress data for many food samples which range from very fluid to semi-solid. Some important deductions can be made from the information contained in Fig. 3. These are as follows:

(a) The shear rate and shear stress conditions associated with viscosity evaluation are not the same for all foods. On the contrary, the conditions range from high shear rates and low shear stresses for

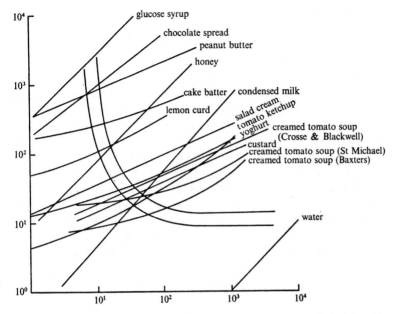

FIG. 3. Shear stress and shear rate bounds for oral evaluation of viscosity with superimposed flow curves for several food commodities.[4] Ordinate: shear stress (dyne cm^{-2}). Abscissa: shear rate (s^{-1}).

very fluid foods to low shear rates and high shear stresses for semi-solid foods. These observations must be taken into account, as will be shown later under (d), when designing viscometric tests to predict the sensory evaluation of viscosity.

(b) The variability of the shear rate–shear stress conditions associated with sensory viscosity evaluation, as discussed under (a), suggests that the stimulus on which the panellist's responses are based is also variable. It is likely that for very fluid foods the stimulus is the shear rate developed at a constant low shear stress of about 10^2 dyne cm^{-2} and for very viscous and semi-solid foods it is the shear stress developed at a constant low shear rate of about 10 sec^{-1}. This deduction is not unexpected since highly viscous foods will not flow readily without the application of stress.

(c) The lower end of the master curve is rather flat. A possible explanation is that at the higher shear rates associated with the viscosity evaluation of very fluid foods turbulent flow is initiated and this gives rise to an apparent increase in viscosity.[5] This means that the recorded shear stress includes a component related to the degree of turbulence developed.

(d) The master curve can be used to predict consumers' comparisons of the viscosities of fluid foods. For example, in Fig. 3 the viscometrically derived shear rate–shear stress plots for creamed tomato soup (St. Michael) and condensed milk intersect on the master curve. This means that in the oral evaluation of these two samples they will appear to have the same viscosity. The same reasoning applies for chocolate spread and peanut butter. On the other hand, the plots for condensed milk and creamed tomato soup (Baxter's) intersect to the left of the master curve. The plot for condensed milk intersects the master curve at a higher shear stress than the plot for creamed tomato soup (Baxter's), so that panellists will judge condensed milk to be the more viscous sample. Similarly the plots for tomato ketchup and yoghurt intersect to the right of the master curve, and from their intersection points with the master curve

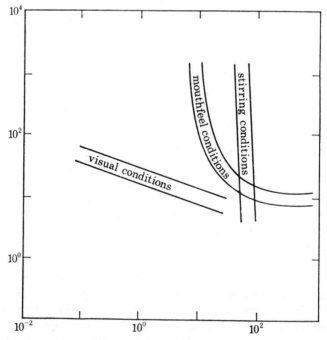

FIG. 4. Shear stress and shear rate bounds associated with non-oral methods of evaluating viscosity.[6] Ordinate: shear stress (dyne cm^{-2}). Abscissa: shear rate (s^{-1}).

it can be deduced that yoghurt will be judged the more viscous sample of the two.

Non-oral Evaluation

Viscosity evaluation is not restricted to stimuli developed in the mouth. A judgement may be made before the food enters the mouth, for example, by shaking the container, stirring the contents or tilting the container. Using principles similar to those described for oral evaluation the shear rate–shear stress conditions associated with evaluation by stirring or tilting the container have been established.[6] The results are summarised in the form of master curves in Fig. 4. They indicate that the shear rate–shear stress conditions vary as they do for oral evaluation but to a different degree. This means that when a series of samples is evaluated for viscosity by oral and non-oral methods the three sets of responses may not place samples in the same order.

Panellists judge viscosity by stirring as the resistance offered by the samples to the stirrer motion so that the situation resembles that in a viscometer. When tilting the container judgement is based on the rate at which samples flow down the sides of the containers.

SPREADABILITY

The criteria used by panellists to evaluate spreadability appear to differ for fluid and semi-solid foods. With salad dressings, mayonnaises, sauces, etc. the majority of panellists base their evaluations on the rate at which the samples spread,[7] whereas with butter and margarine opinions are almost equally divided between the force required to spread the sample and the distance over which the sample spreads.[8] Preliminary observations[7] suggest that the shear rates involved in spreading liquid foods vary with their flow characteristics, higher shear rates being associated with the spreading of the more fluid foods. In this respect the shear rate variability parallels that encountered during viscosity evaluation in the mouth.

Little attention has been paid to the spreadability characteristics of foods so discussion in this section will be confined to parallel studies on pharmaceutical preparations with consistencies ranging from stiff semi-solids to mobile liquids.[9] The spreadability characteristics of these preparations on human skin is a problem of much interest.

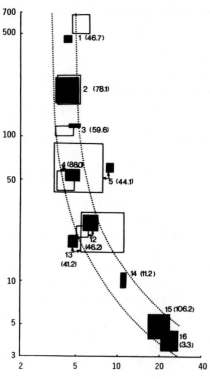

FIG. 5. Shear stress and shear rate bounds associated with the evaluation of spreadability.[9] Ordinate: shear stress (dyne cm^{-2} × 10^{-2}). Abscissa: shear rate (s^{-1} × 10^{-2}).

Evaluation of spreadability involves a longer time than the evaluation of viscosity. The time required is up to 15 sec for very fluid foods and times of 30 sec or more are involved for very viscous foods.[7] In the studies on pharmaceutical preparations a 20 sec time period was assumed.[9]

Panellists' comparison of the spreadability of groups of non-Newtonian lipophilic pharmaceuticals and an appropriate Newtonian silicone oil was simulated viscometrically by subjecting samples to a programmed increase in shear rate from 0 to 1754·0 to 0 sec^{-1} in 120 secs., and also by measuring the shear stress developed at selected constant shear rates which were applied for 20 sec. All measurements were made at 34 °C, which represents the approximate temperature reached by the pharmaceutical during spreading on human skin. The two sets of data were compared as described in the previous section. Figure 5 summarises the findings. As with viscosity evaluation the shear rates and shear stresses associated with the judgement of spreadability vary with the characteristics of the pharmaceuticals. Much higher shear rates and lower shear stresses are associated with the evaluation of spreadability in the more fluid pharmaceuticals.

Parallel studies made with a group of hydrophilic O/W emulsions suggested that the criterion on which spreadability was now judged was the shear stress developed at an approximately constant shear rate of $2000 \, \text{sec}^{-1}$, except for the more viscous samples which were evaluated at a somewhat lower shear rate.[10] However, these observations are not conclusive because a very limited number of samples were examined and their consistencies were not substantially different. The authors of these studies with pharmaceuticals suggest, nevertheless, that sensory evaluation of spreadability may be influenced by the degree of oiliness exhibited by the samples.

CREAMINESS

Creaminess is a textural property which has been studied only orally.[11,12] It implies a very smooth mouth feel with a complete absence of granularity, grittiness, lumpiness, etc. It is associated with consistency limits such that the product is neither too fluid nor too viscous. Optimum creaminess is exhibited when a certain degree of sliminess is exhibited.[12]

A comparison at 60 °C of panellists' and viscometric data for a series of reconstituted powdered soups reveals a relationship between the two sets of data. The precise form of the relationship appears to depend on the fat content, but for both high and low fat contents creaminess is associated with a viscosity in excess of 50 cP.

Other series of non-Newtonian soups were also prepared to which thickening agents such as gums, starches or modified starches were added so that the soups exhibited a viscosity (η) of 100 ± 10 cP at 60 °C at a shear rate ($\dot{\gamma}$) of $49 \, \text{sec}^{-1}$. Previous studies[3] had indicated that this is the shear rate associated with the sensory evaluation of similarly formulated soups. The soups were evaluated for both creaminess and sliminess and the results indicate that optimum creaminess is associated with a certain degree of sliminess. This observation is still valid when soups with a viscosity of 200 cP at 60 °C are evaluated. The flow characteristics of the non-Newtonian soups conformed to the power relationship

$$\tau = k\dot{\gamma}^n \tag{1}$$

where τ is the shear stress, and k and n are constants. A linear relationship is observed between the sliminess rating (R) and the constant n, with:

$$n = mR + C \tag{2}$$

where m and C are constants. A very slimy material is thick, coats the mouth and it is difficult to swallow.[13]

A more recent study[14] with hydrocolloid solutions, honey, butterscotch, and various syrups (chocolate, pancake and vanilla) indicates that the attributes of thickness, smoothness and slipperiness contribute to creaminess. The sensation of thickness relates to the viscous force between the tongue and the roof of the mouth, smoothness is inversely proportional to the friction force developed by contact between the tongue and the mouth, and slipperiness is inversely proportional to the average of viscous and friction forces.

STICKINESS

Regions of the mouth involved in stickiness evaluation are the roof of the mouth, tongue, lips and teeth. Several criteria are involved, the most important probably being the maximum tensile force experienced[15,16] and the evaluation continues over several seconds. Instrumental simulation of this sensory evaluation involves determination of the maximum force developed during adhesive or cohesive rupture between a flat circular metal plate and the sample's surface.[15-17] The speed with which the metal plate is pulled away from the sample's surface greatly influences the statistical significance of the correlation between the sensory and instrumental evaluations, and it improves at the higher speeds of plate removal.

Because the sensory evaluation of stickiness is not instantaneous it is necessary to consider what effect human saliva may have on the instrumental evaluation. Pre-wetting the metal plate with saliva improves the correlation between instrumental evaluation at high speed and sensory evaluation.[15] Furthermore, it reveals much interesting additional information about the mechanism whereby stickiness is evaluated.[16] Most foods exhibit cohesive rupture in instrumental stickiness measurements, i.e. the foods extend as long filaments and rupture occurs eventually within the filaments, because the cohesive forces are weaker than the force of adhesion between the foods and the metal plate. If the foods are viscoelastic, as indeed many are, then cavitation effects appear due to the reduced or even negative hydrostatic pressure developed during rapid extensional flow. This effect introduces a negative pressure, so that the maximum force registered at sample rupture is reduced accordingly. The muco-proteins present in human saliva may reduce the cavitation effects in the same way as certain polymers can in parallel situations.

Non-oral evaluations of stickiness, by drawing the right forefinger away from the food samples' surfaces, do not correlate satisfactorily with the instrumental evaluations. When the finger is withdrawn the skin is elevated and extended so that the pattern of force development could differ from that developed in oral evaluation.[15] This belief is supported by the observation that instrumental data correlate well with sensory evaluations made by withdrawing a plastic spoon out of the samples' surfaces.

Theoretical consideration of the situation where stickiness is judged by squeezing a thin film of sample between two fingers indicates that the predicted[17] stickiness is inversely related to the average velocity (dh/dt) normal to the surface of the moving finger.

$$\text{Stickiness evaluation} \propto \frac{H}{dh/dt} \tag{3}$$

where H, which is a function of the sample, is the distance at which the finger separates from the sample.

$$h = \frac{1}{\left[\dfrac{1}{h_0^{(n+1)/n}} + \left(\dfrac{F_0}{R^{n+3}} \cdot \dfrac{n+3}{2\pi k}\right)^{1/n} \cdot \dfrac{n+1}{2n+1} t\right]^{n/(n+1)}} \tag{4}$$

so that eqn. 3 can be extended:

Stickiness evaluation

$$\propto \frac{H(2n+1)}{n} \cdot \frac{\left[\dfrac{1}{h_1^{(n+1)/n}} - \dfrac{n+1}{2n+1}\left(\dfrac{F_1}{R^{n+3}} \cdot \dfrac{n+3}{2\pi m}\right)^{1/n} t_s\right]}{\left(\dfrac{F_1}{R^{n+3}} \cdot \dfrac{n+3}{2\pi k}\right)^{1/n}} \tag{5}$$

314 *P. Sherman*

where h_0 is the initial thickness of the food sample film, F_0 is the total force, F_1 the normal force developed when pulling the finger upwards, h_1 is the minimum film thickness and is evaluated from eqn. (4), t_s is an average reference time, R is the finger's radius, k and n are the constants quoted in eqn. (1).

MECHANICS OF SENSORY EVALUATION

In the past the emphasis in food texture studies has concentrated on establishing the validity of the Stevens' power relationship[18] for sensory data and data obtained with instrumental methods which often did not reproduce the mechanical conditions of sensory evaluation. More careful design of instrumental methods permits a deeper understanding of the mechanics of sensory evaluation. Thus, on the basis of the facts quoted in the relevant sections, it appears that both the oral evaluation of viscosity in very fluid foods and of stickiness in viscoelastic fluid foods involves at least two mechanisms. Only one of these two mechanisms is specifically related to evaluation of either textural parameter and the other, secondary, process, arises from the conditions in which the evaluation is made. If the secondary process is developed to a significant extent then a question must be asked as to the validity of consumers' evaluations of viscosity or stickiness. The negative hydrodynamic force developed in stickiness evaluations will reduce the maximum force registered by the human senses so that the magnitude of this parameter will appear lower than its true value. Turbulent flow at the high shear rates associated with oral evaluation of the viscosity of very fluid foods will increase the shear stress registered so that the viscosity will appear to be higher than its true value. This problem is not restricted to fluid foods. Similar problems arise when considering some textural properties of solid foods.

REFERENCES

1. Szczesniak, A. S. and Kleyn, D. H. (1962). *Food Technol.*, **27**, p. 74.
2. Szczesniak, A. S. (1971). *J. Texture Studies*, **2**, p. 196.
3. Wood, F. W. (1968). Psychophysical studies on the consistency of liquid foods. In: *Rheology and Texture of Foodstuffs*, SCI Monograph No. 27, p. 40.

4. Shama, F. and Sherman, P. (1973). *J. Texture Studies*, **4**, p. 111.
5. Parkinson, C. and Sherman, P. (1971). *J. Texture Studies*, **2**, p. 451.
6. Shama, F., Parkinson, C and Sherman, P. (1973). *J. Texture Studies*, **4**, p. 104.
7. Romo, E. and Sherman, P. (1976), unpublished observations.
8. Olkku, J. and Sherman, P. (1976), unpublished observations.
9. Barry, B. W. and Grace, A. J. (1972). *J. Pharm. Sci.*, **61**, p. 335.
10. Barry, B. W. and Meyer, M. C. (1973). *J. Pharm. Sci.*, **62**, p. 1349.
11. Prentice, J. H. (1973). *J. Texture Studies*, **4**, p. 154.
12. Wood, F. W. (1974). *Die Stärke*, **26**, p. 127.
13. Szczesniak, A. S. and Forkas, E. (1962). *J. Food Sci.*, **27**, p. 381.
14. Kokini, J. L., Kadane, J. B. and Cussler, E. L. (1977). *J. Texture Studies*, submitted for publication.
15. Boyd, J. V., Parkinson, C. and Sherman, P. (1974). *Proc. IV Int. Congress Food Sci. and Technol.*, **II**, p. 121.
16. Boyd, J. V. and Sherman, P. (1975). *Biorheol.*, **12**, p. 317.
17. De Martine, M. L. and Cussler, E. L. (1975). *J. Pharm. Sci.*, **64**, p. 976.
18. Stevens, S. S. (1970). *Science*, **170**, p. 1043.

DISCUSSION

Harper: How did you define viscosity to your panellists?

Sherman: We did not decide to call this particular parameter viscosity. We asked our consumer panel to judge viscosity and to tell us how they judged it and then to write a definition of what viscosity is. So our use of the term is based on consumer panel studies.

Polydorou: A few years ago I observed that the spreadability function of margarine had similar behaviour to the stickiness function as mentioned in your paper. This was observed through a probe inserted in a margarine production line. This spreadability function is also related to consistency.

Sherman: When a food is spread on a horizontal surface the sample thickness decreases continuously over several seconds. This means that the shear rate to which the sample is subjected increases progressively over this time. Therefore, when stimulating these shear conditions viscometrically one should use a programmed shear rate increase and determine the viscosity after a time corresponding to that taken by the consumer to evaluate spreadability. There is more discussion of this aspect in the published version of this paper.

P. Sherman

Jowitt: Were the consumer panel members previously aware of the meaning of the word 'viscosity' which they were *given* and asked to evaluate? What other forces than viscous ones are involved in the instrumental stickiness measurements described?

Sherman: I will elaborate a little on the history. The work was originally done at Unilever and all the work was initially done there with a texture profile panel of people especially selected and trained over several months, who were then used to this type of work. We then repeated the work, using exactly the same questions and the same terms, on some 200 members of a housewives' group and we got exactly the same response. We used the word 'viscosity' and they seemed to understand what it meant.

Index